PREACHING IN THE
AGE OF CHAUCER

PREACHING IN THE AGE OF CHAUCER

Selected Sermons in Translation

Translated by Siegfried Wenzel

The Catholic University of America Press
Washington, D.C.

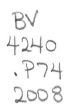
LIBRARY OF CONGRESS CATALOGING-IN-PUBLICATION DATA

Preaching in the age of Chaucer : selected sermons in translation / translated by Siegfried Wenzel.

    p. cm. — (Medieval texts in translation)

    Includes bibliographical references and index.

    ISBN 978-0-8132-1529-7 (pbk. : alk. paper)   1. Sermons, Medieval—England.

    2. Sermons, Latin—Translations into English.   I. Wenzel, Siegfried, 1928–

BV4240.P74 2008

252′.0242—dc22   2007051248

CONTENTS

ACKNOWLEDGMENTS

I wish to thank the respective owners or trustees of the libraries that hold the medieval manuscripts from which these translations have been taken, as well as their librarians and staff, for giving me access to the manuscripts and supplying microfilms of the Latin material. In addition, I am especially grateful to my friend and colleague Professor Richard W. Pfaff for critically reading a first draft of this book and sharing with me his unique knowledge of the medieval liturgy as well as church history in England. Likewise, I am indebted to the two readers of the press for many practical suggestions and corrections.

INTRODUCTION

In a culture without the Internet, television, or even the printed book, the chief, if not the only, medium for spreading information and teaching is oral communication. In western Europe before Gutenberg it was the pulpit that represented the main, and for many people the only, locus from which they would hear the dominant worldview expounded, and oftentimes they would receive with it some information about natural phenomena and amusing stories, though these of course always served the primary purposes of explaining Christian doctrine and of exhorting people to lead good moral lives. Much uncertainty remains, and probably will always remain, about how frequently sermons were preached in late-medieval parishes and about the exact form the preaching may have taken. Yet surviving sermon texts leave little doubt that producing sermons represented a major, if not indeed the major, literary activity in that period, and an activity that was intended to reach the widest and most diversified audience, from popes, cardinals, and bishops, through the clergy, monks, and nuns, to the laity at every social level. Sermons were the medium par excellence through which the dominant system of beliefs and ethics was formulated for and presented to this wide audience. Though this was done in a language that could be understood by the listeners, the majority of surviving sermons have been preserved in clerical Latin. Today much of this extant material is only available in unpublished manuscripts whose scripts and verbal textures pose formidable obstacles for the modern reader. This is particularly true of England, where during the last medieval century (c. 1350–c. 1450) a number of known and unknown authors produced Latin sermons that are accessible only to very determined scholars equipped with a decent command of Latin grammar and vocabulary as well as the patience to solve the myriad puzzles created by poor handwriting and highly abbreviated word forms.

What has survived from this oral and literary activity shows an astonishing variety. To help modern students and general readers gain an impression of the riches as well as the nature of preaching in late-medieval England in an easily accessible form, this anthology offers translations of nearly two dozen Latin sermons and one from a Middle English source. The pieces have been chosen to illustrate a number of things: first, the variety of preaching that was done on different occasions; next, the variety of sermon structures, including both the ancient homily form and the characteristic "modern" scholastic-sermon structure, with several combinations of the two; and last, the variety of styles used by individual preachers, ranging from Wyclif's academic tone, which reads like a lecture, to the mechanical progression by threes and biblical proof-texts as in selection 22, to a more free-flowing, relaxed, and popular style.

During the long period of medieval preaching and sermon making, from the patristic age to the Renaissance, two major types of sermons were created and employed: the ancient "homily" and, beginning around the year 1200, the modern university or thematic or scholastic "sermon."[1] The "homily" concentrates on an extended biblical text and explains it verse by verse, if not word by word. To such literal exegesis may then be added an explanation of the text's allegorical and/or moral meaning. In contrast, the scholastic sermon is based on a single verse or phrase or even word, usually taken from scripture, and then develops from it a larger verbal and notional structure by means of divisions and subdivisions and other

---

1. The two types have often been described and analyzed; see for instance Siegfried Wenzel, *Latin Sermon Collections from Later Medieval England: Orthodox Preaching in the Age of Wyclif* (Cambridge: Cambridge University Press, 2005), 11–16.

means of amplification that often result in a highly sophisticated, even artificial verbal construct (see especially selections 18 and 25). The surviving sermons from this period show that English preachers were familiar with both types and on occasion verbally distinguished between *homilia* and *sermo*.[2] The present selection illustrates this structural variety, ranging from the simple exegetical "homily" (15), through differing combinations of homily and scholastic sermon structure (13, 14, and 6), to the characteristic scholastic sermon with its progression from thema and protheme through the major division and development of the principal parts to the closing formula (see 4, with headnote).

Together with "the word of God," late-medieval preachers were required to preach with regular frequency basic catechetical pieces of church doctrine, the so-called *pastoralia*, which included the Creed, the Ten Commandments, the seven deadly sins, and others. This requirement was spelled out in numerous diocesan constitutions, of which the Lambeth Constitutions issued by Archbishop Pecham in 1281 became the most famous in England, as well as in pastoral handbooks. How a preacher might combine explaining such a catechetical piece with preaching on a biblical text is shown by selections 10 and 12 (the seven deadly sins) and 21 (the Creed).[3]

In order to explain or develop the chosen text, normally taken from either the gospel or the epistle of the day, which would have been read in Latin during Mass just before the sermon, preachers had at their disposal, and certainly used, a variety of aids. These could have been simply commentaries on scripture, such as the *Glossa ordinaria* or the "postils" of Hugh of St. Cher, which went through the Old and New Testament in the order of their books.[4]

---

2. Some examples are given in *Collections*, 257–58.

3. See also *Collections*, 230–33 and 346–53.

4. A postil or *postilla* (from Latin *post illa verba*, "after the words [of scripture]") is essentially an exegetical commentary on scripture. It came to be used for commentaries on entire books of the Bible or on the biblical lections in sermon cycles, where the biblical text is explained phrase by phrase.

Or they could have been gospel harmonies, such as the *Unum ex quatuor* by the Franciscan William of Nottingham (d. after 1330), which consolidated in chronological order what the four gospels report of Jesus' life and teaching, with plentiful commentary. Or, finally, they could have been systematic selections of material from various biblical commentaries now presented in the order of the Sunday gospels, such as the cycle of "sermons" on the Sunday gospels by Philip Repingdon (written probably between 1382 and 1394) as well as earlier model sermon collections.[5] For the further rhetorical development of their message based on the biblical text, other sermon aids could be drawn upon, such as encyclopedias of preaching material (e.g., Bromyard's *Summa praedicantium,* written in the 1330s, perhaps used in selection 21) and especially collections of stories and *exempla* (cf. selection 3).

The first part of this anthology illustrates how the making of a sermon may have progressed from the biblical lection through medieval commentary and postils to an actual sermon text. For this purpose I have focused on the gospel reading for the third Sunday of Lent and chosen three sermons that show very different approaches. This introductory section is followed by nine sermons from the temporal cycle, from Advent and Christmas through Lent, Easter, and Corpus Christi to the Sundays after Trinity (sermons 6–14). Next, I have chosen five sermons in honor of major saints (15–19): the Blessed Virgin Mary (Annunciation and Assumption), Katherine (with two sermons by FitzRalph, showing different degrees of elaboration and recording), and John the Baptist. Last follow six sermons for several special occasions, including an academic lecture in sermon form (20–25). Headnotes to the sermons will give some information about the authors if they are known and about particular features of the respective sermon and its occasion.

5. Thirteenth-century model sermon collections have been studied especially by D. L. d'Avray, *The Preaching of the Friars: Sermons Diffused from Paris before 1300* (Oxford: Clarendon Press, 1985). Repingdom, for instance, draws heavily on the sermon cycles by Jacobus a Voragine, Peraldus, Gorran, John of Abbéville, and others.

In reading the selections one may well be struck by their highly literary quality, shown especially in their formal structure. Preaching in the Christian world is by definition the teaching of faith and morals based on an exposition of the word of God *(verbum Dei)* as it was written and preserved in both testaments of the Bible. This was of course done orally but, whether before or after its delivery, the discourse was "fixed" in writing and given a polished, literary form. One may expect that surviving sermon texts stand at varying distances from their actual delivery, and the surviving material indeed shows much variation in tone and style, ranging, for instance, from the fairly neutral, non-audience-specific pieces in a formal cycle (3, 13, 19) to more "real" or "genuine" sermons that now and then even contain small personal details. Formal cycles, such as that by Felton (3 and 12), were put together for the use by other preachers and hence may be called model cycles or model sermons. They are likely to gather and arrange pertinent material relating to a given lection in a rather faceless manner. In contrast, random collections or individual sermons—although we must suspect that they, too, were written down and collected to serve as models for other preachers—tend to be looser in style, more individualistic in texture, closer to a concrete situation, even endowed with more particular concerns and stylistic features.[6] The difference shows when one compares, for instance, Felton's sermon for the third Sunday of Lent (3) with that by an anonymous monastic preacher on the same gospel (5), let alone with such highly individualized and sophisticated, even witty, pieces as the funeral sermon for Simon with its rhetorical exploration of the tree image (20), the sermon preached at the enclosure of a nun (24), or the introduction of a new university lecturer (25).

The sermons here translated come from collections made in England during the fourteenth and fifteenth centuries. This is the

---

6. A random collection is a group of sermons that do not stand in the order of the church calendar, i.e., following the Sundays, major feasts, and saints' feasts of the church year.

field I am most familiar with and have surveyed comprehensively
in *Latin Sermon Collections from Later Medieval England: Orthodox Preaching
in the Age of Wyclif* (Cambridge: Cambridge University Press, 2005;
hereafter cited as *Collections*). The period from c. 1350 to c. 1450
was the golden age of preaching in (later) medieval England, from
which a substantial though—despite Owst's pioneering work[7]—
as yet relatively unknown body of material has survived. Much of
it remains anonymous, but we do have the names of several outstanding preachers: Sheppey, FitzRalph (17, 18), Waldeby, Repingdon, Brinton (11, 21), Felton (3, 12), Mirk (19), Rypon, Wyclif (14),
Philip (7), Dygon (15), Chambron, Wimbledon (22?), and Alkerton, several of whom are represented in this anthology. The sermons of Brinton, Wyclif, and Mirk, and "Redde rationem vilicationis tuae" by Wimbledon have been edited; the remainder can be
found only in manuscripts or at best unpublished dissertations. In
the latter cases, my translations are based on these manuscripts,
which are identified in the headnotes, together with the siglum and
sermon number I have used in *Collections*. Most are unique copies,
but where a sermon has been preserved in more than one manuscript, I have compared the texts and based my translation on what
seemed to me the best reading. I have tried to stay close to the medieval Latin, in order to reflect the sermons' peculiar stylistic features more or less accurately. In only one of the reported sermons
by FitzRalph (17) and one by Wyclif (14) have I allowed myself
greater freedom in order to produce a readable version of what in
the original texts are awkward or syntactically difficult constructions.

Quotations in the sermons have been identified in the footnotes

---

7. G. R. Owst, *Preaching in Medieval England: An Introduction to Sermon Manuscripts of the
Period c. 1350–1450* (Cambridge: Cambridge University Press, 1926; repr., New York:
Russel & Russell, 1965); and Owst, *Literature and Pulpit in Medieval England: A Neglected
Chapter in the History of English Letters and of the English People* (Cambridge: Cambridge Uni-
versity Press, 1933; 2d rev. ed., Oxford: Basil Blackwell, 1961). Despite their datedness
both volumes contain much sermon material that is still valuable.

as far as possible. Major classical and medieval authors and their works are cited without references to modern editions; for less well-known sources I have added a modern edition, whose publication data may be found either in the respective footnote or in the list of frequently quoted sources. In translating biblical quotations I have drawn on the Douay Version of the Latin Vulgate but have modernized obsolete verb and pronoun forms. In quoting the Bible, late-medieval preachers normally identified book and chapter (except for the Psalms), but not the verse. In case of erroneous citations, I have silently given the correct chapter numbers. To the medieval citations I have, in square brackets, added the verse numbers according to the modern Vulgate Bible; other words within square brackets also are my additions to facilitate the reader's understanding. All biblical citations (especially the Psalms) follow the numbering of the Vulgate.

ABBREVIATIONS

CCCM   *Corpus Christianorum Continuatio Mediaeualis* (Turnhout: Brepols, 1971–).

MED   *Middle English Dictionary,* ed. Hans Kurath, Sherman Kuhn, and Robert E. Lewis (Ann Arbor: University of Michigan Press, 1954–2001).

OED   *New English Dictionary on Historical Principles,* ed. J. A. H. Murray et al. (Oxford: Clarendon Press, 1888–1928).

PG   *Patrologiae cursus completus: Series Graeca,* ed. J.-P. Migne (Paris: Garnier Frères, 1857–87.).

PL   *Patrologiae cursus completus: Series Latina,* ed. J.-P. Migne (Paris: J.-P. Migne, 1844–64).

PART I

FROM SCRIPTURE TO SERMON

This section illustrates how an actual sermon might have been developed from the biblical text read at Mass, for which I have selected the gospel for the third Sunday of Lent. Medieval students of scripture and of preaching would have studied the text (selection 1) with the help of the *Glossa ordinaria,* which furnishes explanations of the biblical text gathered from the church fathers (selection 2). In the thirteenth century and later, such commentary was elaborated, enriched with homiletic topics, and organized according to the Sunday lections by biblical scholars called postillators. Some of their material appears incorporated into the sermon cycle by John Felton, often with acknowledgment (selection 3). The next step would then have been the preparation of a genuine sermon. For illustration I have selected the sermon for the respective Sunday that appears in Felton's regular cycle and two anonymous sermons that demonstrate what individual preachers could do with the inherited material (selections 4 and 5). These examples amply show the preachers' adherence to the inherited exegetical tradition, together with their freedom to select, to shape, and to develop and enrich this material.

GOSPEL FOR THE THIRD SUNDAY OF LENT

THE GOSPEL LECTION for the third Sunday in Lent is Luke 11:14–28. The following is the text as given by Hugh of St. Cher (c. 1235), in *Opera omnia in universum Vetus et Novum Testamentum*, 8 vols. (Venice, 1732), vol. 6, cols. 201rb–203rb, which presents a few minor variations from the modern Vulgate version:

[14] Et erat ejiciens daemonium, et illud erat mutum, et cum ejecisset daemonium, locutus est mutus et admiratae sunt turbae.

[15] Quidam autem ex eis dixerunt: "In Beelzebub principe daemoniorum ejicit daemonia."

[16] Et alii tentantes signum de coelo quaerebant ab eo.

[17] Ipse autem, ut vidit cogitationes eorum, dixit eis: "Omne regnum in se ipsum divisum desolabitur, et domus supra domum cadet.

[18] Si autem et Satanas in se ipsum divisus est, quomodo stabit regnum ipsius? Quia dicitis in Beelzebub ejicere me daemonia.

[19] Si autem ego in Beelzebub ejicio daemonia, filii vestri in quo ejiciunt? Ideo ipsi judices vestri erunt.

[20] Porro si in digito Dei ejicio daemonia, profecto pervenit in vos regnum Dei.

[21] Cum fortis armatus custodit atrium suum, in pace sunt ea, quae possidet.

[22] Si autem fortior illo superveniens vicerit eum, universa arma ejus auferet, in quibus confidebat, et spolia ejus distribuet.

[23] Qui non est mecum contra me est, et qui non colligit mecum dispergit.

[24] Cum immundus spiritus exierit ab homine, ambulat per loca inaquosa quaerens requiem, et non inveniens, dicit: 'Revertar in domum meam, unde exivi.'

[25] Et cum venerit, invenit eam scopis mundatam et ornatam.

[26] Tunc vadit, et assumit septem alios spiritus secum nequiores se, et ingressi habitant ibi. Et fiunt novissima hominis illius pejora prioribus."

[27] Factum est autem, cum haec diceret, extollens vocem quaedam mulier de turba dixit illi: "Beatus venter, qui te portavit, et ubera, quae suxisti."

[28] At ille dixit: "Quin imo beati qui audiunt verbum Dei et custodiunt illud."

❧

[14] And he was casting out a demon, and that was mute. And when he had cast out the demon, the mute man spoke, and the crowds were astonished.

[15] But some of them said, "He casts out demons by Beelzebub, the prince of demons."

[16] And others tempted him and asked him for a sign from heaven.

[17] But he, as he saw their thoughts, said to them: "Every kingdom divided against itself will be brought to desolation, and house will fall upon house.

[18] But if Satan is divided against himself, how will his kingdom stand? For you say that I cast out demons by Beelzebub.

[19] But if I cast out demons by Beelzebub, by whom do your sons drive them out? Therefore they will be your judges.

[20] But if I cast out demons by the finger of God, doubtless the kingdom of God has come upon you.

[21] When a strong armed man guards his court, all things that he owns are at peace.

[22] But if one stronger than he comes upon him and overcomes him, he will take away all his arms in which he trusted and will distribute his spoils.

[23] He who is not with me is against me, and he who does not gather with me scatters.

[24] When an unclean spirit has gone out of a man, he wanders through waterless places seeking rest, and when he does not find it, he says, 'I will return to the house from which I have gone out.'

[25] And when he comes to it, he finds it swept.

[26] And then he goes and takes seven other spirits that are worse than he, and they enter and live there, and the last things of that man are worse than the former ones."

[27] And it happened, when he said these things, that a woman from the crowd said to him, "Blessed is the womb that bore you and the breasts that you drank from."

[28] But he said, "Yes, rather, blessed are those who hear the word of God and keep it."

2

GLOSSA ORDINARIA ON
THIS GOSPEL

The great gloss on the Bible, consisting of the biblical text with
interlineary and marginal comments drawn from the fathers, including Bede and Rabanus Maurus, was put together in the early twelfth
century and became the standard exegetical guide for medieval
preachers. The following is its commentary on Luke 11:14–28.

SOURCE:

Biblia sacra cum Glossa ordinaria . . ., 6 vols. (Antwerp, 1617), vol. 5, cols. 842–46.
Also in PL 114:289–91 and the facsimile reprint of the Strassburg
1480–81 edition of the *Glossa ordinaria* (Turnhout: Brepols, 1992), vol. 4.

LITERATURE:

Beryl Smalley, *The Study of the Bible in the Middle Ages* (Oxford: Basil Blackwell,
1952; reprint, Notre Dame: University of Notre Dame Press, 1964).

✌

And he was casting out: After the words of his preaching, which he
offered to the humble, he also works miracles, so that people who do
not believe him in his preaching would do so when they saw his miracles. Matthew says that this possessed person was also blind. Therefore
three miracles appear in him that were wrought by the Lord: the possessed man sees, speaks, and is freed from the demon. What happened
at that time to one person in the body happens every day in the con-

version of the nations: after the demon and every filth of idolatry has been cast out, they see the light of faith and thereafter their mouths, which had first been silent, would be loosened to praise God.

In Beelzebub: King Ninus, the founder of Ninive, consecrated a statue to his father Belus and established divine honors for him. When the Chaldeans received a duplicate of this statue, they called it Bel. The Palestinians, when they received it, called it Baal, and the Moabites, Beelphegor. But the Jews, who cultivated one single God, in order to deride the gentiles called the image "Beelzebub." Because "Baal" means "man," and "Zebub" means "fly." Hence "Beelzebub" means "the man of flies" or "one who has flies," because of the blood that was offered up in his temple. The Jews also asserted that the prince of the demons dwelled in this image, and they said that it was in *his* power that Jesus cast out demons.

A sign from heaven: Namely, that Jesus would cause fire to come down from heaven, as in the time of Elijah fifty men were killed by fire from heaven;[1] or else that against what was usual in their country during the summer, thunder would be heard, rain would fall, and lightning would flash, as it happened at the time of Samuel;[2] or else they were asking for manna from heaven.[3] But such signs were not wrought by Christ at this time, because the Pharisees would have disparaged him and said that such and similar signs happened through various conditions of the air. Whence the text continues:

But he saw their thoughts. The Lord has the power to see and judge other people's thoughts. It is in the nature of the Jews to ask for signs, whence Paul says: "The Jews ask for signs, the gentiles for wisdom."[4] **But he saw their thoughts.** He responded, not to their words but to their thoughts, and thus he gave in fact a sign of his power in which he looks into the secrets of men's hearts. It is literally true that any solid and strong realm, if it is divided into parts, is reduced to a wilderness and left empty of its inhabitants, and one house will fall on another when the inhabitants of one house are oppressed or pun-

1. 2 Kings 1:9–12.   2. 1 Samuel 7:10.
3. Exodus 16.   4. 1 Corinthians 1:22.

ished by the household of another. What this is leading to spiritually he explains when he adds: **If then Satan is divided in himself.** "If I, as you maintain, cast out demons with the help of the prince of demons, then the devil's realm is divided against itself, and thus the power of his evil cannot stand firm. But since one demon cannot cast out another demon, you say falsely that I cast out demons with the help of the prince of demons. But if what you say should be true, then take care to leave the realm that is thus divided, so that you may not be involved in its fall!" So, let them [the Jews] listen to what follows, namely, in what power the Lord does cast out devils, so that they do not reckon him to be the prince of demons.

But if I cast out demons with the help of Beelzebub, with whose help do your sons cast them out? "Sons" of the Jews he calls the apostles, who with the power they received from the Lord to perform other miracles also received the power to cast out demons. For that casting-out they did not credit the devil but God, because they were aware that they had not learned witchcraft from the Lord. Hence they who "chose ignoble and contemptible things of the world,"[5] in which there was no evil craft, will sit on twelve seats judging the twelve tribes of Israel. Or else he calls them "sons," namely, exorcists of that nation, who by invoking the name of the Lord used to cast out demons. And so he says, as it were: "If their power to cast out demons is attributed, not to the devil but to God, why then does the same deed in me not have the same cause?" **Therefore they will be your judges,** not in their power but by comparison, because they attribute their casting-out not to the devil but to God.

If it is the case that a realm that is divided lies in ruin, the reign of the Father, Son, and Holy Spirit is not divided, because it does not lie in ruin because of some contradiction or external attack. Concerning this realm [Jesus] answered Pilate: "My reign is not of this world."[6] And thus he denies that those who do not put their hope in Christ but believe that demons are cast out with the help of the prince of demons belong to the eternal kingdom. For how can the divine king-

5. Cf. 1 Corinthians 1:28, quoted out of context.
6. John 18:36.

dom remain if faith is split, if the Jewish people exist out of the Law [*ex lege*] and Christ, too, was born in his flesh out of the Law? How can that realm be eternal which is out of the Law if that nation divides the Law when Christ, who existed out of the Law, is denied by the people of the Law? But the realm of the church endures, in which there is one lord, one faith, and one baptism.

But if a divided realm cannot endure, and if the reign of Satan is divided, as you say, because Satan casts out Satan, therefore, etc.

Moreover, if I cast out with the help of the finger of God. God the Son is called the hand or arm of the Father, and the Holy Spirit is called his finger, because of the many different gifts that people receive through the Holy Spirit, just as fingers are separated from each other and there is no harm in the inequality of the members. Granted that the arm is larger than the finger, the arm and the finger are still one body. With this finger the Law was written on the tables. That finger the magi confessed in Egypt.

Then indeed the kingdom has come. That is, God's power to judge, in which he will separate the good from the evil on the day of judgment. Or else, "the kingdom" is blessedness in heaven, as if he were saying: "If I cast out demons in the spirit of God, you should know beyond doubt that the gate to the heavenly kingdom has been opened to those who believe."

When a strong man fortifies his court. As if he were saying: "If, as you are saying, I were casting out demons with the help of Beelzebub, then I would in some measure consent to the devil's works. But I do not consent to him in any way but rather hasten to overcome him and to expel him from my faithful ones." **When a strong man,** the devil, **armed** with many spiritual wickednesses to inflict harm, **fortifies,** by way of servitude, **his court,** that is, the world, which is seated in wickedness,[7] where until the coming of the Son of God the devil used to rule without opposition and badly used his **peaceful** reign in the hearts of the faithless.

---

7. 1 John 5:19.

But if a stronger one. Jesus calls himself "stronger" because he did not consent to the devil peacefully and in his deeds, as they were false-ly accusing him, but he overthrew him with his greater strength and freed the world from his domination. The **arms** of the devil which he took away are the most ingenious subtleties of the devil's spiritu-al wickedness. The **spoils** are the souls that had been deceived by the devil. These Christ **distributed** in his victory, which is a great sign of triumph, because he "led capitivity captive and gave goods to men. . . some as apostles, others as evangelists."[8]

Whoever is not with me, etc. "Indeed my works do not agree with those of Satan, because I myself do not agree in any way with him, but we are totally opposed to each other. For I am humble and be-nign and want to save souls—he is proud and envious and wants to ruin them. I gather powers in my preaching—he scatters and separates from the unity of the church."

And whoever does not gather. These words may be understood as additionally referring to all heretics and schismatics. These are all ex-cluded from the kingdom of God.

When the unclean spirit. "Since you withdraw yourselves from my kingdom by attributing my deeds to the devil, the devil dwells in you, as in his realm, more firmly than before."

Has gone out. The devil went out of the Jews when their people re-ceived the Law and the worship of the one God. And then he passed on into nations that were dry and sterile of the richness of the Holy Spirit and of the love of one's neighbor. But in those nations the dev-il did not find rest, because now he is driven from the hearts of pa-gans who have received the faith of Christ. And so he said: "I will seek the Jews again whom I have left before." And he found that na-tion cleansed with brooms, that is, from the superfluous observations of the Pharisees and the ceremonies of the Law, which are no longer worth anything after Christ's coming. And in order to possess them more firmly, he takes all the demons with him. Thus now the Israel-

8. Ephesians 4:8 and 11.

ites, who blaspheme Christ in their conventicles, are worse off than they were in Egypt before they received the Law, because it is a greater act of infidelity not to receive the one who is coming than it is not to believe that he will come.

These words can [also] refer to any baptized person who after receiving grace neglects to do good works but instead adds actual sins to the original ones. When a person in baptism renounces the devil's pomps and the allure of his former sins, the devil goes out of him and after leaving him wanders through dry places, because the sly tempter searches the hearts of the saints that are free from any softness of dissolute thoughts and of the moisture of lust, if he can set his evil foot there. Whence the text continues:

He seeks rest and does not find it. As he is nourished by evil thoughts and acts, he becomes aware that in the minds of the faithful all his temptations cease. Then he says:

I will return to my house from where I went out. "I will return to the mind of that person from whom I was cast out in baptism, and I will subject my former possession to my accustomed dominion."

And when he finds it swept with brooms. For when the devil, driven by his evil, comes back to such a reprobate, he finds the sinner's mind cleansed from vices in baptism but in no way enriched with good work.

Then he takes seven. That is, all vices together. These spirits are said to be worse than the devil because, while the devil himself is evil, those who, urged by their merits, subject themselves to their vices are not simply evil but try to make themselves appear good when in their hypocrisy they pretend to be virtuous.

And a man's last state becomes. It is better not to know the way of truth than after knowing it to turn back again.

Blessed. Here Mary is praised, who bore Our Lord. In this the depravity of the Jews present [at the miracle] as well as of future heretics who deny Christ's true humanity is confounded, because against the blaspheming Jews the speaker confesses that Christ is the Son of

God and witnesses that he is a true son of a human being, of the same nature as his mother. For unless he were of the same flesh as his mother, the womb and breasts of the Virgin could hardly be called "blessed."

And the breasts. As physicians say, from one and the same wellspring flow both milk to nourish children and seed to engender them.[9] Hence Jesus could be conceived from the seed of the Virgin, as he could be nourished by her milk.

Yes indeed. As if to say: Mary, who carried the Word of God in her womb, is not only praiseworthy but most highly blessed because she observed God's commandments in her deeds. So also all are blessed who conceive the Word of God through the hearing of faith and give birth to and nourish the guarding of a good deed in their own heart and in that of their neighbors.

Who hear. In praise of the church. In contrast the Pharisees are condemned for not seeking to hear and fulfill God's word but rather to blaspheme.

9. Cf. Aristotle, *Historia animalium* 3.20.

3

JOHN FELTON ON THE SAME GOSPEL

A PARISH PRIEST, vicar of the church of St. Mary Magdalene in Oxford from 1397 to 1434, John Felton did not hold a university degree yet became famous as a preacher. By 1431 he had composed a regular cycle of sermons for the Sundays through the church year, almost all based on the gospel readings. As he explained in a short preface to the cycle, he made a *compilatio* "from the crumbs that fell from the tables of my lords—[the masters] of Genoa, Paris, Lyons, Odo, and others,"[1] and evidently noted their names in the margins of his manuscript.[2] Apparently he also drew material from the large sermon cycle of his near contemporary Philip Repingdon, then bishop of Lincoln, without acknowledging such debt.[3] Felton thus gathered as much material for a given Sunday sermon as he could lay hands

1. I.e., Jacobus a Voragine ("Januensis," d. c. 1298), William Peraldus (d. perhaps 1271), Nicholas de Aquavilla (early fourteenth century?), and Odo of Cheriton (d. 1247). Referring to Nicholas de Aquavilla as "Lugdunensis" is odd, since this is the usual appellation for Peraldus, who belonged to the Dominican convent at Lyon and was thought to have been archbishop of that city. But the passages in Felton marked "Lugdunensis" are indeed from the sermons of Nicholas de Aquavilla.

2. But not all surviving manuscripts have preserved all such annotations.

3. Bishop of Lincoln 1404–20, died in 1424. His sermons have been studied by Simon Forde, "Writings of a Reformer: A Look at Sermon Studies and Bible Studies through Repingdon's *Sermones Super Evangelia Dominicalia*" (Ph.D. diss., University of Birmingham, 1985). See also Wenzel, *Collections*, 50–53.

on or saw fit to write up, for the use of poor students and preachers who could not afford to purchase many books, thus creating a model sermon collection. The cycle has been preserved in at least twenty-nine manuscripts.

Having selected a short passage from the gospel lection as his thema, Felton begins the sermon with an address and the invitation to pray, and then gives an introduction to the thema (in this case, by connecting this day's gospel with those of the preceding two Sundays, in a pattern of four kinds of temptation). Next he establishes a division, whose four parts he develops; and he ends with the standard closing formula (for an outline of the main parts of the scholastic sermon structure, see the headnote to selection 4; for other and clearer examples in Felton's collection, see below, selection 12, and *Collections*, 55–57). After developing the four parts, Felton adds some more material relevant to the sermon's general topic, confession.

SOURCE:

Oxford, Bodleian Library, MS Bodley 187, fols. 36ra–39vb (FE-19), with some readings supplied from Lincoln Cathedral, MS 204, fols. 30vb–33vb, where the Oxford manuscript has a defective leaf.

LITERATURE:

Wenzel, *Collections*, 54–57

Alan J. Fletcher, "'Magnus Predicator et Deuotus': A Profile of the Life, Work, and Influence of the Fifteenth-Century Oxford Preacher, John Felton," *Mediaeval Studies* 53 (1991): 125–75; reprinted with additions in Fletcher, *Preaching, Politics and Poetry in Late-Medieval England* (Dublin: Four Courts Press, 1998), 58–118, with edition and translation of two Felton sermons.

The mute man spoke, Luke 11.

Friends: we need God's grace. This is shown in the crafts.[4] As an apprentice in any craft whatever receives its skill from his master or

---

4. In this sermon Felton several times adduces proof from *natura, arte, et figura,* "nature, the crafts, and biblical figures." *Arte,* "art," or better, "the crafts," here and in other

teacher, so a human being receives wisdom from God's word as if from the chief teacher and artisan of all things, for according to Augustine, in the first book of his *Retractions*, there is no other master teaching man knowledge but God;[5] Matthew 23[:9]: "One is your master," Christ. And there is the example of the scribe's pen, which in no way traces a letter unless it is moved by the power and skill of the scribe. The Psalmist says: "My tongue is the pen of a scribe" [44:2], which the Gloss explains is the Holy Spirit. Therefore, pray, etc.

The mute man spoke.[6] Since the devil does not leave off tempting the faithful, and particularly in this season,[7] the church keeps the faithful eager and attentive during these three Sundays so that they may be on their guard against his plots and tricks. Some he tempts but never conquers, namely, spiritual and strong men; their temptation is shown in the temptation of Christ, whom the devil tempted but could not overcome.[8] Others he tempts and conquers and troubles through various vices; such are those who live in sin, and their temptation is shown in the daughter of the Canaanite woman, who said, "My daughter is grievously troubled by a demon."[9] Yet others he tempts and overcomes, but is driven out by contrition and confession; those are penitent men and women, whose temptation is indicated in the possessed man [of today's gospel,] of whom it is said that "Jesus drove out a demon." And still others he tempts and overcomes and is then driven out from them, but he still returns to them; such are those who relapse, whose temptation is shown in the words "When the unclean spirit has gone out of a man," etc.

We should know that wherever the demon's wickedness abounds, divine mercy abounds even more. In that possessed man the demon's wickedness abounded very much, for he held him in his possession

---

sermons refers to human skills and techniques, ranging from agriculture to poetry and painting.

5. Augustine, *Retractationes* 1.12.

6. Some manuscripts of Felton's sermons indicate marginally the source of this paragraph: "Januensis," i.e., Jacobus a Voragine. But Felton's text here and throughout agrees more closely with the corresponding sermon by Philip Repingdon.

7. I.e., Lent.

8. Matthew 4:1–11, in the gospel for the first Sunday of Lent.

9. Matthew 15:22, in the gospel for the second Sunday of Lent.

and had rendered him blind and mute, and according to Chrysostom also deaf. But God's mercy abounded in him because—

> it cast out the demon from the possessed man,
> it gave him back his speech,
> it recovered his sight,
> and it restored his hearing.

By this man who was thus healed we can understand a sinner who is justified, to whom God spiritually gives the four gifts just mentioned.

[1]
First, he casts out the devil from him. A sinner allows the devil to reside in the house of his soul, but Christ casts him out like a bad renter. There are four reasons for which someone may be legally expelled from a rented house: when he does not pay his rent, or when he turns the house to evil use, or when the house threatens to go to pieces and needs repair, or when the owner needs a place to live.[10] For these four reasons the devil can be justly expelled from the house of God. First, because he prevents the sinner from paying rent. God has given a human being three things for which he wants to have rent, namely, his body, his soul, and his earthly possessions. From the body God wants fasting, from the soul, devout prayers, from earthly possessions, alms. But the devil prevents fasting, for to him it is poison, as Ambrose says: "The spittle of a man who is fasting is poison for a serpent."[11] He also prevents prayers, for to him they are a firebrand; Tobit 6[:8]: "If you put a small piece of its heart on the fire, its smoke drives away all kinds of demons." He further prevents almsgiving, which to him is a lance or dart; whence it is said of almsgiving in Sirach 29[:18] that "it

---

10. In Felton's remote source, the second sermon for this Sunday by Jacobus a Voragine ("Januensis"), the four reasons are said to be *secundum iura,* "according to the laws." The reference seems to be to the *Decretals* of Gregory IX (d. 1241), *Extravagantes* 3.28.3, the headnote, which refers to "Abbas" (evidently the commentator Abbot Bernard de Montmirat, d. 1296); see Aemilius [Emil] Friedberg, *Corpus iuris canonici,* 2 vols. (Leipzig: B. Tauchnitz, 1879; repr., Graz: Akademische Druck- und Verlagsanstalt, 1959), 2:521. Some late-medieval preachers were not only familiar with civil and canon law but actually quoted them in their sermons. For some examples, see below, Index, under "canon law" and "civil law"; and Wenzel, *Collections,* 18 and 159–63.

11. Ambrose, *Hexaemeron* 6.4.

will fight against your enemy better than the shield of the mighty and the lance." If someone cannot pay these three kinds of rent, let him at least pay two of them. Augustine says in his Homily 50: "Christians must not say, 'Let us eat and drink, for tomorrow we shall be dead,' but let them say, 'Let us fast, give alms, and pray.'"[12] But if they cannot say "let us fast," let them at least say, "Let us pray"; and if they cannot say, "Let us pray," they should at least say, "Let us give alms." For alms, fasting, and prayer lead to heaven. Therefore Augustine says in commenting on Psalm 50: "If you wish to fly to God, give your prayer two wings, namely, fasting and almsgiving."[13]

In the second place, the devil must be expelled because he turns God's house to evil use. He makes of it a stable of brute animals when in a man's soul brute and even devilish desires take their residence, as he places the filth of all sins in the soul, according to Revelation 18[:2]: "Babylon has become the residence of demons."

Third, he must be expelled because he ruins God's house and it needs repair. God has built the house of our soul from four-sided stones and in a foursquare. Isaiah 9[:10]: "The bricks have fallen and we shall build with square stones," and Revelation 21[:16]: "The city is set in a foursquare." This foursquare is made by faith, hope, love, and virtuous deeds, or the four cardinal virtues. Hence Gregory says: "In as much as you believe, hope; in as much as you believe and hope, love; and in as much as you believe, hope, and love, do good deeds." This foursquare the devil tries to destroy when he strives to carry off faith, hope, love, and good works, as Job 1[:19] says: "A violent wind has come from the desert region and has shaken the four corners of the house." Also, everyone should resist and make a shield of his faith— Ephesians 6[:16]: "In all things taking the shield of faith"—a helmet of hope, and a breastplate of love; 1 Thessalonians 5[:8]: "Let us put on the breastplate of faith and charity, and the helmet of hope of salvation." But on top of all his armor he should place good deeds, as his royal insignia; Romans 13[:14]: "Put on Our Lord Jesus Christ," that is, a good way of life and the deeds of Our Lord Jesus Christ.

And in the fourth place, the devil should be expelled because God

12. Augustine, *Sermon 150.*
13. Augustine, *Enarrationes in Psalmos,* on Psalm 42.

wants to dwell in that house of our soul. The house of our soul has three chambers: one above, namely, our spirit; one below, our body; and one in the middle, our soul. Of these three it is said in 1 Thessalonians 5[:21]: "May he, the God of peace, sanctify you in all things, so that your whole spirit and your body be kept without complaint in the coming of Our Lord Jesus Christ." For God lives in the higher chamber when our spirit, in its higher part, devotes itself to contemplation. For then he comes to such a person and dwells with him; John 14[:23]: "We shall come to him and dwell with him." He dwells in the lower chamber, that is, in the body, when our body is trained in the good and is mortified with regard to carnal desires, according to Galatians 5[:24]: "Those who belong to Christ have crucified their flesh with its vices and evil desires"; and Galatians 6[:17]: "I bear the marks of the Lord Jesus in my body." And God dwells in the middle chamber, our soul, when it is filled with cleanness; Wisdom 7[:27]: "Through nations Wisdom conveys herself into holy souls." "Holy" means the same as "pure." With respect to these three it is said in Psalm 76[:7]: "I have meditated in the night with my heart"—referring to the high contemplation of our spirit; "and I was exercised"—referring to the chastising of our bodies; "and I swept my spirit"—referring to our soul's internal purgation.

[2]

The second gift is that God loosens the sinner's tongue. God gave man a tongue to use for three good things: to praise God—Isaiah 43[:21]: "I have made this people so that they will tell my praise"; to edify his neighbor—Isaiah 50[:4]: "He has given me a learned tongue so that I may know how to uphold with my word him who has fallen"; and to blame himself before God and accuse himself—Job 42[:6]: "Therefore I reprehend myself and do penance." But a sinner does not use his tongue for these three purposes, and thus with good reason he is called mute, Psalm 37[:14?]. He is called mute because he does not praise God but instead blasphemes him through every evil deed. Hence when the Psalmist invites all creatures to praise God, he invites among others dragons, demons, hell, and serpents, as he says: "Praise the Lord, you dragons and all you deeps" [Psalm 148:7]. And further in the same place: "Serpents and feathered fowl" [10]. He never invites the proud, greedy, and lecherous to God's praise, because such people do not praise God but blaspheme him, and therefore they seem to be worse than serpents, dragons, and hell.

A man is secondly called mute when he does not edify his neighbor but instead gives scandal. Sirach 28[:16]: "The third tongue has disquieted many and scattered them from nation to nation." There are three kinds of tongues, namely, a godlike one, which by its nature speaks of things that belong to eternal salvation; as when Peter said to the Lord, John 6[:69]: "You have the words of eternal life." And this is the tongue of the perfect. The second kind is human, which always speaks of the world and of things that belong to our human needs; John 8[:23]: "You who are of this world," etc. "They speak of the world, and the world hears them" [1 John 4:5]. And that is the tongue of the imperfect. The third tongue is diabolical, whose nature it is to backbite and to speak lies; John 8[:44]: "When he speaks a lie, he speaks on his own." That tongue also customarily sows discord, for the devil himself sowed discord between himself and God, and further between God and man. And nowadays he frequently sows discords between people, and this is the tongue of backbiters and slanderers. But people who edify their neighbor speak the first tongue; those who speak of human things—that is, of their worldly business—speak the second tongue; and those who sow discord speak the third tongue. This third tongue does not only disturb neighbors but often breaks up marriages; Sirach 28[:19]: "The third tongue has cast out married women and deprived them of their labors."

The third kind of mute person is the sinner who does not accuse himself of sin in confession, whereas in Proverbs 18[:17] it is said, in another translation:[14] "The just accuses himself in the beginning." Sin has a beginning, namely, evil thought and evil delight. It also has a middle, namely, evil consent. And it has an end, namely, an evil deed. A just person, then, confesses not only his evil deeds but also his consent to evil and his evil thoughts and delights.

---

14. "Other" than Jerome's Vulgate, that is to say, one of the older Latin translations of the biblical texts. The "other translation" here cited reads *in principio*, "in the beginning," for the Vulgate's *prior*. See Petrus (Pierre) Sabatier, ed., *Bibliorum Sacrorum latinae versiones antiquae*, 3 vols. (Rheims: Reginald Florentain, 1743; repr., Turnhout: Brepols, 1976), 2:325.

[3]

The third gift is that God restores the sinner's eyesight. The sign that a sinner has become enlightened is when he can see in front, behind, to the right, and to the left, as is said of the holy animals in Revelation 4[:6] that they were "full of eyes, before, and behind," and roundabout on the right and on the left. One has eyes behind if one considers and reflects on the sins one has committed and has remorse for them; Isaiah 38[:15]: "I will recount to you all my years in the bitterness of my soul." One has eyes in front if one discerns and thinks about God's judgment and fears it; "I am afraid of your judgments," says the Psalmist [118:120], and Job 31[:14]: "What shall I do when God rises in judgment? and when he examines, what shall I answer him?" One sees to one's right when one reflects on how transitory and vain the world's riches are, and hence is not drawn to them with love but rather resists them with disdain; Nahum 3[:7]: "All who will see you will shrink back from you." And one sees to one's left when one perceives how brief and useful the world's tribulations are and thus is not broken by them through impatience or despair. That they are short and useful is said in 2 Corinthians 4[:17]: "What in the present is momentary and light," etc. For this reason (as is said in Exodus 14), when the children of Israel were fleeing from the Egyptians, they had a thick cloud behind them, a shining column before them, and to their right and left the sea like a wall. So, whoever wishes to evade the persecution of the Egyptians, that is, of the demons, must have a dark cloud behind him, namely, constant reflection on his sins, because sins are dark since they render the soul dark; and they are clouds since they hinder our prayers from coming to God; Lamentations 3[:44]: "You have set a cloud before you that your prayer may not pass through." The sea symbolizes the world. It sometimes stands like a wall on the right when it cannot move our mind to intemperance through its prosperity, and sometimes like a wall on the left when it cannot break our spirit by impatience through its adversity. To be thus surrounded by walls the Apostle taught us in 2 Corinthians 6[:7]: "Through the armor of justice on the right hand and on the left."

[4]

The fourth gift is that God restores the sinner's hearing. A sinner is deaf because he does not hear God when he warns him, nor when he bestows on him a benefit, nor when he inspires him, nor when he threatens him. These four God laments when he says, in Proverbs 1[:24–25]: "I called and you refused," that is, when a sinner does not hear God in his warning; "I stretched out my hand," offering you many benefits, "and there was none that took heed," because the sinner does not hear God when he bestows benefits; "you have despised all my counsels," which I inspired in you, because the sinner does not hear God when he inspires him; "you have neglected my reprehensions," because the sinner does not hear God when he threatens. But such a deaf person receives his hearing when he hears God speaking, as in the Psalm [84:9]: "I will hear what the Lord God speaks in me, because he speaks peace to his people."

Now[15] we should notice that the devil is driven from a person spiritually in seven ways. First by hearing the divine word. This is prefigured in 1 Samuel 16[:23], where it is said that "David took the harp, and Saul felt better." The harp symbolizes holy doctrine. Second, the devil is cast out by water, as the devil flees from a drowning man he had inhabited, not wanting to drown himself. This is true of the water of tears and of salutary wisdom. The Psalmist says: "You have crushed the heads of dragons in the waters" [73:13]. He who totally commits himself to study immerses himself in the water of wisdom, etc., and then the devil will leave him alone. This happens to students who at home lead an evil life, but in studying at Paris or Oxford live in a good state. Third, the devil is cast out through prayer. Tobit 6[:8]: "The angel said to Tobit, 'Put a small piece of its heart on the coals, its smoke drives away every kind of demons.'" The smoke from the small part of the heart laid on the coals is the devotion of prayer. A small part of our heart is laid on the coals when our affect is kindled by the fire of divine love. Fourth, the devil is cast out through fasting, just as hunger makes a

---

15. In some manuscripts this paragraph is marginally attributed to "Parisiensis," i.e., William Peraldus. The text can be found in the third sermon for this Sunday by Peraldus.

wolf leave the forest. Mark 9[:28]: "This kind cannot leave through anything except prayer and fasting." Matthew 12[:43]: "When the unclean spirit has gone out of a person, he wanders through dry places, seeking rest and not finding it." Fifth, the devil is cast out by the rod of discipline. Proverbs 22[:15]: "Folly is bound up in the heart of a child, and the rod of discipline will drive it away." We read about blessed Benedict that by flogging he drove the devil from a monk who used to leave the choir whenever the brethren put themselves to prayer.[16] Sixth, the devil is cast out by shouts and much noise, like a wolf. But nowadays people shout more loudly against sheep and lambs than against wolves. Isaiah 58[:1]: "Cry out and do not cease!" Seventh, the serpent from hell is cast out from a man as it were piecemeal: his tail is cast out when one abandons the external deed of sin; his middle part, when one abandons the will to sin or thinking about sin; and his head, when one abandons one's wrongful intention. Sirach 15 [25:22]: "There is no head worse than the head of a serpent"; and 21[:2]: "Flee from sins as from the face of a serpent."

We should know that seven things can lead sinners to confess their sins.[17] First, the great danger they are in. Second is the easiness of healing. Third is the slightness of the vexation [of going to confession]. Fourth is the evil result of remaining silent in this life. Fifth is the evil result of this in the future life. Sixth is the good that comes from confessing in this life. And seventh is the good that comes from it in the future life. The first two points can be proven together. But they cannot be proven except to the eyes of the heart, for they are spiritual and invisible to bodily eyes. We should therefore realize that while someone is in mortal sin, he is without question in the devil's mouth; Job 36[:16]: "He shall save you out of the narrow mouth that is bottomless." The devil's mouth is narrow for those who want to get out, but very wide for one who enters. Having seen how great the danger is, consider how easy is the healing: the very nature of wild animals teaches it, because when they are captured they shriek. You yourself do not have to shriek—it is enough to speak quietly and show your crimes

16. Gregory, *Vita sancti Benedicti* 4 (PL 66:142).

17. The seven things that can lead a person to confession are taken from the fourth sermon for this Sunday by Peraldus and also appear in Repingdon's sermon. Felton reorders several points and adds some material.

to a priest. Furthermore, a person in mortal sin suffers from the most dangerous leprosy, through which he is cut off from the fellowship of God and the angels. He can be easily cleansed of this leprosy by washing himself; 2 Kings 5[:10]: "Go and wash seven times in the Jordan, and your flesh will recover its health." To wash seven times in the Jordan is to confess the seven criminal sins. This washing does not cost much, since it is done by speech alone. "If the prophet had told you to do some great thing," the servants tell Naaman, "you would have done it. How much rather since he has said, 'Wash and you will be clean'?" [2 Kings 5:13]. A person in mortal sin is also in heavy debt and to be handed over to the eternal prison unless he pays off his debt. But one can pay one's debt in large part by a simple reckoning. Therefore, one who does not pay off his debt will justly go to prison; Matthew 18[:34]: "In his anger his lord handed him over to the torturers until he had paid all his debt." Concerning the third point, we should notice that many people are hindered from confessing their sins by shame. But that hindrance is very slight. To be afraid of being ashamed of one's sins which one is sorry for is like being afraid of the Egyptians and the army of the Pharaoh from hell who have already been cast into the Red Sea, namely, by the bitterness of one's contrition. What a strange timidity of those who do not dare speak of the dead! They are very foolish who are afraid that the priest might shudder at their sins. They don't realize that the priest is used to them and thinks of them as nonexistent once he sees and realizes his penitent's good will. In this way Balaam, who was used to portents, did not become terrified at the voice of his ass (Numbers 22). Such people fear their priest may think of them as very evil when they confess horrible sins. But on the contrary the priest may well think they are good, for he knows that by a true confession sins are forgiven, and he can presume that the person who confesses a horrible sin would also confess others he might have. And so he can believe that his penitent is good and, as it were, holy, since his sins have disappeared in confession. Nobody who has washed well is to be believed dirty, and nobody whose sickness has been healed is to be believed ill, nor can someone who has informed on traitors or killed them be believed to be his prince's enemy. Moreover, what harm is there for the penitent if his priest should have a poor opinion of him? Is the sinner worth less for that? Or does the sinner want to sell himself to the priest that he wishes to be thought of great value by him? In the fourth place we should notice that in this life concealing one's sins has many evil consequences, such as being mocked by the demons. For the demons can mock persons who do not dare confess their sins and say: "Look at that fool who lets himself be robbed and does not know how to cry out, what every dumb animal knows how to do!" He does not know how to open the door of his mouth—though it has neither key nor seal—that he may be freed from the danger of imprisonment; a child of seven years could do that! The priest who should free him keeps him in bonds,[18] for the sins he does not confess burden him like a heavy load. Further, he is held in detention in the devil's prison. About the fifth point we must notice that the evil that follows from such silence in the future is one's eternal damnation; Sirach 4[:25]: "There is a shame that brings ignominy," and Nahum 3[:5]: "I will discover your shame to your face and will show your nakedness to the nations," and Jeremiah 20[:11]: "They will be greatly confounded because they have not understood the reproach that will never be effaced with oblivion." On the sixth point we should notice that confession leads to many good things in this life, such as the sinner's disburdening. After confessing a sin that he had been much afraid to confess, a sinner feels as if he has been freed from a great burden. Second is the rejoicing of the heavenly court; Luke 15[:7]: "There is joy among God's angels over one sinner who does penance." Further, the demons' disappointment; Judith 14[:16]: "One Hebrew woman has made much confusion in the house of Nebuchadnezzar." Nebuchadnezzar means "sitting in anguish" and indicates the devil. In his house is made much pain and anguish when someone makes a true confession. Further, rising from spiritual death; Luke 15[:32]: "Your brother was dead and has come to life again." The result of confession, namely, the justification of the sinner, is not less than creating heaven and earth, in Augustine's words.[19] And on the seventh point we should notice that the future good that comes from confession is our eternal glory; Sirach 4[:24]: "For the sake of your soul do not be ashamed to say the truth; for shame brings glory."

18. The Latin of this sentence is not entirely clear.
19. Perhaps Augustine, *Sermo 217*, 11.

We should further know that confession cleanses from the sin of the mouth.[20] This can be illustrated with examples from nature, crafts, and biblical figures. First from nature. Just as some healthy vomiting expels and cleans out slime and impurity from our stomach and gullet, so confession expels the sin and filth of our mouth. Augustine says in one of his sermons: "Our heart is oppressed with the intoxication of iniquity, and confession spits it out. But let it not return like a dog to its own vomit."[21] This is secondly shown by illustrations from crafts. Confession is like a file that cleanses, files, and polishes the tongue after it has become rusty and darkened through undisciplined talk, just as a sword gleams after it has been filed and burnished; Ezekiel 21[:10]: "The sword has been filed so that it may gleam." But there are many wretched and idle people who carry a rusty sword but neglect to file and polish it in confession. These in fact do not fear God, for Ecclesiastes 7[:19] says: "He who fears God neglects nothing." Third, it is shown in biblical figures. In 1 Maccabees 4[:49] we read that Judas made new holy vessels of the temple because they had been defiled by the Gentiles. Judas means "confessing." But the holy vessel of God's temple that has been defiled is a filthy mouth. Judas makes new vessels when anyone who truly confesses makes his mouth new in his pure confession, as it were, and sanctifies what had been made filthy and desecrated through his foolish and vile speech; Isaiah 52[:11]: "Make yourselves clean, you who carry the vessels of the Lord." For our mouth is the vessel of the Lord, which we carry with us and must cleanse in confession. This much in the bishop of Lincoln's *On the Tongue*, part 2, chapter 28.[22]

That delay in confession is ruinous is shown in examples from nature, the crafts, and biblical figures. First in examples from nature, because it torments, it brings harm, and it defiles. First, it torments: just as a wound that is full of poison stings, hurts, burns, and cannot be at rest until it is opened and the poison is taken out, so is it spiritually

20. In the next four paragraphs Felton uses, with acknowledgment, material from the treatise *De lingua*, which in the Middle Ages was commonly attributed to Robert Grosseteste, bishop of Lincoln from 1235 to 1253.

21. Augustine, *Sermo 9.*

22. The quoted material occurs in London, British Library, MS Arundel 200, fol. 108r-v.

with our conscience when it is full of the poison of sin. Gregory says: "For closed sores torment the more; since, when the corruption that is hot within is cast out, the pain is exposed for healing."[23] Delay also brings harm. Our sensitive life is the principle of our senses and motion, such as seeing, hearing, walking, and other actions of our soul. And as it is unnatural for someone to speak, walk, or act unless he has this life, so is it spiritually not possible for a man to have the spiritual sense of loving God, nor the motion of working well, of fasting, and of other similar acts, unless these be grounded on the [spiritual] life in him which comes from true confession and true penitence. Bernard says: "Without confession a just man is deemed to be ungrateful, and a sinner is considered to be dead. Indeed, 'from a dead man confession perishes' as from one who does not exist, Sirach 17[:26]. Therefore, confession is life for a sinner, glory for the just man."[24] And thus in a sinner this life must come before so that the true works of life can follow. Further, delaying confession or penitence defiles a person. Overripe offspring and fruit are considered of less worth and quality; those ripened at the peak of the season, of higher quality and more precious. So it is also in spiritual matters, regarding the offspring and fruit of penance at the beginning of Lent and at its end, or else in one's youth and in one's old age: the first is better and more acceptable to God, the latter of lower quality; the former is more precious, the latter of lesser value. Genesis 30[:41]: "Those that were late become Laban's, and they of the first time, Jacob's." And in the [Mosaic] Law they offered "first fruits to the Lord," Exodus 23[:19].

How ruinous the delay of confession is, is secondly shown in examples from the crafts. First, because such delay is harmful to God. For if someone knowingly receives a traitor to the king in his chamber and, having been warned, will not expel him or delays in doing so, would he not, too, be a traitor and wondrously harmful to the king and deserve fitting punishment? Matthew 12[:45]: "They enter in and dwell there"; Ephesians 4[:27]: "Do not give place to the devil"— and especially if by chance some room has been given him, he must at once be expelled by the fear of God; Sirach 1[:27]: "The fear of

---

23. Gregory, *Regula pastoralis* 3.14 (PL 77:72).
24. Bernard of Clairvaux, *Sermones de diversis* 40.2.

the Lord drives out sin." Further, such delay is shameful. In physical battle it is not shameful if one falls in a strait, but it is most shameful if one lies prostrate, oppressed, and overcome under one's enemy, especially if one had a model and help available to rise and overthrow one's enemy. Thus also in our moral case: it would redound to one's glory if after a fall one were to rise as soon as possible and henceforth act bravely; Jeremiah 8[:4]: "Shall he who falls not rise again, and he who is turned away not turn again?" Such delay is also injurious. For it would be a shortsighted farmer who eagerly puts seed into the soil before he has opened it with his plow and by cultivation made it ready to receive the seed. He would waste a good deal of the seed and of his labor. Thus also in our moral life. To sow seed in the soil is to do works of penance, such as fasting, praying, and the like. Before that, the soil must be worked and opened up with the plow of confession, or else much of the effort of such labor is lost; Deuteronomy 28[:38]: "You will cast much seed into the ground and gather little," and Haggai 1[:6]: "You have sowed much and brought in little." Thus it goes with people who sow the works of penitence while they are in mortal sin and either neglect or postpone making their confession.

Third, how ruinous it is to delay confession is shown in biblical figures. First in the Old Testament. The people of Israel hastened to escape from the rule of Pharaoh, and when the time to leave came, they did not tarry but at the Lord's command readied themselves in every way, as is shown in Exodus 12. Likewise, a sinner must not tarry or dawdle in any way to turn to God through true penitence, especially in this season of escaping from the rule of the devil; Sirach 5[:8]: "Do not delay to be converted to the Lord." For such people are the last to come and bring the king back to his house, 2 Samuel 19[:11]. And further, in the New Testament we read about Lazarus that at the Lord's command "he at once came forth" from the tomb, "he who had been dead," John 11[:43–44]. Thus it must be with a sinner, otherwise his delay or tarrying will be imputed to him as a sin, Deuteronomy 23[:21]. All this is from the bishop of Lincoln's book *On the Tongue,* part 3, chapter 17.[25]

Note[26] about the man near Bristol with a straw in his mouth. Fur-

---

25. Cf. *De lingua,* MS Arundel 200, fols. 143r–v.

26. The verb form *nota* in sermons not only calls attention to something ("no-

ther about the nun who was damned because she was ashamed to confess.[27] Also about the woman from London to whom Christ showed
his heart and made her touch it, whose hands were all bloody when
she woke up.[28] And about the recluse who saw demons and heard one
say that a young girl in the city was ashamed to confess some mortal
sin as she was dying because he was holding her by the throat.[29] And
about a man who had been the devil's companion for a long time, but
after his confession the devil did not recognize him.[30] And about the
demoniac who told many what kind of people they were; to one he
said: "You are such and such a man" and told him many sins. The
man left at once, confessed, and then asked the demoniac: "What do
you say about me?" and the demoniac replied: "I never knew you."[31]
Further, about the hermit who saw a devil reading the names of those
whom he had caused to sin, and the hermit asked him, "Do you have
my name there?" And the devil said, "Yes." The hermit turned away
with grief and firmly resolved to confess, and at once a teardrop fell
from his eye. Then he asked the devil, "Where is my name?" and the
devil said, "Alas, that you have come here. A drop just fell from the air
and deleted your name."[32] Hence the Psalmist says: "Blessed are they
whose iniquities are forgiven and whose sins are covered" [Psalm 31:1],
to which a gloss adds: they are covered [i.e., hidden] from the devil
that he may not accuse, from God that he may not punish, and from
the angels and saints that they may not blush [before them]. Also note
about the slothful king, in *The Deeds of the Romans*, who had three sons
that were as slothful as their father. The first of them said that, if he

---

tice!") but may also signal that the preacher should "tell" or narrate the story that follows. The stories assembled in this paragraph, except for the first, are all well-known
illustrations of the danger of delaying confession and can be found in several *exempla*
collections.

27. Perhaps Tubach, no. 1188.a.4.

28. Tubach, no. 2416, to which other works can be added (see *Fasciculus morum*
497). The story is not always located in London, as here and in the *Speculum laicorum*
(also quoted in P2-22).

29. A version of Tubach, no. 4851.

30. Cf. Tubach, no. 2414.

31. A version of Tubach, nos. 1202.c or 1513 and similar stories.

32. Tubach, no. 4421.

were lying by the fire, and the fire were to touch his feet, he would rather let his feet burn than trouble to pull them away. The second said that, if he were lying in bed and it were raining on his head and his eyes, he would not turn his head for his sloth. And the third said: "If I were being dragged to the gallows with a little rope and had a sword in my hand, I would rather let myself be hanged than raise my hand to cut that rope." And the king said: "There is no doubt that you are my sons, and I shall divide my kingdom among you."[33] This king represents the devil; the first son, those who will not withdraw their love from low pleasures; the second, those who look at women and lust for them but will not withdraw their eyes; and the third, those who are dragged to the gallows of hell by the devil's rope, that is, mortal sin, and will not confess. But the children of God proceed in the opposite way.

Notice further that the devil does his best to prevent one's confession.[34] This can be seen in examples from nature, the crafts, and scriptural figures. First in nature. Note how the wolf particularly, when he has caught a sheep, holds it by its throat, so that it may not call out and thereby perhaps save itself from his power. The devil does the same to the sheep of Christ lest it confess. Second, in crafts. When a thief wants to rob a house where there is a dog, his craft is to give the dog some meat so that it won't bark, and then he enters and takes any precious objects. In the same way the devil. And while this example applies especially to curates who, according to Isaiah 56[:10], are "dumb dogs not able to bark," it can also refer to anyone who is unwilling to confess—as the Psalmist says, "all iniquity shall stop his mouth" [Psalm 106:42]. And third, in scripture. This can be found under the thema "Jesus was casting out a demon." This demon is called "mute" from his having made the man mute. Likewise in a biblical *figura*.[35] 1 Maccabees 7[:26–47] reports how Nicanor wanted to kill Ju-

33. A variant of Tubach, nos. 2896 and 3005; see *Gesta Romanorum* 91, in *Gesta Romanorum*, ed. Hermann Oesterley (Berlin: Weidmann, 1872; repr., Hildesheim: Georg Olms, 1963), 418–19.

34. This topic can be found in many places, including Repingdon's sermon.

35. In sermon rhetoric *figura* refers to a biblical person, event, or (as here) story that is used allegorically to prove a point.

das Maccabee treacherously but did not succeed. Then he attacked Judas openly with his great army, but he fell in battle and his head was cut off. Nicanor means "a standing light" and indicates the devil: as long as he stood [firm], he carried a light, but afterward he brought darkness.[36] And Judas means "confessing," whom the devil tries to deceive if he can close his mouth, so that he may not confess. But "Confessing" must rise against the devil in battle and confess his sins, and thereby cut off his head, that is, his power. Which Christ may grant us. Amen.

36. Referring to the fall of Lucifer, formerly the brightest angel.

4

AN ANONYMOUS SERMON
ON THE SAME GOSPEL

BASED ON BIBLICAL COMMENTARY, postils, or model sermon cycles, preachers could then shape a "real" or genuine sermon. In doing so, they were free to choose their thema and the basic sermon format and to employ appropriate rhetorical devices (see *Collections*, 354–69). This final stage is shown in the following sermon, which comes from a random collection of anonymous sermons that were evidently preached in several small parishes in the English Midlands. Here the preacher draws on several of the commonplaces brought together by Felton and his predecessors in their works on the Sunday gospel, but instead of dealing with the entire lection, he selects and concentrates on a single verse from it, the thema. The sermon is quite unpretentious in its content and style, but it demonstrates neatly the basic structure of a scholastic sermon and its constituent elements, which may be outlined as follows:

[1] Thema
[2] Protheme: an introductory section that opens the sermon, often with an image or even a different biblical text, and then frequently leads to an invitation to pray, commonly the Our Father and Hail Mary.
[3] Restatement of thema
[4] Introduction of the thema
[5] Restatement of the thema

[6] Division of the thema into two or more principal parts[1]

[7] Development of the principal parts

[8] Closing formula: a form of "May he grant us this who [with the Father and the Holy Spirit] lives and rules forever and ever," in the manuscripts usually abbreviated with "etc."

This structure was taught by contemporary handbooks on preaching, the *artes praedicandi*, and was indeed followed universally, with minor modifications used by individual preachers.[2] All eight parts are present in this sermon and have been indicated by numbers in square brackets.

For the collection, see also below, selection 6.

SOURCE:

Cambridge, University Library, MS Kk.4.24, fols. 292vb–294rb (B/2-86).

LITERATURE:

Wenzel, *Collections*, 136–39.

Th.-M. Charland, *Artes Praedicandi: Contribution à l'histoire de la rhétorique au moyen âge* (Paris: De Vrin, 1936).

James J. Murphy, *Rhetoric in the Middle Ages: A History of Rhetorical Theory from Saint Augustine to the Renaissance* (Berkeley and Los Angeles: University of California Press, 1974), 269–355.

❧

[1] **Jesus was casting out a demon, and that was mute,** Luke 11, and in today's gospel.

[2] Dearly beloved, the name "Jesus" is a word of the greatest piety and love, for it means "savior," as Luke 1[:31] says: "You will call his name Jesus, for he will save his people from their sins." Whence the Apostle says in his epistle to the Corinthians 12: "No one can say 'Lord' except in the Holy Spirit" [1 Corinthians 12:3]. Augustine discusses this

---

1. The parts of the division are often "confirmed" with authoritative quotations from scripture or some other source. Such confirmation can be seen, for instance, on pp. 147–52, 196–219, and 257.

2. On sermon form, see also *Collections*, 11–16.

in chapter 10 of his work *On the Trinity:* "No one can pronounce this name 'Jesus' with love and pleasure except in the Holy Spirit,"[3] whereas of something unpleasant people can speak with indifference. But "not everyone who says 'Lord, Lord' enters the kingdom of heaven" [Matthew 7:21], for no one can meaningfully pronounce or hear the word of God except through the grace of the Spirit, for Christ says, "Without me you can do nothing" [John 15:5]. And the Apostle in his epistle to the Corinthians: "We are not sufficient to think anything on our own" [2 Corinthians 3:5]. Therefore, let us pray.

[3] **Jesus was casting out,** etc.

[4] Reverend sirs,[4] the gospel writer tells us today that a man who was mute and possessed by a demon was healed. In Matthew this man is said to have been not only mute but also blind, Matthew 12[:22], and he was healed by the Lord so that he could speak and see. And from this I take the words of my thema, "Jesus was casting out," etc., as already quoted. We can see that in one man three miracles were performed: a blind man sees, a mute man speaks, and a man possessed by a demon is made free. On that occasion this happened in the flesh, but nowadays it happens in the conversion of believers: after the demon has been driven out of them, they first see the light of faith, and then their tongues, which before had been silent, are loosened to praise God. This happens in baptism as well as in the sacrament of penance. Every catechumen is possessed by the demon until the latter is driven out of him by adjurations and exorcisms. So also everyone in mortal sin, until the demon is cast off through penance and confession. In neither case can he see the way of truth until he is enlightened by the grace of the sacrament, nor can he utter the praise of God as he should, because "there is no pleasing praise in the mouth of a sinner" [Sirach 15:9]. Hence in the conversion of such a man our thema is confirmed, [5] **Jesus was casting out,** etc.

---

3. Perhaps Augustine, *De Trinitate* 9.10 (PL 42:969).

4. Address forms like *Reverendi, Reverendi mei,* or *Reverendi domini* would indicate a clerical audience. "Beloved" or *Karissimi,* on the other hand, may be used for an audience of clerical brethren or for the laity. For further discussion of audience addresses, see *Collections,* 9–10 and passim.

[6] In these word we can consider three things:

A name of outstanding worth, **Jesus**;
an act of incomparable power, **was casting out a demon**;
the hiding of truth, **that was mute**.[5]

[7a] First, as I say, a name of outstanding worth is indicated, in **Jesus**. When in Acts 3 Peter had restored the ankles and feet[6] of a man who had a limp from birth to their firmness and was asked by the council in whose name he was doing this, he answered: "In the name of Jesus Christ of Nazareth, whom you have crucified" [Acts 4:10]. And he continued: "There is no salvation in anyone else, nor has another name under heaven been given to men in whom we must be saved" [Acts 4:12]. Bernard comments on this as follows: "If you write something, it won't please me unless I read 'Jesus' there. If you argue or tell me something, it won't please me unless it sounds the name of Jesus. 'Jesus' is honey in my mouth, a song in my ear, a hymn in my heart."[7] And in Acts 5[:41] "the apostles went rejoicing from the presence of the council, because they had been found worthy to suffer reproach for the name of Jesus." The devout pope John XXII granted an indulgence of twenty days to all who at the end of the Ave Maria would say "Jesus," knowing that "in the name of Jesus every knee must bend, in heaven," etc., "and under the earth," Philippians 2[:10]. And Urban IV granted thirty days,[8] so that anyone who has been contrite and has confessed his sins and says the Psalter of the Blessed Mary[9] daily, will have an indulgence of 24 years and 30 weeks; hence the total

5. Formal divisions in scholastic sermons, like the present one, were constructed with much verbal skill and ingenuity, using syntactic parallelism and end rhyme (in Latin as well as the vernacular). Cf. Siegfried Wenzel, *Preachers, Poets, and the Early English Lyric* (Princeton: Princeton University Press, 1986), 82–100.

6. Literally, feet and soles.

7. Bernard, *Super Cantica* 15.6.

8. John XXII (1316–34) and Urban IV (1261–64). On these two indulgences or pardons, see Nikolaus Paulus, *Geschichte des Ablasses im Mittelalter vom Ursprunge bis zur Mitte des 14. Jahrhunderts*, 3 vols. (Paderborn: Ferdinand Schöningh, 1922–23), 2:233–34.

9. The "Psalter of the Virgin Mary," as distinct from the (Little) Office of the Virgin, may refer to a series of verse prayers; see for instance Josef Szövérffy, *Die Annalen der lateinischen Hymnendichtung*, vol. 2: *Die lateinischen Hymnen vom Ende des 11. Jahrhunderts bis zum Ausgang des Mittelalters* (Berlin: Erich Schmitt, 1965), 305–6.

indulgence for one week amounts to 172 years. But the name of Jesus is taken very lightly by the enemies of Christ's cross. Every day and all day long they speak the name of Jesus without reverence, pronouncing it not only idly but also in false oaths. There is no child nowadays who can speak who does not swear by the most holy name of Jesus as well as by all the members of God.[10] For nowadays Christ is dismembered by men's tongues—Hebrews 6[:6]: "They crucify the Son of God again"—whereas in Exodus 20[:7] the command was given, "You shall not take the name of your God in vain," that is, a vow, for in every word a vow is given to God and an oath is doubled. Against this Ecclesiastes 5[:3] states: "A faithless and foolish promise displeases God." And Matthew similarly: "Let your speech be yes, yes; no, no" [Matthew 5:37]. And Sirach 23[:9]: "Let not your heart be accustomed to swearing, for in that are many falls." And again: "A man who swears much will be filled with iniquity, and the scourge will not depart from his house" [23:12]. Let us therefore hold this name of Jesus in great worship and reverence. In this name shines forth his mercy, because, as was said earlier, "Jesus" means "savior." That such swearing by the name or by the members of God is a mortal sin is proven as follows. God forbade our first parent in the state of innocence to eat from the tree of life [Genesis 2:16–17]; since he did eat, it is clear that he committed a mortal sin, and all mankind was condemned for this. But the commandment not to take his name in vain God gave more strictly and sternly than when he forbade him to eat from the tree of life; hence it is a greater commandment. The first commandment he gave to men only once verbally, but the other he gave not only verbally but two times and writing it with his own hand.[11] Now, the greater dignity a thing has, the more serious it is to sin against it. But God's name has a greater dignity than an apple; ergo, etc. Therefore, since all mankind was condemned on account of an apple eaten by one man and sent to hell for five thousand and eighty-three years, how long and how hard will he be punished in hell who offends against

10. In the later Middle Ages, "swearing by the members of God" or "dismembering Christ" with such oaths as "by God's heart" was considered a very grave sin. See for instance Chaucer, Parson's Tale, 591, and Pardoner's Tale, 472–75 and 651–54.

11. Exodus 20:7 and Deuteronomy 5:12.

and breaks this greater commandment a thousand times and more in a year? The prophet says: "The person who sins himself shall die; he will not bear the iniquity of his father, nor will a father bear the iniquity of his son" [Ezekiel 18:4, etc.], but everyone will bear his own burden. Therefore, as I said, let us hold the name of Jesus in great worship and reverence.

[7b] Second, our thema speaks of an act of incomparable power in saying "he was casting out a demon." An example of this is Matthew 17 [:14–17], about the man who brought Jesus his son who had an unclean spirit whom the disciples could not cast out, but Jesus himself drove him out at once. He does the same each time he justifies a person and calls him back from sins. That this is an act of great power is shown by Augustine in his comment on John 14[:12], "He will do greater things than this": "To justify a person is a greater thing than to create heaven."[12] The latter requires only one thing, namely, his will, when "he spoke and they were created" [Psalm 39:9]; but justifying a sinner requires two things: calling him back from sin and stirring him to do good. Both are done through his mercy. The Psalm declares: "His mercy is above all his works" [144:9]. Gregory says: "O God, you show your omnipotence most forcefully in sparing and being merciful."[13] How great it is for us that, after deserving hell for our mortal sin, we can through penance and your mercy return to heaven! In his work *On the Song of Songs* Bernard says: "Because of the gentleness that is asserted about you, Lord Jesus, we run after you, hearing that you do not abhor the poor sinner. You did not abhor the thief who confessed you, nor the sinning woman when she wept, nor the Canaanite woman [who implored you], nor the one caught in adultery, nor him who sat at the custom house, nor the tax collector when he prayed, nor your disciple [who denied you], nor the persecutor of your disciples,[14] nor even those who crucified you."[15] Since God is omnipotent and carries out his omnipotence most fully in being

12. Augustine, *In Johannis euangelium tractatus* 72.3.

13. From the Gelasian Sacramentary, *Liber sacramentorum*, PL 78:181, attributed to Gregory, whence it was used in the collect for 11 Trinity.

14. Saul, who then became the Apostle Paul.

15. Bernard, *Super Cantica* 22.8.

merciful, far be it that anyone should despair on account of his many sins, as Judas did when he fell into the sea of despair and hanged himself. Blessed Augustine says of him: "It was not only the crime he committed but his despair of receiving forgiveness that caused Judas the traitor to perish totally. He was not worthy of God's mercy. In his despair he killed himself and hanged himself. What he did to his body happened to his soul. Just as those who tie their neck and thereby kill themselves, for the flow of physical air no longer enters, so do they who despair of God's mercy stifle themselves inwardly in their despair so that the Holy Spirit can no longer come to them."[16] So far Augustine. But the Canaanite woman, when she came home, because of her faith found her daughter lying on her bed and the demon gone [Matthew 15:22–28].

[7c] In the third place the gospel speaks of the hiding of the truth, because **"that was mute."** The devil renders a man mute so that for shame he cannot make his confession. And this is most dangerous and does not help the weakness of his soul, for the sinner cannot give the devil greater pleasure than by hiding his thought; as is said in Proverbs 28[:13]: "He who hides his crimes will not prosper." Hence, before the mute man could speak, the demon was driven out. The same applies to your soul: first you must abandon sin and have true contrition before you can speak in confession. The *Decretum* says, in *On Penance*, distinction 1: "We must believe that without contrition no sin is forgiven,"[17] because in medicine illnesses are healed by their contraries.[18] As sin arose through illicit delight, so we must be sorry for it in contrition. Hence Augustine says: "It is fitting that our eternal salvation which was shamefully lost through lust must be regained through sorrow."[19] Thus, after the demon had been driven out, the mute man at once spoke.

16. Augustine, *Sermon 352* (PL 39:1558).

17. *Decretum*, De penitentia, dist. 1, c. 87 (Friedberg, *Corpus iuris canonici*, 1:1186).

18. The principle that "contraria contrariis curantur" derives from Hippocrates. In medieval spiritual literature from Cassian on (*Institutes* 12.8), it came to mean that in order to overcome an evil disposition one should practice its opposite virtue, such as humility against pride, etc.

19. Augustine, *De Genesi ad litteram* 3.15.

But we should notice that in confession a sinner must speak in three ways: humbly, truthfully, and with completeness. First he must speak humbly, that is, not defend his sin but confess it in humility, for according to Gregory, "these are the signs of true humility: to recognize one's guilt and to open up what has been thus recognized with the voice of confession,"[20] without in any way defending it, for according to Gregory in his *Morals*, book 33, "When the sum of our sins is defended, it increases; but when it is humbly acknowledged, it is canceled."[21] An example occurs in Matthew about the tax collector. When he said, "God, have mercy on me, a sinner," not daring to raise his head, he went back to his house justified [Luke 18:13–14]. Second, you must speak truthfully and not excuse yourself, for according to Gregory in book 22 of his *Morals*, "he who excuses his sins increases them."[22] Thus our first parents "hid themselves" [Genesis 3:8]. And the offspring that descended from Adam inherited that bitterness. When someone argues about his sin with words of self-defense, he as it were hides himself behind tree leaves. Such people do not deserve forgiveness. Therefore, speak your sin truthfully, so that you may gain forgiveness. We have a biblical figure in David, in 2 Samuel [12:13]. When he said "I have sinned," the prophet came to him at once and said, "The Lord has taken away your sin." And Sirach 4[:24]: "For [the sake of] your soul be not ashamed to say the truth." Third, you must confess your sins in completeness. Augustine says in a sermon: "Let the sinner be careful that in his shame he does not divide up his confession, so as to reveal different sins to different priests."[23] There are some people who hide some sins from one priest in order to confess them to another. This is the same as praising oneself and engaging in hypocrisy. Confession must be integral, so that every demon and every deadly and venial sin may be driven out. Luke 8[:2] furnishes an example, when the Lord drove out seven demons from a sinful woman once and all together. Thus, then, must a sinner confess humbly without self-defense, truthfully without excuses, and completely

20. Gregory, *Moralia* 22.15.
21. Ibid., 33.4.
22. Cf. ibid., 22.15.
23. Pseudo-Augustine, *De vera et falsa poenitentia* 15 (PL 40:1125).

without dividing his sins up, so that he can deserve to receive forgiveness of all his sins, and afterward merit that eternal glory which "eye has not seen, ear has not heard, nor has it entered man's heart, which God has prepared for those who love him" [1 Corinthians 2:9].

[8] May he kindly prepare this for us, he who with God the Father, etc.

5

ANOTHER ANONYMOUS SERMON ON THE SAME GOSPEL

THE FOLLOWING PIECE comes from a Benedictine collection that contains sermons by Oxford student monks of the early fifteenth century. It is addressed to a clerical audience and applies its thema to *ecclesiastici et religiosi*, that is, clerics or churchmen and members of a religious order. The anonymous preacher again chooses a part of the day's gospel reading, the healing of the mute man, but he uses it with a twist, giving muteness a positive meaning and developing the change from muteness to speech in three sections that utilize the medieval commonplace that human speech has three purposes. This is set out in the introduction, which then apparently leads to a request for prayer. The preacher's remarks at the end of the first and third principal parts, to the effect that he has developed his text as best he knows how, may indicate a student speaker, and possibly a Benedictine monk.

SOURCE:
Oxford, Bodleian Library, MS Laud misc. 706, fols. 82–86v (R-17). The unique copy is somewhat garbled.

LITERATURE:
Wenzel, *Collections*, 88–90.
P. J. Horner, "Benedictines and Preaching in Fifteenth-Century England:

The Evidence of Two Bodleian Library Manuscripts." *Revue Bénédictine* 99 (1989): 313–32.

~

The mute man spoke, Luke 11, and in today's gospel.

Reverend sirs, etc. God's immense goodness ordained all things he created in the beginning, both bodily and spiritually, for man's salvation and usefulness. Now, the Son of God, desiring to call back to his own domain man's soul, which he loved above all but which had been made a wretched captive by the devil, became man for that spiritual purpose. Therefore he worked literally a threefold miracle in the man who was possessed by the demon and was brought to him for a cure. For according to what is written in Matthew 12, which somewhat relates to today's gospel, a man was brought to Christ who had a demon and was blind and mute. And Christ healed him so that he could speak and see, because Christ opened his mouth to speak, restored his sight, and freed him from the demon's vexation. By this visible miracle he wanted to teach every Christian spiritually how he could escape from the snares of his enemy, rise to give thanks to his deliverer, work incessantly for his own and his neighbor's edification, and thereby go in safety wherever he wanted. For this, **the mute man spoke.**

For in the first place mortal sin spiritually blinds a man's intellect so that he does not know God; it disturbs his affect so that he loves him less; and it makes him blind both within and without. The second is shown in Saul, who was troubled by an evil spirit, 1 Samuel 19[:9]. The third in Cain, who was led to despair, who did not want to speak about his crime of killing his brother, Genesis 4. But when Christ's grace comes, it illumines our intellect to know him, it frees our affection to love him, and it opens our mouth to speak. According to Aristotle in book 2 of his work *On the Soul,* man was given speech for his own well-being, so that in this he would be superior to all other living beings.[1] Thus he is held to open his mouth in speech for three pur-

---

1. Cf. Aristotle, *De anima* 2.8. For a discussion of medieval views on the function of speech, see Edwin D. Craun, *Lies, Slander, and Obscenity in Medieval English Narrative: Pastoral Rhetoric and the Deviant Speaker* (Cambridge: Cambridge University Press, 1997).

poses: first, he should in speech make his Creator's great deed known publicly; second, he should restrain his neighbor [from sin; and third,] he should reveal his own sin in confession. And thus [pray that I may be inspired] to know how **the mute man spoke.**

Reverend sirs, you should know that we clergymen and religious have been chosen from the Lord's flock especially to praise our God and to edify ourselves as well as our neighbor; and we have been set aside for his ministry so that we might know how to be mute at times in a discreet silence, and then at other times know how to speak. For this reason—

a cleric or religious must be still in internal contemplation in order to speak reverently to God, giving him praise and thanks;

second, he must be still in virtuous discretion in order to speak frequently to his erring neighbor and correct him;

and third, he must be still in true wisdom in order speak prudently and in his confession reveal his own sins and above all admonish others to make their confession.

And then he can open his mouth as is fitting: **the mute man spoke.**

[1]

First, I say, a cleric or religious must be still in internal contemplation in order to speak reverently to God, giving him praise and thanks. Of such a man can be said the words of Lamentations 3[:28], that "he shall sit solitary, and hold his peace: because he has taken it up upon himself," that is, through interior contemplation. For it is very fitting that every cleric and especially every religious should keep a fitting silence, contemplating his God in truth at certain times and desiring to do his will, and at other specific times that are set aside for thus opening his mouth to give devout praise and thanks to his Creator, either in prayer or in reading or in song. Because in these things lies the specific and highest sum of life for an ecclesiastic. As Augustine says on Psalm 88, "if one desires him," that is, God, "even if his tongue is silent, his heart sings; but if one does not desire him, in whatever way he may strike men's ears, in his heart he is mute before God."[2]

---

2. Augustine, *Enarrationes in Psalmos* 86.1.

And thus the Psalmist, in Psalm 50[:17], devoutly says to God: "Lord, open my lips and my mouth shall declare your praise." And Cassiodorus says on those words, "The poor and the needy praise your name" as follows: "Let us see what is that glorious poverty, what that happy need, which praises the Lord even in silence and celebrates the virtue of its patience. A proud man is mute even if he sings a psalm, while 'the poor and the needy praises the Lord' though he seems to be silent."[3] And, so that we may be silent at first and then know how to speak, Solomon in Ecclesiastes 3 marks out a time for silence and a time for speaking,[4] for according to Gregory, in his homily 11 on Ezekiel, "we must learn, not to be silent in speech but to speak in our silence." Hence, according to the same, Solomon placed the time of silence before that of speaking, because, as he says in the same place, that man truly knows how to speak who first has learned to keep his silence well.[5] According to Solomon, Proverbs 10[:19], it is difficult to avoid sin when one speaks a lot, whether it is of good things or evil. And according to our Savior in Matthew 12[:36], in God's terrifying judgment we shall give an account to him of every idle word that we have spoken. Therefore, as is written in Lamentations 3[:26], "It is good to wait with silence for the salvation of God," and so Psalm 38[:3] says: "I was mute and was humbled, and kept silence from good things." And elsewhere the Psalmist prays that a watch be put before his mouth and a door around his lips [140:3]. He does not ask for a wall to be placed around his lips but rather a door, which can be opened and closed, so that when it is shut he will be mute, and then when it is opened he will speak. For "if any man thinks himself to be religious, not bridling his tongue, but deceiving his own heart, this man's religion is vain," as James writes in his epistle [1:26], for true and virtuous speech is the legate and messenger of a true and virtuous way of life. In contrast, a life and mode of living that is given to vice sends before it vain and evil speech as its messenger. Chrysostom says in homily 42 of his work on Matthew: "When you hear a person speak harmful things, do not merely think there is only this much evil

---

3. Cassiodorus, *Expositio psalmorum*, on Psalm 73.
4. "Tempus tacendi et tempus loquendi," Ecclesiastes 3:7.
5. Gregory, *Homiliae in Hiezechihelem prophetam* 1.11.

in him, but rather a much greater wellspring of it. What is said openly is only the overflow of what is hidden in his heart."[6]

From this you can see that it is safer and more virtuous to be frequently silent than to speak. Three philosophers once gave three reasons why it is not useful to speak right away but rather to keep a virtuous silence, namely, Cicero, Quintilian, and Zenocrates. The first derived his reason from nature, the second from the right order of values,[7] and the third from the harm that comes from speaking. Cicero takes his reason from nature when he says: "Nature has given me two ears but only one mouth,"[8] to show that although a man can hear many injuries and offenses, he must speak with patience. We can find an illustration from pagan philosophers in the book *Of Philosophers' Trifles*, where we read that Antiphanes once replied to one who had told him, "So-and-so has said bad things about you": "I don't care," he answered, "because my sense of hearing must be stronger than my tongue, since everybody has only one tongue but two ears." And in a similar way the same book tells that Aristippus said to a person who spoke evil to him, "As you are master of your tongue, so I am master of my ears,"[9] as if to say: just as you can freely say evil things with your tongue, so I can hear them without getting angry. Oh, that religious and all Christians had such a perfect virtue as those pagans! As James 1[:19] teaches us, "let everybody be swift to hear but slow to speak, and slow to anger." The third philosopher, Zenocrates, offers a reason from the harm that speaking causes. To all who spoke evil of him and asked why he alone was holding his tongue he replied: "I have sometimes been sorry to have spoken, but never to have kept silent."[10] He once was curious to test a woman's weakness and

6. Cf. John Chrysostom, *Commentary on Matthew*, homily 42 (PG 57:452).

7. MS: *ex morum premitura.*

8. A similar saying is attributed to Cicero in Bromyard's *Summa praedicantium* L.V.24.

9. Both *exempla* occur in John of Salisbury, *Policraticus* 4.15, in reverse order. The quoted title, "Of Philosophers' Trifles," *De nugis philosophorum*, could refer to several different collections of deeds and sayings by ancient philosophers. The quoted *exempla* do not occur in the *De nugis curialium* by Walter Map (d. 1210). See also below, selection 16, p. 186, and note 6.

10. Burleigh, *De vita et moribus philosophorum*, 266.

seduced his mother with alluring words to consent to the carnal act. Then, compelled by remorse, since he had sinned through his words, he swore off using words forever and bound himself to perpetual silence.[11] This shows that he was sorry to have spoken, but never to have been silent. Therefore, beloved, when we loosen the bridle of silence and engage outwardly in speech, let us speak, not what might harm another person or in any way disturb him or draw or move him to something dishonest or sinful, but what may be to the praise and honor of our Creator and to the salvation of our neighbor. And most especially in this holy season[12] let us deplore the superfluous and vain things that at other times we have uttered in our useless speech. For the Psalmist says, in Psalm 144[:21], "My mouth shall speak the praise of the Lord." When Zechariah was given back his speech, he praised God, as is written in Luke 1[:64]. And so, as you have heard, I have developed a little how **the mute man spoke.**

[2]
In the second place I said that a cleric or religious must be still in virtuous discretion and then speak frequently to his erring neighbor and correct him. From the perspective of such a person it is said in Daniel 10[:15–16]: "I cast down my face to the ground and was silent, and behold, one in the likeness of a son of man touched my lips," namely, through a hidden inspiration of grace for teaching. According to blessed Jerome, commenting on the words "There is a time for silence and a time for speaking" [Ecclesiastes 3:7], the Pythagoreans observed the disciplinary habit of a five-year silence, and after having thus been trained, they would speak. "From this originated their doctrine," he says. "Let us learn not to speak before we have gained knowledge, so that we may then unlock our mouths to speak. Nothing seems to us right except what we have learned, so that after a long silence we may from learners become teachers."[13] Thus every cleric is held to learn in silence if he lacks knowledge; and if he has knowledge, to deliberate with mature discretion what or in what way he should teach his subjects or neighbors, whom he should correct heav-

11. Cf. Tubach, no. 4912.   12. I.e., Lent.
13. Jerome, *Commentarius in Ecclesiasten* 3.6.

ily or lightly, and to improve the one he has corrected with salutary penance, following the example of the one of whom it is written in Acts 18[:25] that, "being fervent in spirit, he spoke, and taught diligently the things that are of Jesus," that is, with the fervor of charity. And as blessed Gregory teaches in his *Pastoral Rule*, chapter 16: "Let the shepherd of souls be discreet in silence and useful in his words, so that he does not speak what is to be kept silent and keep silent what is to be spoken," but always hold the middle way. "For as incautious speech leads to error, so indiscreet silence abandons those whom he could enlighten in their error."[14] Cicero used that discretion, as blessed Augustine reports in a letter to Cyprian: "He never uttered a word that he would want to call back."[15] Therefore, being more spiritual than others in the school of the gospel, any cleric is held, after adopting such discretion, to lead his subject or neighbor when in error to the right way, either with his sound teaching or with his salutary admonition.

But I am afraid that nowadays, regrettably, many fail miserably to carry out this office to which they are bound, either because of their negligence even though they have the knowledge, or because of their lack of knowledge, or because of their perverse way of life. Against the first of these Gregory speaks in his *Moral Commentary*, book 22, chapter 17: "He 'eats the fruits of the earth without money' who takes from the church the stipends for the use of his body but does not provide the ministry of exhortation to his people. What do we shepherds say to this when we think of the coming of our stern judge? We receive the office of herald but eat the church's nourishment without speaking. We demand what is owed to our body, but do not give what we owe the hearts of our subjects."[16] Against the second group the same church father says in his *Pastoral Rule*, as quoted above: "If a priest does not know how to preach, what message will he voice as a mute herald?"[17] as if to say, none. Blind in their ignorance, they do not know how to teach themselves or others, nor can they show the way they must walk

---

14. Gregory, *Regula pastoralis* 2.4.
15. Augustine, *Epistula 143*.
16. Gregory, *Moralia* 22.22. The verse commented on is Job 31:39.
17. Gregory, *Regula pastoralis* 2.4.

to heaven. Rather, they will be prone, not only to fall into vices themselves, but to draw others into many errors as well. The Lord speaks of them meaningfully when he says in Isaiah 56[:10]: "His watchmen are blind," namely, through ignorance, "they are dumb dogs not able to bark," because they do not know how to open their mouths in order to teach. Let such men, if there are any, beware of the danger that truly threatens them on this account, and let them learn diligently how they should rule, admonish, correct, and teach others, lest by chance, as is said in Baruch 3[:28], "because they did not have wisdom, they perished through their folly." But of the third group—those who are judged to be worthless to correct or teach others because of their own evil life—Origen says in his Homily 38 on the Old Testament: "Let the sinner keep his mouth shut, for he who does not teach himself cannot teach another person. In such a case a man is ordered to open his mouth who through his evil life loses the freedom to speak."[18] Thus it is fitting that people who must correct others in their vices and sins should themselves be unbound and free from them. Such the Apostle addresses in his teaching in 1 Corinthians 9[:27]: "I chastise my body and bring it into subjection, lest perhaps when I have preached to others I myself should become delinquent." Therefore, beloved, let us reflect with diligence how pleasing to God and rewarding for our souls it is to curb our erring neighbor from going the path of injustice by means of our heartfelt admonitions and our pure and earnest prayers—our neighbor whose soul is dearer to God than the whole world. For Gregory says in book 3 of his *Dialogues:* "It is a greater miracle to convert a sinner with the word of preaching and the solace of prayer than to raise a dead man in the flesh. In the latter," he says, "flesh is raised, which will die again; but in the former the soul is raised to live forever. If I mention two," Gregory asks, "in which of them do you reckon was the more powerful miracle: in Lazarus, whom the Lord raised in the flesh when, as we believe, he was already faithful, or in Saul, whom he raised in his soul? After Lazarus was raised in the flesh, we hear nothing more of his virtues, for after the resurrection our weak nature can no longer be touched by the things that in holy scripture are said about Paul's vir-

---

18. Perhaps Origen, *In Exodum,* hom. 3.2 (PG 12:310–312).

tues."[19] Therefore, as is commanded in James 2[:12], "so speak, and so do," for as is said in 1 Peter 2[:15], "it is God's will that you put to silence the ignorance of foolish men." Thus, anyone who has been freed of his sins by a cleric's teaching can fittingly state that **the mute man spoke.**

[3]
In the third place I said that a cleric or religious must be still in true wisdom in order to speak prudently and in his confession reveal his own sins and above all admonish others to do the same, for it is written in Wisdom 10[:21]: "Wisdom has opened the mouth of the mute," namely, to denounce and truly confess their sins. For whatever a mute person may say, as long as he is bound by the fetters of mortal sin, he is altogether judged by God, and so a cleric must not only reveal his own sins in confession, as he is required to do, but even more so, he must be watchful in careful attention about the salvation of others, like a careful and prudent physician, eager to see how he can speak to them prudently; in what manners and ways he may be able to lead them to the point where they will open their mouths before a priest in laying open a complete confession of all their mortal sins with the necessary circumstances, and what counsel he should give them afterward to abstain from their sins and what remedy to apply, so that they may not omit carrying out the penance he has given or will still give them. And even if all Christians are bound in the bond of love to do this to one another, a cleric is specifically held to it by virtue of the office he has been given.

Especially in our days it is necessary and useful that everyone who has the knowledge and power apply himself eagerly to this work, for it is certain that the devil, after leading man into mortal sin, uses many and various tricks so that a person will not openly acknowledge his sins, for that is all he needs to bring a man to his perdition. But as the devil perhaps realizes that he cannot shut men's mouths to confess their sins as much as he wants to, it is said that nowadays he sends around his attendants *[satellites]*[20] imbued with pernicious doc-

---

19. Gregory, *Dialogi* 3.17.
20. In the remainder of this paragraph and the beginning of the next, the preacher

trine who, as is said, are trying to thoroughly weaken the perfection of the Christian religion with their perverse and false teachings. In their preaching they openly say many things against the sacraments of the church, which were instituted and ordained both by our Savior and after him by divers other orthodox fathers for the salvation of our souls. And they preach especially against the sacrament of penance and the keys of the church that were given to blessed Peter and the other apostles and their successors, maintaining that it is not necessary for a man's salvation to confess his sins to a priest or someone else, nor that to do so is grounded in any passage of holy scripture, but that it is enough for a man to be truly contrite of his sins, to confess them in his own mind to God, and to do penance for them after the judgment of his own will. But it seems to be completely absurd and unreasonable that a man should be his own judge in any court, above all in the court of his own conscience between himself and God. All doctors of the church speak against such people and their heretical assertions, and mostly blessed Augustine, held the greatest among the others, affirms that making oral confession of one's sins and the powers of the keys of the church are based on the words of Matthew 16[:19] spoken to Peter in the singular: "Whatever you will bind on earth," and so on; similar words are spoken by Christ in the plural to all the apostles together, in Matthew 18[:18] and John 20[:23]. Augustine writes in the third part of his sermons, in *Sermon 54*, as follows: "If you have slept with other women than your wives, do such penance as is done in the church, so that the church may pray for you. Let no one say, 'I do it in private, I do it before God, God knows and forgives because I do so in my heart.' Did then Christ say 'What you will loose on earth will be loosed in heaven' for nothing? And were the keys given to God's church for nothing? We render the gospel useless *[frustramur]*, we render Christ's words useless, we promise ourselves what he himself denies. Do we thus not deceive ourselves?" as if to say, yes indeed.[21] These are the words of that outstanding teacher and

---

speaks against the contemporary Lollards, particularly their denial of private auricular confession. For similar condemnation of Wycliffite teaching in orthodox sermon, see *Collections*, 370–94.

21. Augustine, *Sermo* 392 (PL 39:1711).

chief pillar of holy church. And Anselm agrees with him in his *Book of Similitudes,* Similitude 100, where he proves through a long argument that people who, as has been said, do their penance privately before God and confess their sins to him in this fashion and do penance after their own will are entirely deceived.[22]

On this matter I can adduce many other authoritative sayings, both from other doctors of the church and from the decretals and decrees,[23] but it would take too much time. Yet I plan to speak about this at greater length in the other tongue.[24] Of such perverted teachers is written in Acts 20[:30] that "men will arise speaking perverse things, to draw away disciples after them." Therefore it is very dangerous to those who know, are held to, and can, in defense of our faith and religion, resist harmful preachers of this sort, who try to bring such bad errors into the people, and like dumb dogs, who do not know how to bark, hide in silence. They should in no way allow them to preach to the people but rather expel them from their territories, after the example of Christ who in Luke 4[:42] threatened demons and did not let them speak. Against those who thus are silent to the harm of the Christian people Gregory lashes out, in his *Pastoral Rule,* chapter 39: "Those who see their neighbors' evil deeds and yet hold their tongue in silence are like men who see wounds but withhold medication and cause death because they did not want to heal the sickness they could have healed."[25] Isaiah assumes the character of such a person when he says, "Woe to me that I kept silent" [Isaiah 6:5]. Do not keep silent this way, beloved, but let each of you act according to the bidding of Solomon in Proverbs 31[:8]: "Open your mouth to the mute!" And thus through your own wise and prudent speech "the tongue of the mute will be open," as Isaiah says in 35[:6], that is, open to make a true confession of sins.

---

22. Pseudo-Anselm, *Similitudines* 104 (PL 159:667).

23. Decretals and decrees: the church law collected in Gratian's *Decretum* and the *Decretales* of later popes.

24. Being addressed to the clergy, this sermon was presumably given in Latin, and now the preacher promises to say more about his topic at another time in the vernacular.

25. Gregory, *Regula pastoralis* 3.14.

That these things may be done as is fitting, I have, as you have heard, developed them as I well as I can,[26] so that you may know how **the mute man spoke** and take the holy prophets as your inspiring example, how they formerly spoke to men. Augustine testifies in one of his sermons, saying: "The holy prophets spoke and moved to good things, forbade evil ones, struck fear at the coming punishments, and promised our future rewards."[27] To reach these rewards, may he guide us who, etc.

26. "Taliter qualiter sciui sum prosecutus"; similarly above at the end of the first principal part.

27. Augustine, *Sermo 41.*

PART II

THROUGH THE CHURCH YEAR

The following three sections reflect the organization of sermon series as they occur in medieval manuscripts. When sermons were written or collected in systematic cycles, with one or more pieces for successive occasions in the church year, these were usually separated into sermons *de tempore* and *de sanctis.* The former are sermons for the Sundays of the year, from the first Sunday of Advent to the last Sunday after Trinity; the latter are for the saints, normally from St. Andrew (November 30) to St. Katherine (November 25). Sermons for major nondominical feasts *(de festis),* whether fixed by date (such as Christmas, Epiphany) or moveable (Ascension, Corpus Christi, etc.), could go into either cycle. If sermons for special occasions, such as funerals, the dedication of a church, synods or general chapters, visitation, enclosure of a nun, and so on, are included in cycles, they often appear at the end of *de tempore* sermons.

6

ADVENT

THE CHRISTIAN CHURCH YEAR begins with the first Sunday of Advent. In the medieval church, Advent was a penitential season like Lent, hence this preacher's insistence on penance. His sermon appears in a collection (B/2) that randomly gathers sermons *de tempore, de sanctis,* and for special occasions without regard to their place in the liturgy. Notes in the top margins suggest that these sermons were preached at a variety of small churches in the English Midlands.

In its structure, this sermon combines some features of the scholastic sermon with the older homily form of step-by-step moral commentary on the entire lection. The gospel for this Sunday narrates Jesus' entering Jerusalem, the same as for Palm Sunday, and evidently the liturgy on 1 Advent was also accompanied by a procession. After stating his sermon's leading idea (the way to Jerusalem for us is to abandon sin and go on our way to God) and asking the congregation to pray for him, the preacher refers to the gospel and its main features (Bethany, Bethphage, the spreading of clothes and branches), which he briefly moralizes in what amounts to the introduction to the thema. Then, in the sermon's main part, he states his thema, an Old Testament prophetic prediction of Christ's coming to Jerusalem, and treats it homiletically, without division, by going through the text phrase by phrase and moralizing it. The style of this sermon is succinct and unusually allusive.

SOURCE:

Cambridge, University Library, MS Kk.4.24, fols. 165v–166v (B/2-22).

LITERATURE:

Wenzel, *Collections*, 136–39.

~

Rejoice greatly, daughter of Zion, shout for joy, daughter of Jerusalem: behold your king will come to you, the just one and savior: he is poor, and riding upon an ass, and upon the foal of an ass. Zechariah 9[:9].
An earthly king's wish can be known in various cities by means of his letters. So also Christ's, through his word. Now, it is God's wish that we walk the ways that lead to heavenly Jerusalem. Wherefore David says: "I will keep meditating on your commandments, and I will consider your ways" [Psalm 118:15], as if he were saying: I will not listen to God's word only once but keep meditating on it. Further, when a woman wants to see if she has any blemishes, she looks into her mirror. And a dove sits near water so that, when it sees the shadow of birds of prey, it can escape. The same do the faithful; whence it is said in Canticles [5:12]: "His eyes as doves upon brooks of waters." Let us, then, pray that I may read the Lord's letters so clearly that we may understand and walk in the way of eternal salvation; that we see our sins in the mirror of scripture and wipe them away; and that, when we perceive the shadows of demons in our sins, we may flee to Christ lest we go down to the shadows of hell.

Rejoice, etc. On this day Christ taught us how to walk in the way to our heavenly fatherland, which is signified by Jerusalem. For coming from Bethany he went by Bethphage, and with the people having spread their clothes and branches on the road, he entered into Jerusalem [Matthew 21:1–9]. If we engage in confession, contrition, and satisfaction in our last procession, when Christ will lead his spouse[1]

---

1. In medieval spirituality, Christ's "spouse" was the soul or the church, according to the allegorical understanding of the Song of Solomon (Canticles) and Ephesians 5:23–25.

in marriage, we shall enter the heavenly Jerusalem. Man's soul has left God's court without license, shamefully, through disobedience—for Bethany means "house of disobedience." Now, a physician says, "If you want to be well, you must be obedient and take your medication and follow your regimen." God similarly says, "Do penance," etc. When he says "penance" he refers to our medication, and when he says "do" he refers to our diet, because the soul's food are good works done after giving obedience and having contrition. Confession must be made to the priest, which the Lord indicates by his going by Bethphage, which means "the house of the cheek" and was a small village of priests[2]—hence one must confess to priests. Satisfaction is expressed in the spreading of branches and clothes, which is done through words and deeds, just as sin is committed in words and deeds. The branches are our words. Whence Gregory says: "Many people spread their clothes in the road and cut branches when they excerpt words from the books of the fathers" [i.e., in order to preach]. But we should notice that the children held branches in their hands; in this way we should carry out our words in deeds, so that we may be on Christ's road. By the clothes are understood works, such as mortification of the flesh. Gregory again says: "Many people spread their clothes in the road because they tame their bodies so that they might prepare a way for Christ to their minds."[3]

This coming of Christ, that is, the way he came to Jerusalem, was prophesied by Zechariah in the words mentioned earlier, as he said: **greatly, daughter,** etc. Our soul must be a **daughter of Zion,** that is, engaged in an active and a passive watch,[4] because there is no other creature for whom so many ambushes exist. The wife or daughter of a rich man is often seduced—and mostly by clerics and students running away from schools—with the help of a servant girl.[5] In the same way, man's soul is seduced by the devil with the help of its flesh,

2. This etymology and following information were given by Jerome in his commentary on Matthew and by succeeding commentators.

3. Both quotations from Gregory are in *Homiliae in Ezechielem* 2.5, in reverse order.

4. The preacher is working with the medieval etymology of Zion as "watchtower, lookout," or "watchfulness."

5. Evidently the preacher has a typical fabliau plot in mind, such as *Dame Sirith* and many others.

who flees from the schools unwilling to accept such lessons of grace. The soul is also most fittingly called "daughter of Zion" because, as she is engaged in battle against the devil, she foresees his attacks with alertness, and this is necessary, because "the devil, like a roaring lion, goes about seeking whom he may devour" [1 Peter 5:8], like a proven fighter who struggles with a young boy. Whence Job says [16:10]: "My enemy has beheld me with terrible eyes." But Christ's grace is near to the soul of the man who fights, for God has no other fighter or soldier standing in danger except man. Let us therefore gird our loins in continence, as Moses advises in Exodus [12:11], and let us hold a staff in our hands, the staff of the holy cross, doing good works in penance, "in all things taking the shield of faith," according to the Apostle [Ephesians 6:16]. Furthermore, a mother adorns her daughter so that she might please the bridegroom; likewise prudent watchfulness adorns the soul, that she "may please God in the light of the living" [Psalm 55:13].

Next: **Rejoice.** Some people rejoice in their inner possessions, such as intelligence and knowledge, bodily strength and beauty. This rejoicing made an angel become a devil, namely, Lucifer. Other people in external possessions. This rejoicing made a human being into an animal, namely, Nebuchadnezzar. We must rejoice only in the Lord; hence, "Rejoice in the Lord, you just" [Psalm 32:1].

Then follows: **Greatly.**[6] Presumptuous people rejoice too much. Of lechery they say it was the first sin and was forgiven, and that God does not want to lose his creature, and other such nonsense. They attempt to quash God's justice and hold God a fool when he does not want to correct their excesses. On the other hand, a person who despairs rejoices too little, like Cain. But there is no place for despair since God cannot be vanquished, and God is mercy, hence mercy cannot be vanquished either, as long as a sinner will take his refuge in him. Whence the Lord speaks through Ezekiel [18:21]: "If a wicked man does penance for all the sins he has committed," they will not be reckoned against him. And so we must rejoice **greatly,** which we do when, rejoicing in the Lord, we bring our sins to God's mercy that

6. The Latin term is *satis,* "sufficiently," or, as the following sentences make clear, the right mean between too much and too little.

they may be consumed. Because a sinner, or sin, is like "tow gathered in the congregation of sinners" [Sirach 21:10], and God is fire, as Moses says: "The Lord, your God, is a consuming fire" [Deuteronomy 4:24].

Next: **Shout for joy, daughter of Jerusalem.** First the soul is Zion, like a light in battle, and then she will truly be Jerusalem, when she "sees peace" in her heavenly home.[7] Zechariah thus put things in right order, for "no one is crowned unless he has fought lawfully" [2 Timothy 2:5]. "Jubilation" is the soul's sighing for her heavenly home.[8] Whence Gregory says: "Jubilation is said to occur when the heart's joy cannot be expressed by mouth."[9] Two things cause a pilgrim to sigh: the love for his home and the troubles of his life. So also the faithful soul. Hence it is said in Canticles [2:5]: "I languish with love." And Job says [3:24]: "Before I eat, I sigh." Shout for joy, then, daughter, **behold, your king will come to you.** Christ is called king because he has established his laws, rewarding those who observe them and punishing those who transgress, not by only blinding them as if they were thieves[10] but sending soul and body to hell. And the Lord is **just,** as Rabanus says, "for he does not respect the person of the rich or despise that of the poor."[11]

And then follows: **And your savior.** Christ has three names: "Jesus," "Christ," and "the Nazarene."[12] "Jesus" he was on the cross, where he saved us by pitting himself against the devil so that we might go free. We have sinned, but he was stricken for us. Whence Isaiah says [53:8]: "For the wickedness of my people I have struck him." "Christ" he was in his conception, because "anointed." For there he accepted from the

---

7. The standard medieval etymology for Jerusalem is "the sight of peace."

8. "Shout for joy" in the Vulgate is *jubilate.* In his comment, the preacher uses one of the several medieval meanings of *jubilus* and *jubilare:* the experience of a joy so great that it cannot be expressed vocally, as in the following definition, which is taken from Gregory and repeated in Papias and other medieval lexica.

9. Gregory, *Moralia* 28:15.

10. "Not by only blinding them as if they were thieves" is my tentative suggestion for the text's "non exoccultando tantum uel pugnando in furando."

11. Rabanus Maurus, *Commentary on Ecclesiasticus* 8.5 (PL 109:1015).

12. The etymologies of the three names are "savior" or "salvation," "anointed," and "flower," which the preacher then uses in the following sentences.

Father the fullness of gifts, as anointments that are necessary to us in our sickness. "The Nazarene" he was especially on the day of his resurrection. From his beginning he was a flower on which lay a bountiful spirit; it wilted in his Passion but flowered again in his resurrection; hence, "My flesh has flourished again" [Psalm 27:7]. But that did not happen to a natural man, because after his flesh had wilted, it came to flower again.

Next: **Poor.** Christ taught us poverty as the way to eternal riches. For the devil taught Adam to live so that he would not die forever. Eating keeps us alive, but dainties taken against God's will lead to eternal death. Thus Christ, who is the Truth, taught us in the gospel to die through penance and mortification of the flesh, that we might live forever. The prophet joins "poor" and "riding upon" nicely together, for the way of the poor is plain, but that of the rich, as it were, lies among thorns. A person who is much burdened by his purse cannot ride on an ass as easily as a poor and modest person.

The **ass** indicates the soul. This the disciples loosed, indicating priests leading it to Christ. Let the soul hasten when it is tied up in sins before the devil drives it to its just reward! To this Isaiah admonishes us when he says [58:6]: "Loose the bonds of wickedness." When Christ mounts a simple soul, he renders it composed to rise step by step.[13] An ass is strong in his hind legs; and so is the sinner: when he hears God's word in preaching, he does not repeat it to himself but rather thinks of what is vile and impure. But after Christ has mounted the soul, like an ass it has its ears wide open to hear God's word and is content with vile food, that is, with virtuous poverty. Our procession today is a foreshadowing of that last procession, when rejoicing in Christ we shall go to our eternal home. In this life we make a procession of children, that is, of good works; but on judgment day we shall make a procession of fruits. But a proud man does not join God's procession in this life, for in that no one strides on proudly. He takes pride in carts and horses, but God rides humbly on an ass. Likewise the envious man does not join it, since he tries to get into everybody else's place against God's disposition. The wrathful person does

---

13. Tentative translation for "facit eam compositam vno gradu ascendere."

not join it either, for there is nothing in it that could disturb him. Nor does the greedy person, for he always thinks of his money bags, while in that procession only the praise of the Lord resounds. The sad person does not join, for in that procession there will be nothing but joyful exultation with God's praise.[14] The glutton does not enter, for in his drunkenness he has lost control of his feet, and in his mouth he does not have God's praise but the taste for false delights.[15] And the lecher does not enter because he cannot walk at all when he suffers from kidney flux.[16] All of these will descend in disorder with the devil to that place where there is "no order but everlasting horror" [Job 10:22]. But we, through Christ's grace, let us with Christ mount up to the order of the angels, to enjoy eternal happiness in our heavenly home. Amen.

14. In this sequence of the seven deadly sins, the preacher interestingly uses the sin of *tristitia* instead of the more common medieval *accidia*, following the list established by Gregory the Great.

15. According to common teaching based on Aristotle (*De anima* 2.8), the mouth, or more specifically the tongue, has two natural functions: taste and speech.

16. "Guttas renum patitur," which could also mean kidney stones. In medieval medicine, as in biblical language, the kidneys *(renes)* produce seminal fluid and hence are responsible for sexual lust in the male.

7

CHRISTMAS EVE (NICHOLAS PHILIP)

THOUGH THE RUBRIC AND THEMA MARK this as a Christmas sermon, the preacher's admonitions near the end to prepare properly for the feast "tomorrow" seem to indicate that the sermon was given on Christmas Eve. It occurs among the sermons collected and very probably written by the Franciscan Nicholas Philip in the 1430s. The preacher uses the address form *Karissimi*, "Beloved," consistently and often. This may, though it does not necessarily have to, indicate a nonclerical audience. That this is indeed the case here is made more likely by the popular elements of the preacher's style. Linguistically, it is a genuinely macaronic sermon, which switches back and forth between Latin and English within the sentence structure. One of its peculiarities is that in quoting authorities, including biblical verses, the text often gives them first in Latin and then in a macaronic mixture (i.e., Latin and English), which also slightly expands the source. A brief illustration can be found in note 2 below. Middle English sermon texts follow the same practice of first stating an authoritative quotation in Latin and then translating it with expansions (see, for example, *Middle English Sermons*, ed. Woodburn O. Ross, Early English Text Society, Original Series 209 [London, Oxford University Press, 1940; reprint, 1960], 4, 5, 8, 12, 13, etc.). Here I give only the "translated" form of the relevant quotations.

The sermon has been preserved with two separate prothemes, with the second so marked in the margin. I omit the first. Further, in the unique manuscript the text of this sermon is in spots faded nearly to the point of illegibility. I have tried to render the respective words or phrases in ways that seem true to the context.

SOURCE:

Oxford, Bodleian Library, MS lat. th. d. 1, fols. 61–65v (Q-18).

LITERATURE:

Wenzel, *Collections*, 95–99.

Alan J. Fletcher, *Preaching, Politics and Poetry in Late-Medieval England* (Dublin: Four Courts Press, 1998), 41–57.

⌁

In the Nativity of Our Lord.

Today is born to us a Savior, Luke 2[:11].[1]

Beloved, you know well that when a gold ring or some other precious object that is small drops into the dust and dirt, it can be easily lost and is hard to find again. So did it truly go with the human race, for when it had sinned against God, the heavy burden and weight of sin made it to drop from the height and honor it had in paradise into the dust and dirt of this world. In this dirt it was turned away and hidden from the sight of God. Therefore, after man had sinned, and not before, God said: "You are nothing but dust and earth, and you will return to dust and earth" [Genesis 3:19].[2] But, beloved, you see, when a man wants to have his gold ring again or the precious jewel that he has lost in the dust, he puts his hand in the dust and seeks diligently until he has it again. Now, spiritually speaking, in scripture, by the hand of God is understood Jesus Christ, his own Son, who on this day was born of his blessed mother Mary. You see, commonly a man does all his work with his own hand; and in the same way all the wonderful works that God almighty has done, he has done through his Son. St. John witnesses this in his gospel where he says: "All things were made by him, and without him nothing is made" [John 1:3]. By the word "nothing" we understand sin, for sin was never made by him.

1. Note that the biblical text actually has "to you" instead of "to us."

2. The text reads: "Puluis es et in puluerem reuerteris. þow art nothyng nisi dust and herth, dixit Deus homini; into dust and erth tu reuerteris."

So, when it happened that man, who was such a precious creature and so dear to God, was lost, God in his desire and love to find man again put his own hand in the dust, and that happened when he sent his dear Son to take flesh and blood from the Blessed Virgin. And so it seems to me that what the prophet David desired and longed for has been fulfilled; he had said: "Our soul is humbled in dust, and earth has swallowed up our body; therefore, Lord, rise up, help us and redeem us, for your holy name's sake" [Psalm 43:25–26].

Beloved, if it were possible that the sun, which is eight times larger than the whole world (and as some clerks say, much more), and a small speck of dust could be laid together, the speck would be a small thing and of little value with respect to the size of the sun. Without doubt, so it is between God and his creature. For there was never a speck so small in comparison with the sun as the worthiest creature that ever was, who is unworthy in comparison with the nobility and worthiness of God almighty. So, when it happened that man for the lust and desire he had for the fruit of the tree withdrew himself from almighty God and chose to act against his commandment rather than forego the delicious bite from an apple, he who was only a speck of dust in comparison with God then made his own soul fall into the dust. For that fall God determined that man should die in his body, and in this way earth would swallow up his body.[3] Since it is thus, it seems to me that we have need to make our prayer with the prophet and say as I said earlier, "Rise up, Lord, and help us and redeem us for your holy name's sake."

Beloved, you see that if a man is to rise, he has to be below. But when we ask God to rise, we pray him to come down. This prayer, beloved, God has heard, and he has come down and is risen up again, because he first rose from his mother's womb into this world, then he rose from this world onto the cross to save mankind, and from the cross he rose and ascended to heaven. And there he carried with him our nature to make us lords and heirs of that blissful place. Why, do you think, was all of this done? Know, good men,[4] that he did all this for the sake of his holy name. Of this name the angel Gabriel spoke before he himself [i.e., Christ] was born, when he said to Joseph:

3. In the Latin text the last three sentences have a number of illegible spots.

4. Here "gode men," in English. This may have been the vernacular equivalent of the Latin *karissimi.*

"You shall name him Jesus, because he shall save his people and wash them of their sin" [Matthew 1:21]. In our language "Jesus" is the same as "a savior," and as he did not want to have a name without deserving it, he did the most wonderful deed that pertains to our salvation. For the greatest and most wonderful deed that pertains to salvation is not only to save those who are almost lost or dead, but to save those who are already lost and completely dead. Therefore, to prove that he is indeed our Savior, he would do this wonderful deed. He was on this day miraculously born of his blessed mother, so that it seems to me that I can say the words that I took in the beginning of my sermon:

> To us who were forlorn
> A savior has been born.

As to the development of our sermon, beloved, you must understand that Christ, the Son of God from heaven, overcame three conditions in his birth that every earthly man and woman is afflicted with when he or she is born. As you know, when a person is born into this world he is born in filth and bodily uncleanness; he is further born in the sin of pride, which is spiritual misery; and he is born to woe and disease in sorrow and great sadness. But, beloved, since Christ wanted to be more wonderful in his birth than any other person on earth, it was fitting that—

> in order to turn foul into fair, he was born in cleanness;
> in order to turn high into low, he was born in meekness;
> and in order to turn sorrow into joy, he was born in gladness.

So that in these three ways,

> To us who were forlorn
> A savior has been born.

[1]

First, then, I say that Christ, the Son of God, was born in cleanness. Beloved, as a great scholar says, and it is Eusebius in *The Deeds of the Romans*,[5] in ancient times there was a custom in Rome that the em-

---

5. The preacher seems to be referring to "the father of church history," Eusebius (c. 260–c. 340), but I have been unable to find the cited passage.

peror would never go into battle with his enemies until he had first gone and worshipped an image that he had made in a certain temple in Rome. That image was called the image of Cleanness. And when he had worshipped the image, then he would go and gain victory over his enemies. Now, spiritually speaking, by this emperor of Rome I understand Christ, the Son of God from heaven; by the image of Cleanness I understand Our Lady, St. Mary, who was without any bodily or spiritual blemish of sin. This emperor came to fight for the salvation of his people, against his enemies, namely, the devil and all his angels. But he would not do so until he had first come and done worship to this image of Cleanness. So, when the time came that he readied himself to fight against his enemies, in his coming into this world he gave honor to this image of Cleanness, that is, to his blessed mother, for from the time that God made the world unto our time there was never any woman who received such honor except her alone. For among all the honors that ever a woman had in this world, I ask you, what greater honor could an earthly woman have than that for her holiness and cleanness he who is "king of kings and lord of lords" [1 Timothy 6:15] would take flesh and blood and be born of her? That honor she had before all else for her humility of heart and purity of life. And therefore holy scripture says of her: "You are wholly beautiful, my dear friend, and there is no blemish of uncleanness in you" [Canticles 4:7]. And in as much as this Blessed Virgin, his beloved, was beautiful and pure before Christ came to be born of her, in order that she would not be tainted in his coming but greatly bettered, he preserved her so pure that nature was in awe that she or any woman should be able to bear a child without the blemish of sin or injury to her body. So it is clear that not only she is pure, but also her blessed son was fair and pure, from whose grace and gift she gained all her purity.

Beloved, you should understand that purity can be divided into two kinds: purity of mind and purity of body. If we consider the purity of mind that was in that blessed child, it was he who could say the words of Jeremiah 2[:35]: "I am innocent," so Christ can say, "and without any spot or blemish of sin." And if we consider further the purity of body, he was beautiful and pure, since as a great scholar says, and it is John Damascene, in book 3, chapter 2: "Christ's blessed body was made from the most pure blood and the purest drops of blood that were in the body of Our Lady."[6] Since his body was made in this fashion, we have evidence that not only this child was pure and clean but also his mother was pure, from whom he received this body.

A great scholar, and it is Albumasar in his *Greater Introduction,* tractate 6, difference 1, speaks of a sign and figure for the great purity of this child and his mother. He reports that at one time when the sun was in the sign that scholars call *Virgo,* a virgin was seen rising up into the air who had never been touched by any bodily stain. This virgin was wholly beautiful of sight and carried a child in her arms, who seemed to be the fairest child that ever was, and this child was called Jesus.[7] Spiritually speaking, by this virgin who ascended into the air none other is indicated than the Blessed Virgin, the mother of God, who among all virgins that ever were rose highest in the state of virginity, for when she conceived Christ, she was a virgin; when Christ was being born of her, she remained a virgin; and when she had borne Christ and had become his mother, she was still a virgin as she had been before, so that among all the virgins that had ever been she rose highest in the state of virginity. This blessed woman was also beautiful in sight, for as Alexander says in his commentary on the Song of Songs,[8] the Blessed Virgin was so beautiful, and the beauty of her face of such power and might, that if she had looked on a man who was given to lechery or uncleanness of his body, she would awe him so much and pierce his heart that he would forsake his sin and become a clean person all the days of his life afterward. Holy scripture likens her to a tree called cedar, and to an ointment called myrrh, because as myrrh destroys bugs and cedar drives serpents away, so the beauty of Our Lady's face has quenched and driven away all the lusts and desires and impure thoughts of lecherous men who looked at her. Therefore it seems to me that I can say

6. John Damascene, *De fide orthodoxa* 46 (p. 171).

7. Albumasar or Abu Ma'shar al-Balkhi (d. 886), *Introductorium in astronomiam Albumasaris abalachi octo continens libros partiales* (Venice: Jacobus Pentius Leucensis, 1506), book 6, chap. 2. Albumasar's reference as an authority for the virgin birth occurs in several late-medieval sermons and elsewhere, especially in the pseudo-Ovidian poem *De vetula* 3.626–33; *The Pseudo-Ovidian De vetula,* ed. Dorothy M. Robathan (Amsterdam: Albert M. Hakkert, 1968), 131–32 and 162.

8. Alexander Nequam (d. 1217); his commentary on the Song of Songs is as yet unedited.

of her what is written in Esther 2[:15]: "She was beautiful and well shaped and fairer than anyone can believe." This young woman, on that day, was carrying in her arms the fairest child that ever was born in this world. Of his beauty speaks another great scholar, and it is Jerome commenting on the words "Beautiful above the sons of men" [Psalm 44:3]: "Christ's face was so beautiful and pleasing in the sight of men that his beauty drew many people's hearts to love him and follow him and become good when perhaps they would have been bad if they had not seen him."[9] And therefore, when the Jews had decided to put Christ to death, since they were afraid that his beauty should move men to have mercy and pity on him, at the time of his Passion they disfigured his blessed face with spittle and filth from the sewers in Jerusalem and made him look rather like a devil or tormentor than a living human being.[10] And this was an indication that he was beautiful and pure before he came to be thus disfigured.

Since this blessed child and his mother were so beautiful and pure as I have told you, beloved, this should stir everybody to retreat from uncleanness and other lusts and desires of the body. But I fear, beloved, that there are many in this world who think very little of the purity that was in this blessed woman and her child, because all their joys and all the happiness they have in this world are only in the lusts and desires and uncleanness of the body. But you know, beloved, that if people reflected and bethought themselves right, they would withdraw from that sin and not engage in impurity, because it destroys and ruins people as well as all virtues of which a man might have any profit, in body and spirit. Let us look first at virtues of the body. If a man is beautiful, he loses that beauty. If he is strong, he loses this strength. If a man is prospering in his body, he melts away and vanishes as dew before the sun. And this sin destroys not only bodily virtues but spiritual ones as well, so much so that there is no action a man undertakes while he is in that sin that pleases God, for as St. Gregory says in one of his common sermons: "Just as chastity is not good or great without good deeds, so no deed is good without chastity."[11]

9. Perhaps Jerome, *Epistula* 65, 8.

10. Tentative translation of "and madyn hym lihchere a devlot [*or* deblot?] vel a turmentouur þan ony lyfely man."

11. Gregory, *Homiliae in evangelia* 1.13.

And therefore, for the love of him who was born today in purity for the salvation of us all, if anyone here is in that vile sin, let him free himself of it and make himself clean in anticipation of this holy season. Behold what St. Bernard says in a sermon that he made on the Song of Songs, sermon 24: "Ah, Lord God," says St. Bernard, "how unfitting it is that you, O man, have a body that stands up to heaven and carry your soul down to hell. Truly," says Bernard, "it is a foul thing that your body, which is made of the earth, will lift its eyes to heaven and freely see there the sun, the moon, and the stars, and all the beauty of the firmament, and that your soul, which is a spiritual creature and made in the image of God, will have its eyes set downwards to the lust and desires and impurity of its body. Truly it seems to me," says Bernard, "that man's soul ought to be ashamed that she has such small regard for his creator, who made her such a beautiful creature."[12]

A great scholar, namely, Pliny in book 7 of his *Natural Philosophy*, reports that once there were two philosophers who took such delight in the beauty and fairness of the sun that every day when they could see the sun from its rising to its setting they stood to look at its beauty and clarity.[13] Since there is no comparison between the clarity of the sun, which we see here with our bodily eye, and the fairness and purity of God almighty, who was born today, it seems to me that we are much to blame if for some lust or uncleanness of the body we should turn away from God, whom the angels and the entire company of heaven desire and enjoy to look at for his beauty and purity. Therefore, beloved, since Christ, the Son of God, was born in cleanness, as I have told you, and the cause of his birth was only to save us and be our savior, it seems to me that I can say as I did in the beginning:

> To us who were forlorn
> A savior has been born.

[2]

I also said that in order to turn high into low, Christ, the Son of God, was born in meekness. Beloved, you must know that the Original Sin with which all humans are stained when they are born into

12. Bernard, *In Cantica* 24.6.   13. Pliny, *Historia naturalis* 7.2.22.

this world is a stain of pride that has remained for us from our father Adam, because he was disobedient to the divine commandment. Therefore Christ, the Son of God, in order to destroy this pride and that he himself would not be the recipient of our sin, was born today in meekness. That he who was king of kings and lord of the whole world was born of the most humble woman that ever was, is surely a sign of great humility. God so loves humility and hates pride, as scripture witnesses,[14] that he preferred to be born of a humble woman rather than a great lady. For although in that woman grew and blossomed several different flowers, namely, the rose of charity, the lily of chastity, and the violet of humility, it was the third, humility, through which she conceived Christ. With this agrees St. Bernard when he says, in the first homily on *There Was Sent:* "While Our Lady pleased God with her purity and chastity," says Bernard, "it was nevertheless her humility of heart that was the cause why she conceived Christ when she answered the angel with that humble word, 'Behold, the handmaiden of the Lord; let it be done to me according to your word'" [Luke 1:38].[15] And so, as she stood before almighty God so graciously and humbly that for her humility he wanted to be born of her, I truly believe that Eve never did more for us than the Virgin. The former inflicted harm, the latter healed us. Eve was the cause that we were lost, and the Blessed Virgin, in her humility, was the cause that we were saved.

This humility was not only shown on her part, but Christ himself, too, showed great humility in his birth, for as St. Bernard says in his homily *On Christ's Birth,* "When Christ was to be born," and so on: "When it came about," says Bernard, "that Christ, the Son of God, wanted to be incarnated and be clothed in our nature—whose will could choose what he wanted and do what he wanted—he chose to be born at a time that was most noxious and most grievous to himself, and especially as a child of so poor a mother as her who had no more than a few cloths to wrap him in or a manger where she could lay him."[16] With which Chrysostom agrees, in his second homily of

---

14. The preacher may be thinking of James 4:6 or 1 Peter 5:5.

15. Cf. Bernard, *Super Missus est angelus,* 1.5 (PL 183:59).

16. Bernard, *In nativitate Domini,* sermon 3 (PL 183:123).

his *Imperfect Work*, where he says: "Do you believe," says Chrysostom, "that the kings and shepherds, when they came to look for Christ, found a splendid palace made of marble, as all the other kings have? Do you perhaps believe that they found the king of heaven and earth and the whole world wrapped in silk and costly cloth, or some great ladies to tend to him and be his nurses? Do you perhaps believe that they found his mother with a crown on her head, lying on soft pillows or in clothes of gold? No, no, beloved," so says this scholar, "but do you know what they found? They found an old, forsaken house that was so simple and mean in men's sight that no one would go there to rest or to take his comfort unless he were so overcome with weariness that he could travel no further. In addition," says this scholar, "they found the Blessed Virgin so poorly clothed that she had but one tunic, and that not for display or great array but only to hide the nakedness of her blessed body. They also found that she had wrapped her little child in a few small cloths and laid him in the manger in front of animals, so that the animals' breath could warm the child's body."[17]

Behold, beloved, Christ showed us all this humility in order to destroy our pride and to give us an example to be humble and meek for his love. But I fear that there are many in this world who do not follow Christ or act after his teaching. And this is because they are so overcome by pride that they think of themselves as so worthy and noble that they want to be superior to everybody else beside them. If one were to talk to them about humility, to be gentle in their behavior toward their neighbors, their heart is so full and so blocked with pride that they are beside themselves, and they can't say anything but, "Fie on you, knave, why are you interfering?" And why is this, beloved? Surely because they have no taste for humility or for things that belong to God. Therefore, it seems to me that it goes with them as it does with a lion. Take a lion and lead him into a fair meadow that is

---

17. Pseudo-Chrysostom, *Opus imperfectum* 2 (PG 56:641–642). The "Imperfect Work on Matthew" is a partial commentary on the Gospel of Matthew, which during the Middle Ages was attributed to St. John Chrysostom, one of the major Greek fathers (d. 407). The work has been preserved only partially and in Latin. It was one of the major sources of biblical exegesis in western Europe, and medieval preachers quote passages from it that are not found in the edited text.

full of grass and fair flowers—he takes no delight in it. Why? Because it is not his nature to eat grass. Or take an ox or a sheep and show it partridges, plovers, and all the dainty food man can eat, it does not like it. Why? Because it is not its nature to eat flesh. Truly, beloved, just so it is with the vice of pride. Preach to man about humility, he will not like it, and this because it is not in the nature of pride to be humble, for the two are just as opposed to each other as are white and black. Don't let it be like this, beloved, not like this, but if any of you is stained with this sorry sin of pride, let him bravely pray to that blessed child for mercy in this holy season. You will find him merciful and meek toward you. And if anyone is too bashful to ask God for mercy, let him imagine that God is still but a child. For as you see, if a man is very hard on a child but then gives him a red apple, the child is soon his friend again. Just so does it go with God. Let a man act ever so much against him, if he has the will to give up his sin and make pure his heart, which is formed like an apple, he will no doubt receive mercy. And this is a sign that God is meek and humble toward man.

Of this humility which Christ showed for the love of man St. Augustine speaks in the voice of Christ in his book *Against the Five Heresies,* where he says: "O man, man," says St. Augustine, "you know well that when you were the Father's enemy I made him one with you and reconciled you with him. Thus, should I then find it in my heart to separate you again from him as long as you want to do well and be a good human being? You know well that, when you went astray and wandered off among the mountains and woods, I sought you. I found you among trees and rocks, for you adored them as your false gods. When I had found you, I took you in my arms, put you on my shoulders, carried you, toiled for you, labored for you, did not abandon you for the thorns that I suffered on my head, had my hands and feet pierced for your love to be nailed to the cross. For love I let my side be opened with a sharp lance and my heart be split in two, to give you all the precious blood that was in it. And at the last I gave my own soul for you. What more would you want that I should do for you? All this, O man," Christ says, "I did to knit you to myself, that you would not depart from me."[18] And therefore, beloved, since his com-

18. Augustine, *Tractatus contra quinque haereses* 4.8 (PL 42:1109–10).

ing into this world was not for judgment but that the world might be saved through him, as he himself says in the gospel[19] and as he was born today for that reason, it seems to me that I can say as I said in the beginning:

> To us who were forlorn
> A savior has been born.

[3]

I also said that in order to turn sorrow into joy, Christ was born in gladness. Beloved, you must understand that God creates man in four different ways, as Anselm says in book 2 of *Why God Became Man*.[20] God made a man without man or woman, and thus was Adam created. He made a woman from a man, and thus was Eve made. Then he made a human being from a man and a woman, as we all have come into being. And finally, he made a man from woman without another man, and that was himself as he was born on this day. If we look at man's first creation, when Adam was made, we do not find in scripture that there was any joy in his creation. When God made Eve from one of Adam's ribs, we do not find that there was any joy. If we go further, when God made man from a man and a woman, as we have been made, I believe that commonly there is not much joy but rather a great sorrow and sadness which the mother has for the pains on her part; and the child, as soon as he is born and comes into this world, he cries and weeps and shows much sorrow. If it is a boy, he begins his lamentation with "A" for Adam; if it is a girl, she begins her lamentation with "E" for Eve. However, beloved, when Christ was born, it did not happen like this at all: there was no sign of sorrow but only of joy and bliss, so much that the angels in heaven rejoiced, men on earth rejoiced, and all the four elements showed that they had joy and delight in their natures at Christ's birth. For as holy scripture testifies, the night that Christ was born, there came a host of angels together with the angel who brought the shepherds the news of Christ's birth, and they sang "Joy and bliss to God on high, and peace on earth to men

---

19. John 12:47.
20. Anselm, *Cur Deus homo* 2.8 (PL 158:406).

who have good will." Creatures without reason also showed a kind of joy at Christ's birth, for as Orosius says in his *History of the World*, about the time that Christ was born, the Emperor Octavian of Rome saw a circle of fire around the sun, in which a beautiful maiden was sitting who carried an absolutely beautiful child in her arms. The same scholar says of the earth that the vineyard of a country called Engadi budded forth against the course of nature and bore leaves, flowers, and fruit, and all this in the night that Christ was born.[21] About the air there are various similar stories. But the *Legend of the Saints* reports that the darkness of the blessed night vanished and it became such a fair and bright weather as on any day of the year. The same book also tells that the water in a fountain at Rome turned into oil and flowed into the water of the Tiber.[22] Thus it is seen that creatures endowed with reason, such as angels and men, and creatures without reason, as these four elements, made joy and bliss.

And since all these creatures had joy and mirth when Christ was born, it seems to me that we, too, ought to be glad and make joy as much as they did. But there are many in this world who think they are making joy and mirth in this holy season, while in truth, if they bethought themselves rightly, it is not joy but a great sadness, in so far as it displeases God. For some men's joy will be in singing dirty song, speaking foul words, playing foul games and going after the souls of people around them. Some there are to whom all their joy will be in having noble drinks, rich clothes, and to be merry in their bodies. But their poor soul goes all ragged and torn, it wears its old clothes on Christmas day; it goes full of sin, full of the wretchedness that it has lain in ever since Easter till today.[23] Let the soul be bathed and washed clean and made pure as the body is, and afterward put on a new coat for tomorrow, where the body will perhaps have one too. That man would be well at ease tomorrow . . . .[24]

21. Orosius's world history is here quoted by its common medieval title, *Ormista*, i.e., Or[osii] m[undi] ist[ori]a.

22. Iacobus a Voragine, *Legenda aurea* 6 (Christmas, 43–47), which reports all these signs of the birth of Christ, including those attributed to Orosius and others.

23. "Since Easter" because of the mandatory confession before the Easter communion.

24. These last sentences are largely illegible in the manuscript.

And so, beloved, for the love of him who was born on this day for our salvation, make such joy that your souls come to a better state by it and not a worse one. And then God will say to you what he said to his disciples, in John 16[:22]: "I will see you again, and your heart shall rejoice; and your joy no man shall take from you." This joy is the joy of heaven. May he lead us to this joy who lives and reigns without end. Amen.

8

CHRISTMAS

THIS SERMON APPEARS in a preacher's notebook whose entries were written from the early to the late fifteenth century. The scribes copied sermons from different sources in random order, many with English phrases and verses. They include Thomas Wimbledon's famous sermon *Redde rationem vilicationis tuae* ("Render an account of your stewardship," Luke 16:2) in Latin. The Christmas sermon here translated was apparently copied very early in the fifteenth century.

SOURCE:
Cambridge, University Library, MS Ii.3.8, fols. 143–44 (A-45).

LITERATURE:
Wenzel, *Collections,* 175–81.
Ione Kemp Knight, ed., *Wimbledon's Sermon "Redde Rationem Villicationis Tue": A Middle English Sermon of the Fourteenth Century* (Pittsburgh: Duquesne University Press, 1967).

⁓

Sermon for the Nativity of Our Lord.

Ah, ah, ah, Jeremiah 1[:6].

By way of introduction we should notice that this word "Ah"[1] can be fittingly used as the thema on the feast of Christ's Nativity for

1. The text speaks of the *letter* A, because in Latin the thema is "A, a, a."

three characteristics that are found in Christ. "Ah" is a short and small word, and Christ, as can be found in the doctors of the church, was the smallest and shortest human being, because while other humans do not have their souls infused from God until four months after their conception, Christ was a true human being from the first moment of his conception on, and hence he was small and short according to the verse, "The Lord made a short word over the earth" [Romans 9:28].[2] This is one reason. Further, "Ah" marks the beginning in every language, because every alphabet, whether Latin, Hebrew, or Greek, begins with A. In the same way Christ is the beginning of creation, as he himself testifies in Revelation 1[:8]: "I am Alpha and Omega, the beginning and the end." Alpha in Greek is the same as A in Latin. And this is the second reason. The third is that the letter A is the beginning of our salvation and redemption, as is shown in the angel's greeting in Luke 1[:28], "Ave, Maria," etc. And thus it is clear how for these three reasons "Ah" may be taken as the thema for Christ's Nativity. But since in his nativity only three persons were present, as is reported in the authoritative books, namely, Mary, Christ, and Joseph, "Ah" is taken as our thema three times.

For the further development we should notice that "Ah" is commonly spoken for three causes: for well-being, for woe, and for wondering.[3] Thus,

> Mary could say "Ah" for her well-being,
> Christ for his woe,
> and Joseph for his wondering.

---

2. The modern Vulgate reads, "Verbum breviatum faciet Dominus super terram." But the form used in this sermon, "Verbum abbreviatum fecit Dominus," was standard in the Middle Ages, well known especially from the very popular work by Peter the Chanter that began with these words; see John W. Baldwin, *Masters, Princes, and Merchants: The Social View of Peter the Chanter and His Circle*, 2 vols. (Princeton: Princeton University Press, 1970), passim, and especially 2:246–65.

3. The Latin text of this sermon uses English phrases regularly for its divisions and subdivisions, often with rhyme or, as here, alliteration: "for wele, wo, and wonder." In the classification proposed in *Macaronic Sermons*, this would be type B1.

[1]

For the first chief part I say that Mary could say "Ah" for her well-being. As we can see, a woman finds her joy and prosperity in four things: in her bloodline, her wealth, her beauty, and the fruit of her body; in English:

in gret blode,
in myche gode,
in grete bewte,
and in frut of body.

Now, among all women, these four conditions are most truly found in the Blessed Virgin in her present delivery. For Mary was descended from great blood, namely, from many kings, as is clearly shown in Christ's genealogy in Matthew 1, and this on the part of her parentage. She was likewise of good and noble blood on the part of her son, since she was the mother of God and of a human being. This much for the first condition. Further, the Blessed Virgin possessed a wealth of riches, for in this birth she became queen of heaven, lady of the world, and empress of hell. And so any sinner can say of her what is written in the Book of Wisdom 7[:11–12]: "Now all good things came to me together with her," that is, the Blessed Virgin, "and innumerable riches through her hands, and I knew not that she is the mother of them all." This much for the second reason. In this birth Mary also had a blessed fruit, namely, when she gave birth to Christ, her first-born son, who was most powerful, wise, and benign. This is proven by Aristotle in book 4 of his *Physics:* "Everything in the middle must share in the parts of either extreme."[4] Since the Blessed Virgin's son is the person in the middle between Father and Holy Spirit, and since the Father in his nature possesses power and the Holy Spirit benignity, it follows of necessity that the Son shares power with the Father and benignity with the Holy Spirit. So, when he is called "wisdom of the Father,"[5] it follows that what I said earlier is correct [that Christ is the most powerful, wise, and benign]. Hence it is justly

---

4. Perhaps Aristotle, *Politics* [!] 4.9.
5. A standard medieval definition, from Augustine, *De Trinitate* 8.11, etc.

said in Luke 1[:42]: "Blessed is the fruit of your womb." This much for the third reason. Finally, the Blessed Virgin was the most beautiful of all women, for it is of her that blessed John speaks in Revelation 12[:1] when he says that "a great sign appeared in heaven: a woman clothed with the sun, and the moon under her feet, and on her head a crown of twelve stars." Thus Mary was beautiful in her appearance. But she was even more beautiful in her faith, for in faith and humility did she conceive Christ and give birth to him. Among the Greeks, in the life of blessed Dionysius, the story is read that blessed Dionysius was burning so strongly in love for her that he often implored blessed John the Evangelist in his prayers that he would show him the Virgin in actuality. On one occasion he was granted his prayer, and as he entered the oratory where the Virgin was in her prayer, so many rays of light came from her that, overcome by the extreme brightness, his eyes failed him and he could not stay. Then, when his powers had somewhat returned, he said that unless the faith of the church had held him firm, he would have thought there was no other god [but her]. And this much for the fourth condition. As we reflect on these things, Mary, the mother of God, could quite rightly say "Ah" for her wellbeing. And this has been our first chief topic.

[2]

In the second place I say that Christ could say "Ah" for woe. This can be shown in three ways. When he was born, although he was the son of the Most High, he was not wrapped in purple and fine linen,[6] he was not placed in a manor house or castle where the children of lords are commonly placed, but he was put in a stable and wrapped in a poor cloth of his parents. He did not have fire or a midwife, nor any of the other things that were necessary for such a childbirth, but as it were, he suffered great pain from nakedness and lack of any help. Hence, such a great lord in such need could rightly say "Ah" for the woe he suffered in his beginning. Then in his following life, Christ also suffered many things, in both words and blows, as is openly shown in many places in holy scripture, as when people said to him "You have a demon" [John 7:20, etc.] and "You give testimony

---

6. Probably an allusion to the rich man of the parable, Luke 16:19.

to yourself, and your testimony is not true," in John 8[:13]. Likewise he suffered many blows, as at the time of his Passion; and also in his death he sustained much suffering and pain, because he was accused falsely, against reason, and condemned with shouts. All his enemies were his judges. And his friends abandoned him and fled, all but the Blessed Virgin and John the Evangelist, whom he saw weeping and in great pain for him. So, if Christ at the time of his birth thought of how much weariness and pain he would suffer in his entering, going through, and leaving his life, he could well say "Ah" for woe. And this has been my second principal part.

[3]
In the third and last place I say that in this childbirth Joseph could say "Ah" for wonder. This can be demonstrated in many ways. First, Mary was his wife and yet gave birth without having slept with him. Second, he saw her give birth without pain. Third, he who was God and man wanted to subject himself to Joseph and obey him. Fourth, in this birth Joseph saw that the first was the last when God became man, for among all things man was created last. He also saw the bread go hungry, for Christ was the living bread that came down from heaven, yet, "when he had fasted for forty days and forty nights, he was hungry" [Matthew 4:2]. He also noticed that in Christ's birth, what was short became long, man became God, what was feeble was made strong (for our faith was made strong in our believing the article[7] of his incarnation), and sorrow was turned into song, when that great prophet came into the world for whose coming the patriarchs, prophets, and other holy fathers of the Old Testament had called out in their suffering. And thus, finally, Joseph saw a wondrous move, namely, from heaven to earth, when God descended; a wondrous setting, when God was clothed in humankind; and a wondrous knitting together, when virginity was joined to motherhood. In thinking of these things, Joseph could indeed say "Ah" in wonder.[8]

7. Article: referring to the "articles of faith," the individual phrases that make up the (Apostles') Creed, here: "[I believe] in Jesus Christ, his only son, our Lord, who was conceived by the Holy Spirit, born of the Virgin Mary." See Brinton's sermon in selection 21 (p. 243).

8. Again, the two distinctions here end in rhyming English words: "schort was

And thus, through Christ's nativity—

> All our wonder and all our woe
> Has turned into well-being and bliss also.

namely, our eternal joy. May Jesus Christ bring us to that joy. Amen.

---

turned into longe ... , febul was made stronge ... , sorow was turned into sownge";
and "a wonder flytting ... , a wonder settyng ... , and a wonder knytting."

9

ASH WEDNESDAY

THE THEMA OF THIS ANONYMOUS SERMON is taken from the epistle for Ash Wednesday, and its topic, penance, spelled out in the margin, deals with the main concern of preaching during the season of Lent. The sermon provides a good example of the medieval view of mankind's spiritual history, from creation and fall through Christ's redemptive death to the future bliss. It also furnishes instruction about the required pre-Easter confession, how in preparation for it penitents must examine their consciences, and how the priest confessor must inquire about their sins.

The sermon has been preserved in a collection evidently made at the Benedictine priory at Worcester, whose cathedral library still owns the book. At least a dozen different hands copied sermons (167 in all) randomly into it in the fifteenth century, and often copied the same sermon twice. The sermons are *de tempore, de sanctis,* and for special occasions in random order, including many for a monastic audience as well as university sermons.

SOURCE:
Worcester Cathedral, MS F.10, fols. 132rb–133v (new foliation; W-72).

LITERATURE:
Wenzel, *Collections,* 151–58.

᷎

For Penance.

Be converted, Joel 2[:12].

Reverend sirs, in Holy Writ I read of two lords who are always contrary and set against each other, so that nobody can please both at once. And yet everybody in this world serves one of these lords. The first lord is the prince of justice, the king of peace, King Solomon, the king of ages,[1] that is, "superior," and the lord of eternal heavenly bliss, God himself. The second lord is that proud Nebuchadnezzar, the king of Babylon, evildoer and master of endless confusion, the devil of hell. These lords are constantly at strife for the lordship over the city that lies between Jerusalem and Babylon, which is called Jericho. This name means "moon," which in holy scripture often stands for instability and signifies this world, which is always unstable, waxing and waning just like the moon. But according to Augustine on the Psalter,[2] this city does not wholly belong to one lord, but part of this city is under the rule of the king of Jerusalem. These are good people who reflect on the things of heaven and try with all their powers to keep themselves from sin, and if they should fall into sin, confess it in humility and turn to God, and ask for his mercy and forgiveness. "Theirs," as Christ witnesses in the gospel, "is the kingdom of heaven" [Matthew 5:3]. Others belong to the king of Babylon, and those are people who have only a taste for earthly things, who prefer earthly happiness to Christ, who "seek the things that are their own, not the things that are Jesus Christ's" [Philippians 2:21]. They all have their dwelling and heritage in Babylon, in the reign of the devil, which is hell.

And since this city of Jericho, as it were, lies in the middle between these two realms, each of their lords has his soldiers in this city in order to extend his rule and convert people to himself. On one side, God has his stewards to increase his lordship. They are holy people, such as the apostles, martyrs, confessors, virgins, and all who follow their way of life. Some of these are constantly at work through the example of their good life, others through their preaching, to convert

---

1. *Rex seculorum*, tentative reading of *rex osirl'm*; cf. Revelation 15:3.
2. Augustine, *Enarrationes in Psalmos*, on Psalm 64:1–2.

people from sin, move them to practice virtues, and lead them to the reign of Christ, which is heavenly bliss. On the other side, the devil has his angels and evil men, who day and night move people to vices and sins through their temptation and bad example, in order to lead them to Babylon, the place of the devil. If you want to understand the household of that lord in detail, take good heed and you will hear about the cursed fellowship of his officials. First, Pride is the steward of his house, a great master over the others, and he commands many people in his livery, which are garments with decorated edges, pointed shoes, short clothes that hardly cover their loins, swords of vengeance hanging on their sides. He also commands women who with their long tails sweep the ground, wear their heads like temples with horns made of the tall turrets of their hair, have their faces painted that they might appear more splendid, and use scornful speech, disdain the poor, and utter pompous words. These and similar things are the livery and signs by which those are known who are the devil's retainers with his steward. The treasurer of his court is Avarice, who collects gold generously and distributes it with a tight fist. His attendants are those who in buying and selling exceed a reasonable profit, who praise their wares beyond their worth, who lend money at usurious rates, who hide defects from the buyers, or who deceive their neighbors in any other way for their own gain. The justice is Wrath, who judges nothing correctly, nor does he carry out any rightful order but rather his personal vengeance. His officers are inclined to evil; they fight, quarrel, speak evil, and murmur with vindictive men. The doorkeeper is Envy, for according to holy scripture, "through the envy of the devil, death came into the world" [Wisdom 2:24]. Envy's office is to open the door to evil and to keep out everything that is good. His servants are those who rejoice at other people's injury and are sad about their good fortune. The hosteller or guest-master is Lechery, who has many retainers and sends many souls to hell. The chamberlain is Sloth, who hangs up curtains and brings in soft pillows, so that on holy days people may lie long in their beds. Drunkenness is the butler and Gluttony the cook—indeed an evil cook, who poisons many, for gluttony kills more people than does the sword.

These are the devil's seven chief officials and men's mortal enemies in the city of Jericho, who labor night and day to extend the devil's lordship. And indeed, however much God's ministers exert themselves in preaching and teaching, the lordship of the devil is being extended more than that of Christ. There are more citizens of Babylon than of Jerusalem; there are more evil men than good ones. And therefore, as a remedy against this, the church has ordained that in this coming holy season of Lent the word of God should be preached and taught to the people more than at other times of the year, to make them leave that cursed company and the house of that false tyrant, the devil, that I have spoken of, and then lead them to the court of him who is the true lord and king of the whole world, in as much as he has created all things from nothing. Such preachers will tell you that it is written: we are "preaching to you to be converted from these vain things, to the true God, who made heaven and earth" [Acts 14:14]. And therefore, that I may truly [free you] from the devil, [pray with me,] etc.[3]

Be converted, as in the beginning. Reverend sirs, you should understand that after God, our Lord, had made and formed humankind from nothing in his own image and likeness, for the great love he had for it, he put it on the right path of virtues, on the highway of innocence and original righteousness, so that man might be a good pilgrim toward the holy land, toward the promised land, to this home of eternal bliss above. And lest the darkness of ignorance hinder him and lead him astray from this way, he ordained as his guide and leader the bright star of clear reason and discretion, in whose light he would, wherever he might be, be able to see whether he was progressing well or not. But the ancient fiend of humankind, wanting to harm it, interfered with the light of this star, darkened a large part of his reason, and caused such a cloud of sin to fall before his eyes that humankind could not see clearly and perceive its way, so that, after what the prophet Isaiah says, "they hardly knew the way of peace" [59:8]; and Isaiah immediately adds the cause: they sinned against the Lord and turned away so that they did not walk behind their God [cf. 59:13]. And right after the star of man's reason lost its light, it was no wonder that man at once, through the devil's temptation and guidance, went off the path of virtue and the good life, lost

---

3. The sentence, at the end of the protheme, seems to contain the formal invitation to pray. As is often the case in other sermons as well, it is abbreviated: "Et ideo vt recto modo a diabolo, etc."

the way that was to lead him to heavenly bliss, and fell into the wasteland of vices and sin. He had been on the high hills of pride and right away fell into the valley of greed. Sometimes he lost himself among the sharp thorns and scrub of wrath and envy; sometimes he was in such darkness far from God in the deep mires of gluttony and lechery that he could not go farther. In this fashion, this wretched pilgrim went into the wasteland and well out of his way until he was all weary, just as the prophet says: they wandered "where there was no passing and out of the way" [Psalm 106:40].

And there was no one who could teach man the right way, until the second person in the Trinity, Christ the Son of God, had mercy and compassion on them and said through his prophet: "I will return and have mercy on them and will bring them back to their land," Jeremiah 12[:15]. And when he saw that the time was ripe, he came down to be man's leader and guide to go before him in his own person, that he might go before him and bring him out of the dangerous place. And so that we might recognize him better and follow him in the darkness of this world, he dressed himself in a white tunic, he took flesh in the blood of the Virgin Mary and clothed his divinity in the tunic of our human nature. And since in the land where man was thus wandering astray there was no straight path of virtue but it was all full of thorns and the scrub of sin, he took the sword of the word of God and, with his teaching and preaching, cut down the thorns and scrub, flattened the mountain of pride with his humility, and filled the valleys of greed with his generosity and almsgiving. And thus, with many labors and much solicitude, he prepared for us a straight way of perfection and virtue and gave us the law of the gospel, which, if anyone will keep it, will lead him to the bliss of the eternal kingdom of heaven. And so, after God our Lord of his grace and goodness had prepared for us the way and put us in it, he went before us with the example of a good life, and what he taught, he fulfilled in his action. He relit the star of our reason through the light of faith so that we might not go astray; and he gave us the staff of hope that we might not become weary; and to comfort and sustain us he put in our pilgrim's bag the provisions of charity and love. In this way our guide in his infinite mercy and piety converted us and put us on the right path to the Promised Land, the kingdom of heaven, which in the beginning of the world he gave our forefathers in paradise, so that we might take possession and ownership in it with him without end, as he promised in the Old Law through his prophet Jeremiah, 30[:3]: "I will cause them to return to the land which I gave to their fathers, and they shall possess it." Therefore, if through evil and sins we turn from the way in which God has now put us, God calls to us out of mercy with the words that I have chosen as my thema: **Be converted,** as I said in the beginning.

But perhaps you want to say now: "Sir,[4] you say well. You have told me how God turned us from our wretchedness and made for us a way to heaven. But it is commonly said that 'this way' that leads to heaven 'is strait' [Matthew 7:14], and that many stray from it. Therefore I ask you, teach me how I must keep this way so that I do not stray from it and take a crooked way for the straight one." Certainly, I will tell you. You must walk in it as the Israelites did when they went out of the land of Egypt toward the Promised Land, toward the city of Jerusalem. Here in our world, what is this desert? It is a solitary place and without human comfort. By that is understood the sacrament of penitence, in which one abstains from food and drink and does not take bodily comfort but rather is sorrowful and weeps for one's sins. That is the desert through which we must travel. But perhaps you ask me how long you should travel through this desert of penance? I say as the children of Israel said to Pharaoh: "We will go a three days' journey into the wilderness" [Exodus 3:18, etc.]. These three days are nothing else than the three parts of penitence:

contrition,
confession,
and satisfaction.

I will now talk to you briefly about each of these parts as God will allow me, and soon come to an end.

[1]

The first day's journey that we must travel is contrition, and to be sure, unless we travel this journey well, we shall never come to our heavenly home, for as our teachers say, by the laws that now ap-

---

4. "Sir," *domine* (the vocative case of *dominus*, "lord"), was the usual way of addressing a priest in the Middle Ages.

ply God cannot and will not give man bliss unless man have remorse and sorrow for his sins. Therefore Augustine on the Psalter, where he deals with the verse "Justice shall walk before him" [84:14], says: "Man's first act of justice is to punish himself for being evil and make himself good."[5] This is the way for God to come to him. Contrition can be likened to water that is sprinkled on limestone. Just as it dissolves the limestone, extinguishes fire, and produces smoke, so contrition softens the hardness of man's heart, extinguishes the fire of sin, and produces the grace of the Holy Spirit. But for true contrition two things are necessary: sorrow for the crimes one has committed and the firm intention to abstain [from sin]. For contrition is commonly defined as voluntary sorrow for one's sins with the intention of abstaining from them. What powerful effect such contrition has is shown in an exemplum.[6] We read in *The Lives of the Fathers* that Paul, a disciple of blessed Antony, saw a man enter a church who was as black as an Ethiopian. Two demons were leading him and rejoiced, while a good angel followed him from afar as if in mourning. After a little while he saw the same man leave the church whiter than snow. The two demons were far from him and weeping, while the good angel now was close to him and most joyful. The holy father was astonished at the man's sudden transformation and asked him how, when he entered the church, he was blacker than pitch, but when he left, whiter than snow, etc. In the hearing of many people the man replied: "I have for a long time lived a wretched life in many great sins. But when I just now heard the words of Isaiah [1:16–17] read in the church: 'Wash yourselves and be clean, take away the evil of your devices from my eyes: cease to do perversely and learn to do well,' as soon as I heard them, I promised God in sorrow and anxiety for my sins that I would leave my former sins and serve him with a pure heart."[7] Learn from this story how true contrition with the intention to keep from sin is the first way to God.

But perhaps you say: "Sir, my sins are so enjoyable, so pleasing and delightful that I cannot find it in my heart to be sorry and sad for

5. Augustine, *Enarrationes in Psalmos*, on Psalm 84:16.
6. The text reads *in erumpna*, which must be a scribal error for *in exemplo*.
7. *Verba seniorum* 23 (PL 73:1047).

them." I will tell you a remedy against this. You should be like the peacock, according to what scholars who deal with the nature of things say.[8] When the peacock sees his own feathers—some shining as bright as gold, as those around his shoulder, others the color of sapphire as blue as the firmament, as are those around his chest and neck, and others still full of open eyes, as are his long tail feathers—he takes such joy and delight in their beauty that he raises his tail like a wheel, struts in pride, and fans his feathers so that one can hear the sound from far away. But notwithstanding all this pride and gamboling, as soon as he looks at his feet, how vile they are and black, he draws in his tail and walks humbly with a sad face. Truly, whoever you are, whatever gay feathers of precious clothes and array you have and however proud you are as a peacock, whatever delight you find in any sin, whether it is lechery or greed or anything like that—look at your feet, that is, the end of your body, your final point. Think what your end will be if you were to continue your sins, and your reward for them. "The end" of sin "is death," says the Apostle [Romans 6:20–21], not only death of the body but of the soul, eternal damnation in the pit of hell. Who has his heart so hardened in sin that he will not turn back? If he were to think intimately of the pains of hell, whose heart would not be struck by sorrow if he reflects on how ugly sin is which deforms the image of the Blessed Trinity in his heart and changes it into a picture of demons? Add to this the shame for your sin, how shameful it is that God and the holy angels see all the vileness of your sins and will make them public in that fearful judgment, to your greatest embarrassment, unless they are wiped out in penance. Let all this be your feet, and without doubt, when you look at them and reflect in your heart how much wretchedness comes from your sins, you will be contrite and sorrowful for them.

So, then, as the holy days of penitence lie before you, leave your sins through true contrition and penance, and from your heart **be converted** to God. For in Sirach 17[:20–26] it is written: "To the penitent the Lord has given the way of justice. Turn to the Lord and forsake your sins. Turn away from injustice. Tarry not in the error of the

---

8. The simile is found in many sermons and handbooks—for example, Bartholomew, *De proprietatibus rerum* 12.31.

ungodly." If you repent this way, you will be converted to the good, and thus you will travel well on the first day's journey to the bliss of heaven.

[2]

The second day's journey that we must travel in the desert is confession. However much sorrow you may have for your sins, unless you make confession if you have the opportunity and a priest available, you will not be freed from your sin. Through confession any unclean spirit and any human soul is cleansed from every stain of sin. Therefore Augustine says, in his book *On Penance:* "Confession saves the souls, restores virtues, and overcomes the demons. It closes the mouth of hell and opens the gates of paradise."[9] But in order that confession may have these effects, two things among others are necessary. First, confession must be well prepared, and second, it must be made with completeness. How confession should be prepared we learn from the example of those who must give an account. We can see that when a bailiff is called to give his account, before he goes to it he diligently checks what he has received and his expenses, the place, the village, the time, and what he has spent in other business. He gathers it all together and puts it in writing, so that his accounting may be confident and efficient. So it is also with our spiritual accounting. Before we give it, we think how we have spent our life (which is worth more than money) since we have been last to confession, in what place, what village, what society we have lived, if anyone has moved us to sin, if we have led anyone to sin; where, when, how, how often we have failed, whether in falling into the seven sins or by misusing our five senses and not practicing the seven works of mercy as much as we could. These items, in the order of the sins, we will recall in our memory and write in our heart before we go to confession in order to give an account of our life. If those who go to confession were to do thus, they would find many things that at this moment they pay no attention to, because they examine their conscience as they should. There are some people who come to confession so lighthearted and merry as if they set no store by it, and when they show up, they have little

9. Pseudo-Augustine, *Sermones ad fratres in eremo* 30 (PL 40:1289).

or nothing to say but ask their confessor, "Ask me, sir." What an astonishing thing and bad misuse! People will diligently think how they can achieve their foul[10] thoughts and evil desires, but they don't think ahead how they should show their sins so that they may be healed of them. Alas, that they seek hell with greater attention than heaven! Alas, you Christian, how will you be excused before God, that strict judge, when on judgment day you will give an account of your every thought and deed that you have ever done in your life? If a bailiff who had been selling from the profit of a large estate came to his auditor and said, "Sir, ask me what you will, I have not given it any thought until now," his auditor will want to reproach him of his negligence and condemn him for being in arrears. How, then, will you answer before God, the highest auditor, you who can faultlessly count five hundred dollars[11] but perhaps of five hundred sins can hardly count fifteen? Such negligence is inexcusable, such cursed ignorance, that a man who is so skilled in counting dollars is found to be so incompetent in counting his sins. And therefore, people who are thus through their negligence separated from God our Lord, the prophet advises them to get words of shrift and confession and turn back to him: "You who have fallen down by your iniquity, take with you words and return to the Lord," Hosea 14[:2–3].

And although it sometimes happens that some people who have fallen into sin are negligent of their salvation and do not know the words to express their confession, the confessor should nevertheless support them humbly, comfort them, and help them. Just as a clerk helps the bailiff to make his account, so must the priest ask his penitent about the Ten Commandments and the seven deadly sins with their branches and circumstances in order, and inform him in any of these as best he can.

I have told you how people before their confession should call to mind their sins. Now I say that all sins that come to their mind should be told to the priest in their entirety. You must know that, just as a fox, when he catches a goose or hen to carry it to his hole, if he can he slashes its throat so that it cannot cry out, lest by its cry it be tak-

---

10. *Mingentos* in the manuscript.
11. *Denarios,* literally "pennies." I have upgraded to more modern standards.

en away from him—so that deceitful fox, the devil, wanting to drag Christians to the hole of hell, takes pains to literally stop their throats and prevent their tongue and speech, lest by confession they are taken out of his power. Sometimes he fills them with shame of confessing. Thus we read that as someone was asking the devil what he was doing among the people, he said: "I give back what I have taken from them. I took shame from them and I give it back. Before Lent I took shame away from people so that they would sin without hesitation. Now during Lent I give them back their shame so that no one may purge himself from his sins through confession." Not only through shame but in many other ways does the devil prevent a man's confession. Whence Gregory says in a homily: "When a wretched person falls into sins, the devil moves him not to confess them, and he says, 'Your sin is light and small, God's mercy is great, and you will be able to live a long time yet.' And he does all that so that he may ruin you and lead you into despair." But take heed of such preaching. The devil is that cursed fox who preaches thus that he may destroy you and take away your spiritual medicine. And therefore man carries the remedy for all the diseases of his soul in his tongue. There is no mortal wound that, if the tongue touches it in true confession, does not at once get healed, and if the tongue does not touch it, then it can in no way be healed, as is truly said, "Death and life are in the hands of the tongue" [Proverbs 18:21]. For when the tongue conceals sins, it brings death; when it reveals them, it brings life. In our physical life we see that in people who are coming to their life's end, when their tongue falters, they are near death, and it does not help to give them medicine. But if someone loses speech altogether, men despair of his health. If after this he should recover, it is considered a miracle. In the same way, if a sinner loses his speech, so that he cannot confess his sins, it is a great miracle if he will ever be saved. So then, as long as you are well and alive, before you fall into spiritual death through sin, beg for God's mercy, and without doubt he is so merciful and gracious that he will forgive you. This the prophet affirms when he says: "While you are alive and in health, you shall confess and praise God and glory in his mercies, for great is God's mercy and his forgiveness to them that turn to him," Sirach 17[:27–28]. Thus, with the tongue of confession, **be converted** to your Lord, as I said in the beginning.

[3]

The third day's journey that we must travel in the desert is satisfaction. However much you have been contrite and confessed your sins to God, unless you receive penance for them and do it, all will be of no avail. For a worthy satisfaction two things are necessary: discretion on the part of him who imposes it, and obedience on the part of him who receives it. The priest confessor who imposes penance should bear himself like a surveyor who measures the land or other things. Like a surveyor, who takes his measuring stick and compass and measures with them the length and breadth, the curvature and angles of things, a confessor, after hearing the complete confession, should, with the compass of discretion and the measuring stick of his reason, measure the circumstances of the sins and the conditions of the sinners, so that he is able to give each illness its appropriate medicine. And therefore says Augustine in his book *On Penance:* Discretion is greatly necessary to the confessor, "that he may consider the quality of a sinful deed with respect to place, time, perseverance, the character of the sinner," how old he was, what education he had, whether he was in orders, from what temptation he acted, how often he has committed it in deed.[12] When all these things have been considered and weighed, the confessor in his discretion should enjoin a penance that corresponds to the sin. This enjoined penance the penitent must receive in obedience and carry out in its totality. However much a person may show his wounds to a wise physician, and however good a plaster he may receive, unless he takes it and puts it on his wounds, he will never be healed by it. In the same way, however much a man may show his sins to a skillful spiritual physician—a discreet and wise priest—and however salutary a penance he may receive from him, unless he will apply it and carry it out in deed, he will never be healed by it. And as I said before, the priest must have discretion, so that he may enjoin a penance that is appropriate to the sin. For some sins bodily mortification is appropriate, for others almsgiving, and for yet others subduing the flesh and devout prayer. This

12. Based on Pseudo-Augustine, *De vera et falsa poenitentia* 14 (PL 40:1124), this passage became a commonplace in later medieval literature, such as Peter Lombard, *Sententiae* 4.16.2 (4:337) and *Decretum*, Causa 33, d. 3 (De penitentia), c. 5 (Friedberg, *Corpus iuris canonici*, 1:1238).

is allegorically indicated in Mark 9[:28]: "This kind of demon can go out by nothing but fasting and prayer."

Now, my lords, for a brief recapitulation of my entire discourse, that my sermon will be more deeply impressed on your memory, as well as in confirmation of the three parts of my sermon: I find that once there was a demoniac who one day was in church. At the elevation of Christ's body the demon cried out through his mouth: "Oh, how small in the form of bread, and how great is your power!" After Mass the demon was conjured by the priest to say why he was troubling people and what his name was. He answered: "We are three demons who trouble this man for his sins, and we have three names that correspond to our actions. I, the first, am Hardheart, the second is Stopmouth, and the third Closepurse. My office is to harden men's hearts that they may not be contrite for their sins. The second demon's office is to stop people's mouth that they may not confess. And the third demon's office is to close men's purses and keep them from giving alms that they may not through almsgiving make satisfaction for their sins. Whoever does these three things shall be ours forever."[13] If you want to drive out these three demons, I will tell you of three things that are contrary to the works of these demons, namely, contrition, confession, and satisfaction. If we take on these three, however often the three demons Hardheart, Stopmouth, and Closepurse have led us away from God and the right path of virtue this year, we return to him after the three days' journey I have talked about, so that he himself can say to us truthfully what is written in holy scripture: "Come to me again after three days," 2 Chronicles 10[:5]. That is to say: after you have made satisfaction for your sins through these three parts of penitence—contrition of heart, confession of mouth, and satisfaction in deed—I shall go before you and lead you into my bliss, where you will rule with me forever. To that bliss may he bring us who lives and reigns with the Father and the Holy Spirit. Amen.

13. A popular *exemplum*, probably originating in the Lenten sermons of Jacobus a Voragine (sermon 46) and used by Robert Holcot (sermon 58, with English), Repingdon, Felton, and the anonymous sermons J/5-6, P2-28 (with reference to the *Speculum historiale* of Vincent of Beauvais and English names), and R-30 (with English), with various English forms of the three names. The story is illustrated in a wall painting in Oberambach, Pfalz (Germany).

10

GOOD FRIDAY

IN THE LATE-MEDIEVAL CHURCH the Good Friday liturgy took a special form, quite different from the normal Mass (in fact, on this day the Eucharist was not celebrated). It included reading the Passion according to John, a series of intercessory prayers with genuflections, worshipping or "creeping to" the cross, and a communion service with the preconsecrated hosts brought in from a side chapel or similar place. Sermons for this occasion tend to be quite long and focus, in one form or another, on Christ's suffering and death.

This concentration is well illustrated by a sermon that on internal evidence was made for Good Friday ("hodierna die"). It utilizes a number of commonplaces on the Passion, such as the *exemplum* of Christ the Lover-Knight, Christ's wounds as protection against or healing of the seven deadly sins, and his seven words on the cross. Much of this material can also be found in meditative texts, such as Pseudo-Bonaventure's *Meditationes vitae Christi* or Ludolf of Saxony's *Vita Christi*, and in fact like the latter this sermon goes through the canonical hours, connects them with features of the Passion, and then recommends moral topics for meditation at these points, all of it under the image of the nightingale, who sings more and more exuberantly until it dies. These topics are also found in other Passion sermons, often in different combinations or with different developments; a good example is the Passion sermon by Nicholas Philip, edited by A. G. Little, "A Fifteenth-Century Sermon," in Little, *Franciscan Papers, Lists, and Documents* (Manchester: Manchester University Press, 1943), 244–56.

Again like other sermons on Christ's Passion, this Latin sermon contains a large number of English verses that translate its thema, the division, and then various liturgical or meditative Latin verses. Instead of rendering them into awkward modern lines, I present them, together with the rhymed thema and division, in their original Middle English form.

SOURCE:
Cambridge, Jesus College 13, part 5, fols. 83v–90v (J/5-19).

LITERATURE:
Holly Johnson, "Preaching the Passion: Good Friday Sermons in Late Medieval England" (Ph.D. diss., University of North Carolina at Chapel Hill, 2001).
Wenzel, *Collections*, 140–45.

⮑

What has he done, why shall he die? 1 Samuel 20:32.

>   Wat hath ys man do
>   Þat he schal dyȝe 300?

Beloved, Augustine in book 10 of *The City of God*, chapter 19 or 20, and Valerius Maximus, book 5, chapter 4, report that when Codrus, the king of Athens, saw his whole country being laid waste, he consulted his god about what should be done. His god answered him that he would not gain victory over his enemies or save his realm unless he himself would die. A similar response came to his enemies, namely, that if King Codrus should die, if they were to kill him, they themselves would be overcome. Therefore they forbade that anyone should kill the king. But King Codrus changed his royal clothes, entered the battle, and gratuitously provoked his enemies, so that he was at once killed by them and through his death overcame his enemies and saved his people.[1] In like manner it was the case that humankind could not be called back to heaven in justice unless Christ died. Gregory affirms

---

1. A favorite story for medieval preachers, including *Fasciculus morum* and Brinton; see Tubach, no. 1136. From Augustine, *De civitate Dei* 18.19 and Valerius Maximus 5.6.ext. 1.

this in book 17, chapter 15, of his *Moral Commentary:* "In order to gain eternal life it was necessary that the guilt of our first parent be deleted, who willingly became bound to suffer death. But this guilt could not be deleted except by a sacrifice. Brute animals were not worthy victims for rational man, therefore a human being had to be found to be killed, a rational host for the rational sinner. But since a stained host could not purify the stained sinners, it was necessary that that human being who was to purify humans from sin was himself free from sin. And so," says Gregory, "the Son of God came for our sake into the womb of the Virgin Mary and became man and offered the sacrifice for us. He offered his body as a victim without sin, which could die in its human nature and purify in justice."[2] Thus Gregory.

Now, this noble knight, Christ, seeing that his people could not be saved unless he himself died, and seeing that through his death he would destroy the devil's power, as he could not suffer and die in his royal garment, that is, in his divinity, changed his garment and put on the clothes of human nature, in which he was unknown. In these he entered the battlefield and was killed, and thereby, through his death, he saved humankind and overcame the devil. Now, if you ask why the Son suffered death rather than the Father or the Holy Spirit, I answer as follows. Vegetius, in his book *On Military Matters,* says that in the military game that is called Round Table each knight hangs out his shield on his tent, and when someone's shield is touched by a challenger, he would be armed by a virgin and step out for combat.[3] In the same fashion, figuratively, in the three divine persons was power, which is attributed to the Father, wisdom, attributed to the Son, and clemency, in the Holy Spirit. Now, since in his sin man did not desire to have God's power or his clemency but only his wisdom or knowledge, which is attributed to the Son—as the devil said to him, "You shall be as gods, knowing good and evil," Genesis 3[:5]—it was fitting that Christ, called into battle, should arm himself with the arms of our mortality from

2. Gregory, *Moralia* 17.30.

3. For this "game" of the Round Table as a sermon topic, see Wenzel, *Preachers, Poets, and the Early English Lyric,* 234n68; and Lawrence Warner, "Jesus the Jouster: The Christ-Knight and Medieval Theories of Atonement in Piers Plowman and the 'Round Table' Sermons," *Yearbook of Langland Studies* 10 (1996): 129–43. The reference to Vegetius seems unique and questionable.

the Virgin and thus enter the combat. Consider that Christ redeemed man not only through mercy but also through justice. For this there are many reasons. First, because our first parent committed sin through the deceit of the devil and through his own volition. In so far as he sinned through his own volition, he was put in hell with justice, but in so far as the devil had deceived man through fraud, he was detained there unjustly. Now, since the devil detained man unjustly because of his fraud, Christ freed man as an act of justice. But since man was held justly [because of his own volition], in freeing him God granted man mercy. The second reason is this. Although the devil had a right on all who descended from Adam, since Original Sin was in them, in Christ, who was conceived by the Holy Spirit, the devil had no right, because in him there was no sin. Now, since the devil laid hands on Christ unjustly to kill him and deliver him over to the Jews, the devil justly lost what before then he had justly owned. For injustice cancels justice. The third reason is this: A buyer justly owns what he has bought. Now, Christ bought us with a great price, namely, his own blood. Therefore, he freed us justly from death. The fourth and most powerful reason is taken from civil law. The law of the *Digest* "On Rescinding a Sale," in paragraph "Any thing sold in good faith," says that when something is sold for less than half its just price, it should be considered as not bought, and the seller can claim it back.[4] With this agrees canon law, in book 3 of the *Decretals*, "On Selling and Buying Goods," chapter *When our beloved sons*, where it says that the canons of Beauvais wrote to the pope against the abbot and brethren of Charlis because the latter had bought, without the chapter's knowledge, a forest called "Black" from someone for ten pounds while it was worth forty marks. In his rescript the pope committed the case to a bishop and dean for determination. At last the dean proceeded to determine the case, and finding that the aforesaid brethren had bought the forest for less than half its just price, he judged that the sale was void and that the forest belonged to the church of Beauvais, and he declared the canons to be its

---

4. Justinian, *Digest* 18.1.54 (in the collections of ancient Roman laws ordered by the emperor Justinian and promulgated in 533, also known as *Pandects*). The preacher seems to be citing a gloss or commentary, perhaps that of Accursius; see Justinian, *Corpus iuris civilis Iustinianei*, 1:1719.

owners.[5] A similar case can be found in the same passage. Now, our forefather Adam sold his soul, which was most beloved by God and of the greatest price, to the devil for some transitory pleasure and for nothing. Christ reclaimed it and bought it back with full justice. As a biblical figure, it is said in Leviticus 25[:47–48] that "if the hand of a stranger or a sojourner grows strong among you," that is, the action of the devil and his fraudulent work, "and your brother being impoverished sells himself to him," the latter may be redeemed by any relative. Now, Christ is our relative, and his blood justly redeemed us who had been sold through our sin. And since through his death Christ has sanctified man and redeemed him in justice and mercy, the Apostle says in 1 Corinthians 1[:30]: "Christ is made for us by God wisdom, and justice, and sanctification, and redemption."

There is a story about two brothers, one rich and the other poor. One day a stranger came to the house of the poor brother. Since he had nothing to serve him, he went to his rich brother to buy food for his guest. He gave it to him with the stipulation that, if he were not to pay for it by a certain day, the rich brother would have a strip of skin from his back down to his feet. The poor brother agreed. But as he was unable to pay at the stated time, he was led to the judge so that he might lose a strip of his skin. As he was on his way to the judge, the son of the king met him, and when he heard where he was going and for what purpose, he said: "Will you sell me your blood?" The poor brother agreed. And with this purchase, the king's son said to the rich brother: "Do not shed the blood that I have bought!" When the rich brother saw that he could not get a strip of skin without shedding the blood that had been bought [by the king's son], he let him go free.[6] These two brothers are man and the first angel, who after his sin became the devil and was richer and more powerful in his natural gifts than man. Then a stranger came to man, namely, Temptation and Suggestion from within him. When our forefather wanted to nourish him, he bought from the devil forbidden fruit, with which he stilled his appetite. But since man could not repay, the devil wanted to

---

5. *Decretals* 3.17.3 (Friedberg, *Corpus iuris canonici*, 2:518–19).

6. I am not aware of other occurrences of the particular trick story. For other medieval antecedents of *The Merchant of Venice*, see Tubach, no. 3867.

detain mankind like a strip of skin for all time eternally, if possible. But the noble son of the Eternal King bought man's blood, and in this way the devil could no longer possess the strip of skin. Further, to redeem this blood Christ shed all of his own blood. All our veins come together in our hands and feet, and so all his blood was shed in the piercing of his feet and hands. Further, the blood between his skin and flesh was driven out through blows and wounds. And lastly, in the piercing of his heart and sides he shed all his blood. Some scholars believe that a man's life is in his blood; and thus, in order to give us his life, Christ shed all his blood, as I have said. Others believe that the primary location of life or the soul is in the brain; and Christ's brain was shed through the crown of thorns. A third group believes that life resides mainly in the heart; therefore, that Christ might truly give us his life, his heart was cut in two. In this way Christ gave his life and died, so that he could say the words of Genesis 25[:32]: "Lo, I die." And since he gave his life for us to justify and reform us, after the words of the Apostle in Romans 5[:10], "we have become reconciled with God through the death of his son." Therefore Christ could say "Lo, I die," add: for you. Now since the Blessed Virgin Mary, who knew Christ best, knew how he had been conceived and been born, and knew that he was without sin and guilt, and that Christ's life was without blame before God and men, she could in her lament ask the question of our thema: **Why shall he die,** that is, my son?

For the development we must know that Christ died for us for three reasons:

First, for to destruyyn þe deuelys my3th,
second, for to makyn vus strong in fy3th,
and third, for to restoryn vus to owr ry3th.

[1]

For my first main part I say that Christ died for us to destroy the devil's might. You must understand that to overcome the devil Christ had four encounters with him.[7] The first was in the desert after his fasting, when the devil tempted him to gluttony; but Christ resisted

---

7. "Bella of arest," fights in which there is no direct contact with the enemy (MED).

him bravely and defeated him—yet the devil was not yet fully overcome. But notice here the false trick of the devil: he began to tempt Christ with the last temptation that he had brought to Adam, gluttony, thinking he might thereby overcome him. The second combat was on the pinnacle of the temple, where he tempted him with pride; but in this he did not win either. As he saw that he was not succeeding, he started the third combat when he took Christ to a mountaintop and showed him all the kingdoms of the world, tempting him with avarice; since men easily incline to that, he thought he could easily overcome him. But in all these combats Christ carried the victory. But this was not yet the end, because unless Christ died, the devil would retain the power of men that he held earlier. So a fourth combat followed, on Mount Calvary, when in order to triumph completely over the devil, Christ mounted the horse of the cross, with the helmet of sharp thorns on his head, and the corselet of his bloody and red garment on his body; his spurs were the nails in his feet, his lance the one by which his heart was cleft in two. And in this way Christ destroyed the devil with his seven armies, that is, the seven deadly sins, which Christ suffered in seven places so that he might uproot them more clearly, as I will explain later on. We find a biblical figure for this in Ecclesiastes 9[:14–15], where it is said that "there was a small city and few men in it. A great king came against it and surrounded and besieged it. In the city was found a wise and poor man, who saved the city through his wisdom, and later on nobody ever remembered this poor man." The great king was the devil, who came to the city of man's soul with seven armies, the seven deadly sins, and besieged it for many thousand years, that is, from the time of Adam until Christ. But then a poor and wise man was found in this city, Christ, who freed the city through his wisdom. Yet afterward none of the Christians, as it were, remembered Christ, but instead, like the ungrateful Jews, they render evil for his good deeds, adding sin upon sin.

Now, today the church, in her office and in holy scripture, remembers that God conferred ten solemn favors on the Jews, for which they returned evil deeds on this day. The first favor was that he led them out of Egypt, where under the rule of Pharaoh they were afflicted with divers labors, doing slave work with clay, straw, and brick, as is reported in the beginning of Exodus [1:14], and in order to lead

them away he worked many signs. But see what gratitude for that favor they showed on this day: him who freed them from their enemies
they bought today from Judas the traitor for thirty shillings so that
they might hand him over to his enemies and death. And him who before had released them from the bonds of slavery in Egypt, the chief
priests today led in fetters. Such ingratitude Mother Church today
rightly reproaches when she sings in the person of Christ: "My people, what have I done to you," etc.[8]

> My folk, now ansuere me,
> qwat haue I to the gylt?
> qwat my3th I more a doon for te
> þan I haue ful-fylt?
> Owht of Egypti I browht the,
> the þou were in woo.
> þow dy3thest a cros now for my deth
> os I were thy foo.

> [My people, now answer me: what wrong have I done to you?
> What more could I have done for you than I have already
> done? I brought you out of Egypt, where you were in pain.
> Now you made a cross for my death, as if I were your enemy.]

This indeed was great ingratitude. The same, and an even greater, ingratitude is shown by Christians who are alive and by sinners who
crucify Christ. Whence Augustine says on Psalm 7: "The evil of those
men who crucified Christ has reached its end. But the evil of those is
greater who do not want to live right but hate the precepts of truth,
for whom Christ was crucified."[9] And this is no wonder, for through
his sin man kills what God loves more than the whole world, man's

---

8. These are the Reproaches (*Improperia*), which could be chanted during the vener-
ation of the cross in the Good Friday liturgy. They consist of an antiphon ("Popule
meus, quid feci tibi? Aut in quod contristavi te? Responde michi") sung at the beginning and between a number of stanzas that set God's favors shown to the Israelites
in the Old Testament against Christ's sufferings. The writer of this sermon has translated everything into English stanzas of four lines. For other renderings of the *Improperia*, as well as other Passion lyrics used in sermons, see Wenzel, *Preachers, Poets, and the
Early English Lyric*, chapters 4–5 on John of Grimestone.

9. Augustine, *Enarrationes in Psalmos*, on Psalm 7:9.

soul. For when God gave the devil power over Job's body, out of love he forbade him to touch his soul. Just as a noble lord of this world guards the more precious jewels himself, while he gives the common ones to his servant for safekeeping, so, according to Chrysostom in homily 3 of his *Imperfect Work*, God has given temporal goods to both good and evil people for safekeeping, but their souls he has kept for his own protection, according to the Psalm [96:10]: "The Lord preserves the souls of his servants *[sic]*." And notice that God showed in his passion that he loves men's souls more than himself, which I prove as follows. Any merchant loves the thing he buys more than the money with which he buys it. But the Son of God bought man with himself; ergo, etc. Therefore Bernard says: "He would not have given himself for me unless he loved me more than himself."[10] And for that reason those who are so ungrateful that they give their souls, God's jewels, to the devil can be compared to the ungrateful Jews.

The second favor that God conferred on the Jews was that he led them everywhere as their guide, going before them and showing them the way. Therefore, God alone was their leader of old. But see how badly they returned that favor on this day, for today they all denied him and said: "We have no king but Caesar" [John 19:15]. And while he led them on the right way through the desert, they led him to Annas and Pilate. Therefore the church makes lament in the person of Christ:

> My people, etc.
> My folk, ansuere me ouer al
> I ledde the and fore the 3ede.
> Alas, wy art thow so onkeende
> Now at my most nede?

[My people, etc. My people, answer me. I led you above all and went before you. Alas, why are you so unkind now in my greatest need?]

The third favor that God conferred was that they crossed the Red Sea dry shod, while Pharaoh and his army drowned in the sea. "Pha-

10. Perhaps Petrus Cellensis, *De disciplina claustralis* 25 (PL 202:1140).

raoh's chariots and his army he has cast into the sea" [Exodus 15:4].
But for this favor the Jews, like ungrateful people, today bound Christ
to a column, scourged him, and spat in his face. And therefore the
church makes lament:

> My folk.
> In þe see drye I made the gon
> os yt were in londe
> wit scorgis thou hast now broke my bon
> and bownde me wt harde bonde.

[My people. I made you walk dry in the sea as if it were on
land. Now you have broken my bones with scourges and bound
me in a hard bond.]

It is the same with us: for by the Red Sea we understand the blood of
Christ or baptism reddened with the blood of Christ, which allows
us to go dry shod to the kingdom of heaven. In this baptism the devil and his army are drowned. But when we sin, for this favor we deny
our baptism through mortal sin, we scourge Christ through wrath and
envy, we bind him to the column through avarice and greed, and we
spit on him through uncleanness and lechery.

The fourth favor was that God fed them in the desert with manna
for forty years and made rain fall from heaven. But in return the Jews
clamored that he should be crucified. And so the church says:

> My folk.
> Fourty ȝar I sente the awngeles fode
> from heuene
> for thys ȝe nayle me on the rode
> and cryyn with gret steuene.

[My people. For forty years I sent you angels' food from
heaven. For this you nail me on the cross and shout with a
great voice.]

It is the same with Christians, whom God nourishes many times with
his body and blood, the manna that is more precious than any other manna. But they despise God in their sinning and not only crucify
him, as I said before, but as far as their will goes, kill him. Whence

Chrysostom says in homily 35 of his *Imperfect Work:* "Every evil person, in as much as it lies in him, lays hands on God and kills him, for when he provokes God's anger, blasphemes, and despises his commandments, does he not kill God, if this were possible, so that he may sin more freely?" as if to say, yes, indeed.

The fifth favor was that he everywhere overcame their enemies, for the Jews prevailed against all. But today they repaid him badly when they jeered at him, mocked him like a fool, and treated him with dishonor. And therefore the church makes lament:

> My folk.
> Al thy fon I slow for the
> and made the greeth of name
> lytel tellyst now of me
> but dost me ruth greeth shame.

[My people. I slew all your enemies for you and gave you a great name. Now you set little store by me but cause me very great shame.]

The sixth favor was that God gave them his commandments and rites, and promised them the Promised Land if they observed them. But today the Jews acted against him and against his commandments. He had commanded them not to give false testimony against one's neighbor, and not to kill the innocent. But they accused him with lies in three things. First they accused him that he made himself a king. But they lied in this, since, when they wanted to make him king, he fled [John 6:15]. Second, they accused him that he forbade to give Caesar tribute; but that, too, was false [Matthew 22:16–21]. Third, they accused him that he said he was the Son of God. That was true, but for a truth nobody should die or be condemned. Hence they killed him falsely. And therefore the church says:

> My folk.
> Ryth lawes I gaf to the
> in trewthe that þou schuldyst stonde;
> falsly þou demyst now me
> w'touten lawe of londe

[My people. I gave you right laws so that you should stand in truth. Now you judge me falsely against the law of the land.]

And this is said against false judges, who under the influence of petitions or gifts falsely judge their neighbors. But there is no doubt that, just as the Jews were condemned by God for not observing his commandments (as is said in Deuteronomy 11[:28]), so these people will in the end carry God's condemnation. They are "Susanna priests," who do not have God before their eyes.[11]

The seventh favor was that he led them into the Promised Land, which was flowing with milk and honey, where they lived in complete abundance and fruitfulness. But today the Jews repaid him badly when they nailed him on the cross with nails of iron, which in the Law was a most shameful torment. Of this Mother Church makes her lament in the person of Christ:

> Mi folk, ansuere me.
> With gret blisse I brouth the
> to the land of beheste
> now on the cros þou hanggest me
> and naylest wonder faste.

[My people, answer me. I brought you to the Promised Land with great bliss. Now you hang me on the cross and nail me to it most firmly.]

A *figura* for this appears in the gospel, where it is said that a man planted a vineyard and sent his servants, and so forth [Matthew 21:33ff.]. This vineyard was God's Law. The first servant whom he sent was Moses, who for forty years tried to find the fruit of the Law in them, but in vain. Another servant was David, who with his psalms invited them to the good, but without success, as they said, "What do we have to do with David?" [1 Kings 12:16]. The third servant was the choir of prophets who corrected the people; but they persecuted and killed them. At last, God the Father sent his Son, Christ, but the false Jews, knowing that he was the heir, killed him. Thus they returned his favor badly.

11. Reference to the story of Susanna and the two elders, Daniel 13.

The eighth favor was that, when they had no drinking water in the desert and nearly died of thirst, God commanded Moses to strike the rock twice with his rod, and abundant water flowed forth [Numbers 20:11]. And in another place he made for them bitter waters sweet [Exodus 15:23ff.]. But that favor they repaid him badly today, for they gave him vinegar mixed with gall to drink. Of which the church says:

> Mi folk, etc.
> Holsum water I sente the
> owthe of the harde stoon;
> esyl and attyr thou drunk to me,
> other hadde I noon.

[My people, etc. I sent you healthy water out of the hard rock. You gave me vinegar and poison to drink—I had nothing else.]

The ninth favor was that after they had been led out of captivity, he made them kings and freedmen, and so on, from their own kind, such as Saul and David, etc. But they repaid him ill, like ingrates, when today instead of golden crowns they put a crown of thorns on his head. Of this the church laments:

> Mi folk, etc.
> Worthi kyngges I haue the mad
> of thyn owen brood;
> wit thornes thow hast crowned myn heed,
> yt rennyt al on blood.

[My people, etc. I made worthy kings for you from your own nation. Now you have crowned my head with thorns, it flows all in blood.]

The tenth favor was that when he went before them in a pillar of fire at night and a pillar of cloud by day, wherever the children of Israel were, it was light and tranquil [Exodus 13:21]. But they repaid him badly for this favor when they killed him who is the true light and treated him most shamefully. Of this the church makes lament:

> My folk, etc.
> Bysylyche I 3af the ly3th

> bothe be day and ny3th;
> for thys þow hast me doon to deth
> al 3ens the ry3th.

[My people, etc. I eagerly gave you light both by day and night. For this you have put me to death, against any justice.]

Just as these Jews received many favors from God and repaid them badly, so also do Christians repay him even more badly. Consider how often you were in tribulation, in anxiety, in illness, and you would be free of them rather than have all the goods of the world, and you promised God to emend your life, but right after you were freed to your earlier state, you reversed yourself. But fear God's vengeance in the end! Augustine says in his book *On the Marvels of Holy Writ* that because the Ninevites, who repented and deserved God's mercy, afterward returned to their former sins, God changed forty days into forty years and then destroyed them. In the same way, etc.

Christ, who thus in his Passion defeated the devil through his five main wounds, was foreshadowed in David, who killed Golias with five stones, as is reported in 1 Samuel 17[:40]. For this reason, when the Blessed Virgin, his mother, saw the Lord of glory thus treated, who had raised their dead, healed their sick, fed the hungry, given light to the blind, and taught those without knowledge, could therefore rightly lament and say about Christ, her son: **Why shall he die?**

[2]

For my second main part I said that Christ died to make us strong in fight. As I touched on earlier, before Christ's death the devil fought man with a sevenfold army, the seven sins. To strengthen man against them, Christ suffered pain in seven places. Therefore, a devout writer, addressing humankind in the person of Christ, says as follows:

> Wyth the garlond of thornes kene
> myn heed was bowonden, that was wyl sene.
> The streem of blod ran[12] be my cheke.
> Thou proud man, therfore be meke.

---

12. Ran: i an, MS.

[With the garland of sharp thorns was my head surrounded,
that could be well seen. The stream of blood ran on my cheek.
O proud man, therefore be meek!]

Against wrath he suffered the nail in his right hand, and thus he says:

> Whan thou art wroth and wylt ham wreche,
> beholde the leere þat I the teche.
> Th[r]owygh myn ryth hand the nayl yt good.
> For3eef therfore and be nowth wroth.

[When you are angry and will have vengeance, behold the
lesson I teach. Through my right hand goes the nail. Therefore,
forgive and be not wrathful!]

Against avarice he suffered the nail in his left hand, and thus he says:

> Th[r]owygh my left hand [þ]e nayl is dreue.
> Thenk therof 3yf thou wylt leue,
> and help the powre with almesdede,
> and Good of heuene schal 3eld thi mede.

[Through my left hand the nail is driven. Think of it if you
want to live, and help the poor with almsgiving, and God in
heaven will give you your reward.]

Against sloth he suffered the nails in his feet, whence he says thus:

> Rys vp, slaw man, owt of thy byd!
> Behold my feeth, how yt arn bled,
> qwow yt be nayled onto the tre.
> Thank me therof, yt was for the.

[Rise up, slow man, out of your bed! Behold my feet how
they are bloodied, how they are nailed onto the cross. Give me
thanks for that, it was for you.]

Against envy, which is rooted in the heart, he suffered the lance that
opened his heart. Wherefore he says:

> Wyt thys spere that was so gryl
> Myn herte was stongge, so was my wyl,

> for loue of man that was me dere
> enviows man of loue to lere.

[With the spear this is so cruel my heart was stung—it was my will, for love of man who was dear to me, to teach you, envious man, of love.]

Against lechery he suffered being scourged in his whole body. Whence he says:

> Beholde, þou man, with reuful herte
> thys scharpe scorges knottys smerte,
> my blodi bak qwow y ys betun,
> and leet [look?] at me thy lust to letyn.

[Behold, man, with rueful heart the painful knots of these sharp scourges, my bloody back how it is beaten, and look at me to leave your evil desire.]

Against gluttony he suffered thirst, and therefore he says:

> In al my thyrst vpon the rode
> the Jewys me goue thynggis vn-gode,
> esyl and galle for thyrst to drynke.
> Glotun, therof I rede the thynke.

[In all my thirst on the cross the Jews gave me bad things, vinegar and gall, to drink for my thirst. O glutton, I advise you to think of this!]

And thus God fully defeated the devil's army through these seven bloodlettings. If we were to keep these in mind, we would never sin in any of the seven deadly sins. For as the Apostle says in Hebrews 9[:14]: "The blood of Christ shall cleanse our conscience from dead works, to serve the living God."

A story[13] has it that there was a lord and king who had a most beautiful daughter. He loved her most dearly, and in token of that he made her his heir, on the condition that if she ever committed a car-

---

13. The *exemplum* of Christ the lover-knight, which exists in many places and varying forms; cf. Wenzel, *Preachers, Poets, and the Early English Lyric*, 233–38.

nal sin, she would lose her heritage. She later sinned in lust, lost her heritage, and became an exile. Now, this happened to come to the ears of a valiant knight. He took pity on her, left his own country, and traveled to hers to regain the woman's heritage. He entered the battlefield in order to fight for her against her enemies, defeated them, and gave her back her heritage, yet nonetheless he died in his blood on the field. The woman reflected on this, and lest through some light provocation she were to fall again into a similar wrongdoing, she hung up the knight's arms and bloody shirt in her bedchamber, so that in remembering her gratitude to this knight she would never return to sin. And in order to do this with greater constancy, she wrote these words in her bedchamber:

> I haue in loue and freysch in mynde
> the blod of hym that was so keende.

[I keep in my love and fresh in mind the blood of him who was so kind.]

With these words she always answered any flatterers who tried to seduce her to sin, and in this way she kept her heritage. In moral terms: The father of this woman was our Father in heaven, who had a most sweet daughter, man's soul, whom he loved so much that he gave her all paradise as her heritage, but with the proviso that she would lose it if ever she ate the forbidden apple. Because she ate it, she lost her heritage and was sent in exile to earth. A knight, Christ, heard of this lost girl. He left his own eternal home, entered the girl's country, that is, the world, and took flesh from the Blessed Virgin, and entered the battlefield on Good Friday to fight for her. He won the victory over the devil and reinstalled the girl to the joy of heaven, but himself died and lost his life. Now, following the example of this woman, the girl should fill her soul and bedchamber with meditation on the Passion of Christ, and when she is tempted by the devil to some sin, say the words of that woman I recited earlier, namely: "I haue in loue," and so forth. And without doubt, she would never again sin or lose her heritage. In this we can easily see how man is made strong through the Passion of Christ. And thus the Apostle says in 1 Corinthians 15[:22]: "As in Adam all die, so also in Christ all shall be made alive."

Some devout person imagines that at the time of Christ's Passion, in its beginning, there was a great debate between Christ's divinity and his human nature. His divinity wanted and said that Christ had to die. But his human nature argued against it. Its first reason was: "You, God, decreed in the Old Law that it is illicit to kill the innocent, nor must an innocent be killed. I am innocent of any sin, both original and actual, as I was conceived of the most pure drops of the blood of blessed Mary. Therefore it is unjust and against the Law that I should die." But his divinity replied: "The giver of the law is above the law. I gave the Law, and therefore I am above it. And insofar as you are innocent and without sin, you are a worthy sacrifice to my Father for humankind. And therefore you shall die." And his human nature argued again: "God is merciful on sinners. Be, I pray, even more merciful on me who have never sinned, and since humankind can be saved as easily through a single drop of my blood as through my death, accept some of my blood and spare my life." But Divinity replied: "Even if all humankind can be saved through the shedding of a single drop of your blood, yet, so that I may gain man's love and that he may be more strongly bound to me, you shall shed all your blood and die." And Human Nature argued again: "God, you knew from the beginning how ungrateful, how false mankind is, despite all the favors and benefits you bestowed on them. Thus, even if I die and shed all my blood, they will be false and more ungrateful than before, since they have a greater reason to be grateful." And God replied: "Even if they are ungrateful, I shall maintain my favor[14] and you shall die." And Human Nature said: "That is unjust!" To which God replied: "What I want to fulfill is not unjust."[15] And Human Nature said: "God, in the Old Law you commanded with the threat of a curse that no one should offend his father or mother, nor should he give cause for offense. But if I die, my mother will die for grief. Therefore it is against the Law if I must die." Now, when God heard about his mother according to his human nature, that she would have to die, he could no longer debate but went to Mount Olivet and prayed to his Father that "if it might be, the hour might pass from him" [Mark 14:35]. "And

14. The Latin here puns: "Etsi ipsi sint ingrati, ego ero gratus."
15. "Non est iniustum quod ego volo esse completum."

his sweat became as drops of blood, trickling down upon the ground" [Luke 22:44]. And as he was praying further, at last God decreed that for love of man his human nature should die.

When Human Nature heard this,[16] it appealed to the law of nature and its judgment, asking that he might be judged according to this law. In this law there are four judges or justices, and two advocates. The judges were Noah, Abraham, Isaac, and Jacob, and the advocates Treason and Reason. Treason pleads that he should die, saying: "Christ is a traitor to God the king, because such was God's statute in the beginning, and still is, that Adam and his whole offspring should die. Now, Christ belonged to Adam's offspring, therefore he should die. Since Christ spoke against that statute when he said, 'If any man keep my word, he shall not see death forever' [John 8:51], he contradicted the divine statute and therefore should die as a traitor." To which Reason replied: "It is true that Adam and every human being who descended from Adam through the common way of sin had to die. But this one [i.e., Christ] did not come that way, since he was without sin, as was his virgin mother. Therefore he does not have to die." Now, to establish the truth in this, the jury was called, that is, the twelve patriarchs, the sons of Jacob. They all agreed that Christ had to die, and so Joseph brought their verdict to the judges: "Just as I was sold into Egypt for thirty pieces of silver for the salvation of my people, so Christ will be sold to the Jews." Thereupon the judges gave judgment. The first, Noah, said: "Just as no human being was saved in this world except through my ark, so none will be saved except through Christ's cross and death." The second judge, Abraham, said: "As I killed the calf [Genesis 18:7], whose blood was shed seven times, so Christ the Son of God will be killed for man's salvation." The third judge, Isaac, said: "As I was bound and put on the altar as a sacrifice [Genesis 22], so Christ will be bound and offered up for mankind." And the fourth judge, Jacob, said: "Just as I saw a ladder

16. The preacher continues to develop the struggle within Christ with another dramatic image in which Christ's human nature appeals to the three laws, the law of nature, the Mosaic Law or Old Testament, and the law of grace. The same image appears in a sermon by Nicholas Philip (Q-39), edited by A. G. Little, "A Fifteenth-Century Sermon," in Little, *Franciscan Papers, Lists, and Documents* (Manchester: University of Manchester Press, 1943), 248–51.

reaching up to heaven, and the Lord leaning upon it, and angels going up and down this ladder [Genesis 28:12–13], so Christ will rest on the cross, through which men will go up to heaven."

After this judgment had been given in the law of nature, Christ appealed to the law of Moses. In that law were the same advocates as before and four [different] judges: Isaiah, Jeremiah, Ezekiel, and Daniel. Treason said that Christ must die because he acted against the Law, as he healed people on the Sabbath, when it was not permitted to work. Reason replied that it was more fitting for Christ to heal a man than for someone to save his ass or ox. And since the latter was allowed, the former was even more firmly permitted.[17] But the jury of the twelve prophets agreed that Christ had to die. Jonah took their judgment and reported: "Just as I was in the whale's belly for three days and nights, so Christ will lie dead in the earth." Then the first judge, Isaiah, gave his judgment: "Like a sheep he shall be led to the slaughter, and he shall be dumb as a lamb, and he shall not open his mouth," Isaiah 53[:7]. The second judge, Jeremiah, said: "He shall give his cheek to him that strikes him, he shall be filled with reproaches," Lamentations 3[:30]. Ezekiel said, 12[:12–13]: "His face shall be covered, that he may not see the ground with his eyes. I will spread my net over him, and he shall be taken and die." And the fourth judge, Daniel, said: "As I was brought near death by my enemies in the lions' den and yet escaped [Daniel 6], so Christ will be brought to death by the Jews, will go down to the lions' den of hell, and will free those who are captives there."

And as Christ is thus condemned to death by the law of Moses, he appeals to the third law, that of grace and of the Christians. In this jury are the twelve apostles, who declare with one mind that Christ was to suffer and die [cf. Acts 17:3], for they say that it was God the Father's will not to spare his own son but to hand him over in our stead.[18] They affirmed this not only in word but also in deed, when one betrayed Christ, another denied him, and the rest took flight. In this law are four judges: Annas, Caiaphas, Herod, and Pilate. They all say: "He is guilty of death" [Matthew 26:66]. And since two of

17. Cf. Luke 14:5.
18. A patristic commonplace; see Augustine, *De Trinitate* 13.11.

them were high priests of the church,[19] it is clear that the clergy and the religious establishment had abandoned him, nor could his clerical status save him, and so nothing was left but death. For the two high priests sent him to Pilate, Pilate to Herod, and Herod sent him back to Pilate. In the end Pilate gave a false judgment against him and condemned him to death. And in this way Christ was condemned to death by all three laws, and he was first bound, then scourged, afterward mocked and reviled, and finally crucified.

Yet when Christ saw death come near, that he might not leave those whom he loved without consolation, he gave them what he had and bequeathed it as his legacy.[20] Therefore Ambrose says in a sermon: "When the author of piety[21] hung on the cross, he left his legacy, giving to each appropriate works of piety: his persecution to his apostles, his body to the Jews, his spirit to his Father, a bridegroom to the Virgin, paradise to the thief, hell to the sinner, and the cross to Christians who do penance." The parchment on which this testament is written was his most chaste body, which was drawn on the cross like parchment on a stretching frame. The ink with which it was written was his precious blood. The quills were the lance and nails. Five large seals hung on this testament, namely, his five wounds. This testament was not closed up but is wholly open. And as soon as it was written, it was probated. Since the Apostle in Hebrews 9[:17] says that "a testament is of force after men are dead," in order to confirm his testament to the fullest, Christ died. But the Blessed Virgin was standing beneath the cross and saw her son suffer so many pains and reproaches that he had not deserved—no wonder that in her distress she cried out, **Why shall he die?** Namely, her son.

---

19. Annas and Caiaphas. They are called "episcopi ex parte ecclesie."

20. Christ on the cross issuing a legacy or testament or "the charter of salvation" is another commonplace in late-medieval meditations on the Passion; see Emily Steiner, *Documentary Culture and the Making of Medieval English Literature* (Cambridge: Cambridge University Press, 2003), 50–53 and passim. In connection with it, Christ is usually compared to a book or charter of parchment.

21. *Auctor pietatis* occurs frequently in the writings of St. Ambrose's contemporaries Chromatius of Aquileia and Peter Chrysologus.

[3]

For my third main part I said that Christ died to restore us to our right, which is the joy of heaven. From scripture and elsewhere it is manifest in many ways that God expelled Adam from paradise and put a threefold guard on the way to paradise, namely, an angel and a sword that was flaming and two-edged [Genesis 3:24]. These guarded the gate of paradise so that Adam would not reenter. Now, for man's return to paradise Christ removed the angel in his incarnation, when he reconciled angels and men. And as in the sword were two properties, namely, sharpness and the flame, both had to be destroyed so that the way was open. Now, natural philosophers say that the sharpness of a sword cannot be better removed than by bathing it in the hot blood of a lamb after it has been killed. In this way, in order to destroy the sharpness of the sword at the gate of paradise, Christ shed his blood like an immaculate lamb. That the blood might be quite hot, he suffered death at a youthful age, at thirty-three years, when a man is at the height of his manhood. But a flame cannot be better extinguished than with water, and therefore Christ in his death shed water from his side, with which he extinguished the flame of the sword and called us back and restored us to paradise. Natural philosophers also say that, when a nightingale dies, as it naturally feels its death coming, in the middle of the night it looks for a thorn bush, flies to it, and begins to sing very sweetly. About the first hour, near daybreak, it raises its voice louder and opens its throat and beak wider. About the third hour it knows no limit in its song, so much does its joy increase, and the more it sings, the more fervent it becomes. About the sixth hour, as the sun rises higher, its voice loses its power more and more. At that point its voice breaks and nearly stops with its effort. But at the ninth hour, it folds its wings, bends it neck, and sings so much that its veins rupture. And pressing itself against the thorn, it dies.

In the same way, our nightingale, Christ Jesus, when he knew he had to die, began his song near midnight. For when Christ was captured in the garden at the false counsel of the princes and Pharisees and false men, and in their evil plan was betrayed, accused, and falsely sold, then he began his song, the same that religious sing in their Matins: "Blessed is the man who has not walked in the counsel of the ungodly, nor stood in the way of sinners" [Psalm 1:1], for he knew that their counsel would lead to death. At the first hour, he was led to Pilate and they accused him falsely, struck him, bound him, and spat on him. They did all this against their law, for he had not deserved any of this as he was innocent. And thus Christ sang more loudly, as we use to sing at Prime: "Blessed are the undefiled in the way, who walk in the law of the Lord" [Psalm 118:1]. At the third hour, they cried out against him without mercy, "Crucify!" clothed him in purple, pierced his head with a crown of thorns, and laid a cross on his shoulders. Then, as he knew that they acted against their own law, Christ submitted himself to the eternal law which decreed that he should die and patiently suffered all these things, singing even more loudly: "Set before me for a law the way of your justifications, O Lord, and I will always seek after it" [Psalm 118:33], as if to say: I will always be ready to fulfill your law and your will until death. At the sixth hour, Christ was nailed to the cross with the thieves and was fed gall and vinegar; and then he cried out even more loudly to humankind: "My soul has fainted after your salvation" [Psalm 118:81],

> For thy sawle-sauyng
> My sawle makyt his endyng.

At the ninth hour this nightingale cried out so loud that he gave up his spirit. But what then was the last song of this nightingale? Certainly: "Your testimonies are wonderful, therefore my soul hath sought them" [Psalm 118:129], as if he were saying to the Father:

> Thy wondyrful wil and wytnesse
> My sawle hath sowht in bitturnesse,

in the bitterness of death. And in this way our nightingale died.

In this fashion the mortal nightingale, which is our human soul, should at these five hours sing louder and louder in contemplation and rise up to God. The first hour is Matins, when the soul should for God's sake overcome its vices, despise the world, and adhere to God. And the devout soul should reflect that what men seek in sins[22] they will more truly find in God, according to Augustine. (Say here the de-

22. Possibly a line has dropped out.

velopment found in the preceding sermon, in the second main part.)[23]
To avoid sins and the counsel of sinners, let this be the song of your
soul: "Blessed is the man who has not walked," etc. Note that such
contempt of the vices merits God's blessing, and thus the soul says:
"Blessed is the man," etc. When the soul has thus overcome the vices,
it behooves her to rise and sing more loudly in observing God's commandments and to practice the virtues through constant love of God.
And at that hour she will sing, "Blessed are the undefiled in the way,
who walk in the law of the Lord," for fulfilling the commandments
likewise merits God's blessing; hence she says "Blessed," etc. And even
if the commandments may seem hard to observe, without doubt if
one fosters a faithful love of God, they will seem easy.

Beloved, in ancient times there was an image of Love,[24] marvelously painted and fashioned. First of all, it was made of purest gold,
in sign of its preciousness, for good love is a precious jewel. Just as
fire, when it is placed in the hearth, comforts and does no harm because it is put in its proper place—but when it is put on the roof of
one's house, it burns the house, for it is not put in the proper place
ordained for it—just so it is with love. That image was further fashioned in the shape of a woman, for women are more fervent in love
than men and do not restrain their passions as much. Moreover, the
image was clothed in green color, which is most durable and always
new. Such must love be, without wearying. On the forehead of this
image the words "Far and near" were written. Now, the proverb says,
"Out of sight, out of mind." In order that such falseness may not be
found in love—namely, that the farther people are apart in body, the
less they are close in mind—these words "Far and near" were written
on the image's forehead. On its chest was written "Death and Life,"
in token that those who are friends in life must not be separated in
death; for one should be an even greater friend in death than one was

23. Such cross-references to other sermons in the same collection, directed to the
preacher, are not uncommon. In this collection, however, as it stands, there is no
"preceding sermon" that fits the reference.

24. The use of such "images," antique paintings or statues representing vices and
virtues, in late-medieval preaching has been studied by Beryl Smalley, *English Friars and
Antiquity in the Early XIVth Century* (Oxford: Basil Blackwell, 1960). This particular image can represent love, Christ, friendship, or gratitude. See ibid., 180n1.

in life. In life we could help ourselves, but no longer so in death. On the hem of this image was written "Winter and Summer." This indicates prosperity and adversity, meaning that true love must last equally in the time of adversity as in prosperity. We have many friends in prosperity but few in adversity, as the Wise Man says in Sirach 6[:10]: "There is a friend a companion at the table, and he will not abide in the day of distress." And above all, this image has an open wound in its side as a sign of love. Blessed Augustine says that there are three signs of love, namely, good gifts, pleasant words, and the sharing of each other's secrets. But nowadays many are cheated through gifts, deceived through pleasant words, and so on, as is shown in Joab and his cousin Amasa, in 2 Samuel [cf. 20:9, etc.]. Therefore Augustine mentions the third sign of love, sharing each other's secrets, because one would not do that unless one truly loved another person. Now, Christ loved us in all these ways, as is manifest; therefore, let us love him in turn in the same way. And thus his commandments will without doubt seem to us quite easy.

At the third hour we should raise our voice even more in prayer, petition, and good deeds, for it is not sufficient to abstain from sins and observe God's commandments if the soul does not engage in good deeds and prayers. And that God may grant you to work well in good deeds and in his law, sing the third song: "Set before me for a law the way of your justifications, O Lord, and I will always seek after it," that is, I will always seek the law of the Lord and the way of just deeds through good occupation and devout prayer. (And speak here about prayer if you wish, as you find it in the preceding sermon, part one.)[25]

At the sixth hour cry out and sing still more loudly in meditating on Christ's Passion and death, reflecting on this verse: "My soul has fainted after your salvation," etc. "For my sowle sauyng," etc. In this meditation you should pay attention, as blessed Bernard says, to how the Jews pressed thorns on Christ's head, which was so dear to the angels; how his face, that was so "beautiful above the sons of men" [cf. Psalm 44:3], was disfigured with the spittle of the Jews; how his eyes, shining more brightly than the sun, darkened in death; how his

25. See note 23.

ears, which hear the angels' song, hear the insults of the Jews; how his mouth, which taught the angels, is fed with gall and vinegar; how his feet, whose footstool was adored "for it is holy" [Psalm 98:5], are nailed down; how his hands that formed the heavens are stretched and nailed on the cross; how his whole body is scourged, his side pierced by a lance. And what more? Nothing was left but his tongue, so that he would pray for sinners and commend his mother to his disciple. So far Bernard.[26] These things, then, the sweet nightingale of our soul should remember of Christ's Passion.

At the ninth hour the soul, like the nightingale, must raise its song most loudly and meditate on the glory of heaven that God has prepared for her; on the divine gifts he has offered you; how he has created you above all things, has ordained heaven and earth for you; how he has placed you in the number of the faithful, has made you healthy and well, given you sense and many other things, has often heard you in your needs and weaknesses and freed you, has forgiven your sins, and preserved you from mortal sin. For all these things Chrysostom says in book 1 of *On Compunction:* "Even if we die a thousand times and if we practice all virtues of the soul, we do nothing worthy of what we have received from God."[27] And therefore you should raise your voice high and sing: "Wonderful are your testimonies" or your works to me and your gifts, "and therefore my soul has sought them," through continuous remembrance and thanksgiving. Therefore, just as Christ the nightingale offered himself to the Father with his fivefold song, so you should offer your soul to God in the way I have described.

Ovid tell us in *Metamorphoses* 10—and Theodulus alludes to it in the verses "The mountain ashes struggled, their tops bent down, to follow," etc. ["Orpheus through the woods as he was singing his songs"][28]—that when Orpheus, the best harp player, had married Eu-

26. A similar version of this devotional commonplace occurs in Petrus Cellensis, *De disciplina claustrali* 6 (PL 202:1110).

27. John Chrysostom, *Ad Stelechium de compunctione* (PG 47:418).

28. Theodulus, *Ecloga*, lines 189–90; in Francesco Mosetti Casaretto, ed., *Teodulo, Ecloga: Il canto della verità e della menzogna* (Florence: Galluzzo, 1997), 14. For the patristic and medieval allegorization of Orpheus as Christ, see John Block Friedman, *Orpheus in the Middle Ages* (Cambridge, Mass.: Harvard University Press, 1970).

rydice, and she with her companions was eagerly gathering flowers in a garden, a serpent bit her in her foot and she died from the poison. In his grief for his recent bride now dead, Orpheus dared to descend to hell and the dark places, and there he played his lyre so sweetly that the dead souls began to weep. At last the gods of the underworld were moved by the sweetness of his song, and Eurydice was given back to him. Morally speaking, this Orpheus is Christ, the son of God the Father, who in the beginning led Eurydice, that is, man's soul, through his love and charity in marriage. But a serpent, the devil, right after her marriage, that is, after her first creation, while she was gathering flowers, that is, as she longed for the forbidden apple, bit her in his temptation, killed her through her sin, and sent her to hell. When Orpheus, Christ, saw this, he took a harp and descended to hell and delivered the souls of men. What was this harp? Certainly Christ's Passion and torment, for if he had not suffered, he would not have freed the souls from hell. The wood of the harp was the cross on which he hung; its black hide, Christ's flesh with its blood blackened by the heat of the sun. On this harp were strings of three kinds: tenor, middle, and treble. The tenor strings were the ropes with which he was drawn to Mount Calvary; the middle strings, the ropes by which his hands and feet were pulled to the holes in the cross; and the treble strings, the scourges with their knots by which his whole body was scourged. The pins were the nails, and the plectrum was the lance. On this harp Christ played seven very sweet songs to comfort sinners, which were the seven words he spoke on the cross.

His first song was "Father, forgive them, for they do not know what they are doing." In this the sinner is given great comfort when he sees God's clemency as he prayed for his persecutors and sinners. He prayed for them not only on the cross but also in heaven. Whence Bernard says: "Man, you have a sure access to the Father: the mother shows her son her bosom and breasts, the Son shows the Father his sides and wounds. There cannot be the least refusal where so many signs of love come together."[29]

29. Arnaud of Bonneval, *De laudibus beatae Mariae Virginis* (PL 189:1726). The Virgin's appeal to Christ by showing her breast(s) is quoted in many sermons and represented in many works of visual art. Cf. Wenzel, "A Latin Miracle with Middle English Vers-

> Suer help hast thou and prest
> qwer the modyr hyr sone schewyt hyr brest,
> the sone hys fader hys blode syde
> and alle hys wowndes opennyd wyde.
> Ther rw may be noo waryngge
> qwer is of loue so gret toknygge.

[You have sure and prompt help where the mother shows
her son her breast, the Son his Father his bloody side and his
wounds opened wide. There can be no denial where there is
such a great token of love.]

For this reason Jerome says that when Judas hanged himself, he offended Christ more in his despair than in his betrayal.[30] The second
word and the second song was: "Today you shall be with me in paradise." By this word, too, the sinner is given great confidence in God's
mercy. For Christ did not say these words to his mother or the apostles but to the sinful thief who was hanging by his side. Notice, then,
how easily he gained heaven, and do not despair of God's mercy. But
do not trust presumptuously in God's mercy, for as Augustine says,
"The sinner is also struck with this punishment that at his death he
forgets himself who during his life forgot God."[31] The third word
and song was "Woman, behold your son." That was a most painful
word, because when Christ turned to his mother, he did not dare say,
"Mother, behold your son," referring to himself, so that he would
not kill her, but rather referred strangely to John. Whence Chrysostom says: "Oh good Jesus, your most sweet mother, who nursed you
so sweetly and diligently and suckled you so sweetly, you now address
rudely! But at that point it was not the time to speak with sweetness
and call to mind the nature of a mother. For I believe," says Chrysostom, "that if Christ had spoken so sweetly, the Virgin's heart would
have cracked."[32] His fourth song was "O God, my God," etc. This

---

es," *Neuphilologische Mitteilungen* 72 (1971): 77–85; and Wenzel, *Preachers, Poets, and the Early English Lyric*, 118–19.

30. This commonplace can be found, for example, in Augustine, *Sermon 352* (PL 39:1558) or *De civitate Dei* 1.17, etc.

31. Augustine, *Sermon 220*, 5, on Holy Innocents (PL 39:2153).

32. Thus in Ludolf of Saxony, *Vita Christi* (*Landulfi . . . euangelistarum et euangelii totius*

word Christ did not speak in his divinity, which wanted Christ to die, but in his human nature, which naturally shrank from death. The fifth word or song was, "I thirst," not for bodily drink but for men's souls, for whom he thirsted more that for his own life. Whence Bernard says: "Why are you thus thirsting, Jesus?" etc.[33] The sixth word was "Into your hands, O Lord, I commend my spirit." In this word Christ showed his great humility in commending his soul to his Father, and to us he showed a great lesson, that we should be humble and also eagerly commend our souls to God, for if he did so who did not need to, so much more should we. And the seventh word was the last, which completed all others, when he said "It is consummated." That is to say: I have fulfilled it all, for I have overcome the devil, I have made you strong in battle, and I have restored you to your heritage by my blood and death, so that you are now free to enter the heritage of the kingdom of heaven. A sign of this appears in 1 Kings 22[:36], where it is said that after Achab's death, "the herald proclaimed through all the army saying: 'Let every man return to his own city, and to his own country.'"

Thus, after Christ died in battle, all have become free and are restored to heaven. The prophet Hosea confirms this in chapter 13[:14]: "I will deliver them out of the hand of death," namely, out of the devil's hand and might, as I said in my first main part; "I will redeem them from death," strengthening them in their spiritual fight, as I said in the second part; and "O death, I will be your death; O hell, I will be your bite," that is, by taking them from you and restoring them to their right, as I said in the third part. May he make us partakers of that hereditary right, he who lives and reigns eternally. Amen.

---

anni interpretatio et expositio ac super ipsis meditatio) (Milan, 1488–89), part II, chapter 63, attributed to Chrysostom, as elsewhere in medieval texts.

33. Probably Bernard, Sententiae 3.1.

II

EASTER (THOMAS BRINTON)

THOMAS BRINTON, Benedictine monk, doctor of canon law, and bishop of Rochester from 1372 to 1389, left a collection of Latin sermons that he had preached on various occasions before the clergy or the people or a mixed audience, in his cathedral, in his monastery, in London, in other establishments, and evidently even at the papal court at Avignon. This Easter sermon, for which its editor suggests the date of 1383, may have been addressed to a monastic audience (as the protheme with its remarks about rising at night for liturgical offices suggests) or a mixed one. As here, Brinton often commented on moral abuses of his time, on political upheavals such as the Peasants' Revolt, and on heretical Lollard teachings; see further selection 21.

SOURCE:

Thomas Brinton, *Sermons*, ed. Mary Aquinas Devlin, O.P., Camden Third Series 85–86 (continuous pagination) (London: Royal Historical Society, 1954), 2:492–96 and 466 (BR-107 and end of 101).

LITERATURE:

Wenzel, *Collections*, 45–49.

William Brandt, "Church and Society in the Late Fourteenth Century: A Contemporary View," *Medievalia et Humanistica* 13 (1961): 56–61.

On Easter Day.

I have risen. Taken from Psalm 138 and recited in today's Mass.[1]

After the order established by Mother Church, we rise especially at two times in order to pray and to praise God. First at midnight, for three reasons: first because Christ, with whom the fullness of grace has come down from heaven, was born at midnight; second because in the middle of the night the impediments from visible things cease which during the day distract people; and third because Christ rose in the middle of the night. To show that this is true, we read in the *Gospel of Nicodemus* that, when the Jews learned that Joseph of Arimathea had laid Jesus' body in a recently hewn grave, they rose up in such furor against him that they caught him and shut him up carefully in a small house of stone, planning to put him to shameful death after the Sabbath. But lo, in the middle of the night of his resurrection Christ came to him in the house that was taken up by four angels, kissed him, led him out of it with the seals left intact, and sent him free and safe to his own country.[2] From these things we may conclude that those who rise at midnight to sing, say, or hear Matins commemorate and honor Christ's birth, resurrection, and coming for the judgment. Would that all who are bound to rise at this hour were as fervent and willing to praise God as we read about an elderly monk in the *Lives of the Fathers.* As he would not miss saying Matins at a single midnight, his brethren asked him how he could endure so much labor in his old age. He replied: "To me, to serve God is not labor but delight." And they said: "But since the Apostle says, 'Let your service be reasonable,' you must work with reason so that you do not destroy the substance of your body." To whom he replied: "Believe me, brethren, when Abraham saw how God rewarded the labors of his saints, he regretted that he had not worked more."[3] To conclude, the monk could certainly say to God with the Psalmist: "I rose at midnight to give praise to you" [Psalm 118:62]. We rise to praise God a second time in

---

1. "Resurrexi" is the first word of the introit in the Mass for Easter Sunday, taken from Psalm 138:18.

2. *Gospel of Nicodemus* 12.1 and 15.6; in M. R. James, trans., *The Apocryphal New Testament* (Oxford: Clarendon Press, 1924).

3. The source note given by Devlin is not to this story.

the morning, and this for many reasons. First, because in the morning God created the angels, who as soon as they were created burst out in praise of God. Second, because the lark, when it praises God in the morning, wherever it alights after its song, it finds its pasture for the day. Third, because manna, the food of the angels, could only be gathered in the morning [Exodus 16]. Therefore, because Jacob, who rose in the morning and struggled with an angel, deserved to be blessed by him [Genesis 32:24–29], let us, who have struggled against our vices during the past Lent, pray in the beginning of this sermon that we may deserve to receive eternal blessing, etc.

I have risen, as before. In order that our rising from sin to grace may correspond to Christ's resurrection from death to glory, three things are necessary above all, namely, that we rise:

> quickly,
> openly,
> and perfectly.

[1]

We must rise quickly for three reasons: first because of the devil's malice who stands against us, for as blessed Gregory says, when a wretched man falls into sin, the devil urges him not to confess, assures him that his sin is light and excusable, predicts a long life, and suggests that he keep still and not rise, so that in this way he may foster in him contempt of God and despair for himself, and the person thus misled may remain so firmly in his sin that he does not even think of rising. An example is Judas, who first committed theft, secondly betrayal by knowingly handing over his Lord, thirdly apostasy when he withdrew from Christ and the holy fellowship of the apostles, fourthly despair, and fifthly homicide, first in himself by hanging himself, and then in Christ, whom he sought to hang on the gallows. But beware that you do not despair, however much you may sin, for Anselm says: "We do an injury to divine mercy when we despair of it in whatever our wretchedness may be, because in comparison with God's mercy every evil is like a spark amidst the sea."[4] Second,

---

4. On this image, which was attributed to various authors, see John A. Alford, *Piers*

we must rise from sin quickly because of the sin that defiles us. Just as heavy things drawn through water appear light to the person who draws them, so when they are put on land they are so heavy that they almost weigh him down, for at that point he begins to notice their weight. In the same way, people who draw along an evil life at first do not notice the weight of their sins, because they draw them through the waters of delight and pleasures; but when death comes and dust returns to dust, then they feel that unconfessed sins are heavier than any rocks. All the rocks in the world, if they are tied to a sinner's neck, could not draw him to hell, whereas the smallest mortal sin can do so through its weight. Hence let the sinner conclude of his situation what is written in Lamentations 1[:14]: "The Lord has delivered me into a hand from which I cannot rise." Thirdly, because of Christ's benignity who calls the sinner's soul to grace: "Arise, make haste, my friend; come, you shall be crowned" [Canticles 2:10 and 4:8]. In this verse Christ comforts the sinner's soul in four ways. First, penitence renews his friendship, "my friend"; second, it stirs the soul to go to grace, "arise"; third, it speaks against dangerous delay, "make haste"; and fourth, it promises an eternal crown, "come, you shall be crowned." As a biblical *figura:* when Peter slept in the jail, an angel said to him three times, "Arise quickly," Acts 12[:7], as if to say—since one fittingly says "Arise!" to a person who is lying down, or sitting, or sleeping—O soul who are lying in delights, arise, because of the malice of the devil who stands against you, with respect to my first point; O soul who are sitting in darkness, arise, because of the weight of sin that defiles you, with respect to the second; and O soul who are sleeping in filth, arise, because of Christ's benignity who calls you to grace, with respect to the third.

How pleasing it is to God and how fruitful for the sinner to rise quickly from sin is shown plainly in a chronicle about a cleric in England, who was a canon at a major church and a relative of his bishop. He was in carnal love with the very beautiful daughter of a Jew. She told him that she was so much loved by her father and so carefully guarded that they could not get together except in the night of

---

Plowman: A Guide to the Quotations (Binghamton, N.Y.: Medieval and Renaissance Texts and Studies, 1992), 47–48.

Good Friday, because at that time the Jews suffered a flow of blood and were thus preoccupied with other things.[5] The cleric came to her that night and slept with her till morning. And when her father rose and found him with his daughter in the room, he thought to kill him but was afraid because he was the bishop's relative. Nonetheless he shouted at him: "You bad Christian, where is your faith? I would kill you if I didn't fear the lord bishop." And so he was thrown out of the house in confusion. Now, when the bishop was about to celebrate on Holy Saturday, the cleric, who as hebdomadarian[6] was to read the lesson, was afraid to serve at the altar on such a day. He was also afraid, out of shame, to confess. But as he stood in his vestments before the bishop and was overcome with shame, lo, the Jew entered the church with a great crowd in order to complain to the bishop about that cleric. Seeing this the cleric spoke to God in his heart: "Lord, whose nature it is to have mercy, and whose mercy is above all your works, even if I have deserved death in your justice, I ask for your great mercy, that in it you deliver me in this hour. If you will do so, I firmly promise to rise from my sin and never commit it again as much as I can." What else? As the Jews got ready to accuse the cleric with one mouth, they suddenly became so mute by God's power that they could not speak at all. And when the bishop saw the Jews with their mouths agape and not speaking, he thought they had come to make fun of the divine office, and he had them thrown out of the church to their confusion. But the cleric, who thus experienced divine mercy in himself, confessed his sin to the bishop and entered the religious life, while the girl was baptized and became a nun, so that in the end the cleric could say to God with the Psalmist: "Lord, you have proved me and known me; you have known my sitting down and my rising up" [Psalm 138:2].[7] So much for the first part.

---

5. The ultimate source explains: "At that time [i.e., Good Friday] the Jews are said to suffer an illness which is called 'flow of blood.'" Caesarius of Heisterbach, *Dialogus* 1:92.

6. Someone who holds a (church) office for a week.

7. The story, in several variants, is Tubach, no. 2811.

[2]

In the second place I said that like Christ's resurrection our rising from sin must be open, giving clear evidence. We rise from sin openly when a person who had been proud becomes humble, the wrathful man meek, the lecher chaste, the glutton sober, and when the greedy person or usurer makes manifest restitution. To prove this, lo an example from nature. Natural philosophers tell us that the panther, a very beautiful animal of many colors, after he is sated with food hides in his den and sleeps there for three days. When he rises from his sleep, he seeks a high place and roars. With this such a sweet smell comes from his mouth that all the animals come to him and follow him steadily, all except the dragon, who when he hears his voice hides in the caves of the earth.[8] To our purpose: The panther is Christ, "beautiful above the sons of men" [Psalm 44:3] and multicolored in virtues. Speaking of physical beauty, the beauty of Absalom was ugliness compared to his divine beauty. The wisdom of Solomon was foolishness compared with his divine wisdom. And so with the other virtues. When he had become sated with the torments he suffered in every part of his body, from all the people, from every element, in every one of his senses, he hid as it were in his den when he descended to hell in his soul, while his body rested for three days in the tomb. After his resurrection the sweetest smell came from his mouth, when in his appearance to many he manifested the glory of his resurrection and strengthened them in faith. When good Christians hear his voice, they seek him eagerly and follow him. They show openly that they have risen by a true resurrection from the death of sin through the worthy reception of the Eucharist and good works and continued perseverance, saying about themselves in truth the words of the Psalm [19:9]: "We are risen and are set upright." But the dragon, who hides in the caves of the earth, signifies carnal men who know nothing but what is carnal and earthly. Against them the Apostle says in Colossians 3[:1–2]: "If you are risen with Christ, seek the things that are above. Mind the things that are above, not the things that are upon the earth."

8. The same story with moralization in *Fasciculus morum*, III.xx.170–88 (p. 275). Cf. *Physiologus*, ed. Francis J. Carmody (Paris: E. Droz, 1939), 124 (though not close).

Such people, for the most part, are like the dead man whom Simon Magus boasted to have raised, who seemed to have only wagged his head because of his charms.[9] When they hear good words, they nod their heads but do not give up their sins. For what adulterer, after leaving his concubine, now clings to his lawful wife? What usurer makes restitution of what he has unjustly acquired? What unjust retainer[10] or perjurer abstains from what he has committed? What [merchant] who uses false measures with which he deceives his neighbors or poor pilgrims breaks them up or burns them? And further, of those cursed rebels whose dangers I have more often than enough exposed in my sermons, which of them confesses with contrition and truth and does penance in his deeds, since "sin is not forgiven," etc.[11] [i.e., unless one makes restitution]? Surely we are worse than many Ninevites, because they humbled themselves under God's scourges, but we presume beyond measure and are proud. They put on sackcloth, we, precious garments. Their king and elders heard Jonah's preaching and became afraid and for fear left their sin, but our elders and lords do not fear God or respect man. On the contrary, those who ought to defend Mother Church and her laws and privileges unto death are the first to persecute her. For that, Christ with good reason threatens us in Matthew 12[:41]: "The men of Nineveh shall rise in judgment with this generation, and shall condemn it: because they did penance at the preaching of Jonah. And behold a greater than Jonah here!" For words that Christ spoke in the gospel about the future have quite plainly been fulfilled in our days, namely: "Nation shall rise against nation, and kingdom against kingdom; and there shall be pestilences, and famines, and great earthquakes in places. And all these are the beginnings of sorrows" [Matthew 24:7]. And immediately following he says: "Many false prophets shall rise and seduce many" [24:11]. "False prophets" I call those who teach and affirm false things about the

---

9. *Legenda aurea*, 372.

10. *Manutentor.* In fourteenth-century England the practice of "maintaining" a retinue of frequently riotous and oppressive servants became a major social evil that is often criticized in moral discourse and in Middle English "political" poetry; see MED under "maintenour."

11. *Decretals* (Friedberg, *Corpus iuris canonici*, 2:812–13); from Augustine, *Epistula 153.*

church's sacraments. First, about baptism, when they say that a bishop or priest who is in mortal sin cannot baptize or administer the sacrament. About confession they say that as long as one is rightly contrite, external confession is superfluous and useless. About the Eucharist they say that the substance of material bread and wine in the sacrament of the altar remains after consecration. To their first affirmation I answer that without baptism there is no salvation, and that baptism can be given by anyone, as long as it is given in the form taught by the church. To the second, I reply that if confession was neglected without reasonable cause, it deprives a person of the right of church burial (*Decretals*, On penance and remissions, canon "Omnis").[12] As a *figura* of this: when Christ had healed a leper, he commanded him to show himself to the priest.[13] As Ambrose says in his book *On the Sacraments*, before the words of consecration, there is bread on the altar; but after consecration, by the power of the words bread becomes the body of Christ. And thus what was bread before consecration is now the body of Christ after consecration.[14] Further, recently those false prophets have been preaching and affirming that the cross of Christ and images must not be worshipped. This is manifestly false. Hence, against these pseudo-prophets that have risen against the church and assert and preach their errors with lies, the church can legitimately conclude with the Psalmist that "unjust witnesses have risen up against me, and iniquity has lied" [Psalm 26:12], for their sayings have been publicly condemned. This much about my second main part.

[3]
On the third part[15]—and this is the last one—I said that we must rise from the night of sin perfectly and without relapse. Just as "Christ rising from the dead dies now no more, death shall no more have do-

12. The famous canon *Omnis utriusque sexus*, mandating annual confession and communion, issued at the Fourth Lateran Council; Friedberg, *Corpus iuris canonici*, 2:887–88.

13. Matthew 8:4.

14. Ambrose, *De sacramentis* 4.

15. Sermon 107 here has a reference to an earlier sermon, whose text will be followed to the end: "On the third part—and this is the final one—I said that our rising from sin must be perfect without relapse, and so on. On this matter, see above in sermon 101, on the thema 'He has risen in the night' [Proverbs 31:15]."

minion over him" [Romans 6:9], so a sinner who has once risen from the death of sin must never want to relapse, as far as it lies in him, and eagerly reflect that in the same flesh in which we live we shall rise again in the end. For as Job says: "I believe that my Redeemer lives, and in the last day I shall rise out of the earth, and in my flesh I will see my God," etc. [Job 19:25–26]. An example occurs in nature: When the phoenix, who lives for many years, senses that his powers fail, he makes a nest from aromatic twigs. When in summer these twigs are lit by the heat of the sun, he willingly enters his nest and is set on fire and burned to ashes. From these ashes a small worm is born within days, which soon grows feathers and takes again the shape of a bird. Spiritually speaking, by this phoenix I understand a just man. When he has lived for many years, he fashions for himself a nest of aromatic twigs, by putting together a bundle made up of the good works he has done in his life, in the firm hope of being saved eternally, as scripture says, "the just man has hope in his death" [Proverbs 14:32]. Without doubt, if the bundle of good works is set afire in his life by the heat of charity, and when then his spirit is in death separated from his body and his flesh turns to decay and decay into ashes, from these ashes the just man will at last rise again in his body and soul to receive his reward from the Lord. And thus his body, which in life was a burden to this soul, will after his resurrection be his glory. Which, etc.

12

EASTER OR CORPUS CHRISTI
(JOHN FELTON)

EASTER SERMONS very often dealt with the Eucharist and with receiving Holy Communion, whose mandatory annual reception was
normally undertaken on Easter Sunday. The same topics also form
the subject for sermons on the feast of Corpus Christi, later in the
church year. The following piece occurs in the systematic cycle by
John Felton (see above, selection 3) for Easter Sunday. It was copied separately into a collection perhaps made by or for Benedictine
monks at Cambridge (see selections 10 and 24), where it is marked
"de Corpore Christi." Several of its topics are characteristic commonplaces of eucharistic sermons, such as the qualities of the host
set against the seven deadly sins and eucharistic miracle stories. Another topic of the same kind is the "Virtues of the Mass," in selection 21.

Felton here follows the normal scholastic structure more closely than in his earlier sermon above (3), with protheme, introduction
of the thema, division, and development of the three parts. This text
also contains some English elements, but in contrast to selection 10,
here they have only structural functions.

SOURCE:

Oxford, Bodleian Library, MS Bodley 187, fols. 47ra–49ra (John Fel-
    ton, FE-23); collated with Cambridge, Jesus College MS 13, part 5, fols.
    126v–128 (J/5-36).

LITERATURE:

Wenzel, *Collections*, 54–57 (on Felton), 140–45 (on collection J/5), and 377–80 and passim (on eucharistic sermons).

Alan J. Fletcher, *Preaching, Politics and Poetry in Late-Medieval England* (Dublin: Four Courts Press, 1998).

~

He who eats this bread shall live forever, John 6[:59].

In chapter 17 of book 4 of *On Christian Doctrine*, Augustine shows that if in one's teaching one wishes to persuade, to delight, and to bend [one's listeners' wills], one must devoutly ask God that one may be heard intelligently, freely, and obediently.[1] Likewise, Chrysostom on Matthew, homily 20, says that just as it is not possible that the earth becomes fruitful from rain alone but needs the wind to blow over it, so it is not possible that doctrine alone improves a person but that the Holy Spirit must come into his heart. Therefore, having commended all and each that are to be commended in this sermon,[2] let everyone say with devout mind an Our Father and a Hail Mary.

He who eats, etc., as before. In English:

Who-so ethet of þys bred,
he sal leue and neuer be ded.

About the manna, which was a type of this bread, people asked in Exodus 16[:15]: "What is this?" How much more can this question be asked about *this* bread! Now, in the schools of theology a question is usually answered by means of conclusions, and so I offer three conclusions that answer this question. The first is this: Although here appears to be material bread, it yet is not so, but it is the flesh and blood of Christ. In English: "Þow þer seme materyal bred, 3yt þer ys noyn, but þer ys crystis flesshe and hys blode." The first part of this answer rests on the teaching of the church; the second appears in the Sequence:

1. Augustine, *De doctrina christiana* 4.17.

2. In the *commendatio*, which is often found in monastic and other sermons, the preacher asks the congregation to pray for a series of people, including the king and social and ecclesiastical superiors, benefactors, the dead, and all Christians. See also below, selections 16 and 23.

> Hear what holy church maintaineth,
> That the bread its substance changeth, etc.[3]

Notice that only priests, not the laity, receive this sacrament under the species of wine, because anyone who receives the body of Christ receives both Christ's flesh and blood. Therefore, the Sequence says:

> Yet is Christ, in either sign,
> All entire confessed to be.

The second conclusion is this: Although there appears to, etc.; but what is there is Christ's body, which was put on the cross. In English: "Þow þer seme, etc., but þer ys Crystis body þat doyn was on þe rode." Here the first and the second part are based on the words of Augustine in one of his letters, which are put into canon law, *On Consecration*, distinction 2, "Not the body [which you see will you eat]." There it is written that the same body of Christ is received invisibly by the faithful that was visibly put on the cross.[4] The third conclusion: Although there appears, etc.; but this is a spiritual nourishment and food. In English: "Þow þer seme, etc., but þer ys gostly fode." The first part is evident, and for the second we have the quoted thema. Therefore I say that here is the flesh and blood of Christ, etc.

For the further development you should notice that I intend to show—

first, how all the liberal arts go wrong about this sacrament, and how in this sacrament are seven qualities that are opposed to the seven deadly sins;

second, how all human senses go wrong about this sacrament except our hearing, and how the unknown food becomes known;

and third, I plan to show through examples from nature, the crafts, biblical figures, and stories how this miraculous transforma-

---

3. From the sequence for the Mass for Corpus Christi, "Lauda Sion Salvatorem." A sequence is a rhythmic composition recited or sung at Mass after the reading of the epistle. "Lauda Sion" was composed by St. Thomas Aquinas for the feast of Corpus Christi.

4. *Decretum*, De consecratione, d. 2, c. 45 (Friedberg, *Corpus iuris canonici*, 1:1330–31).

tion of bread into Christ's body takes place, and how the same substance is a healing remedy for one man and poison for another.

And this will be the subject of our collation.[5]

[1]

First, then, we should know that grammar is mistaken about this sacrament. For there is a rule in grammar that a short syllable can sometimes become long, but a long one can never become short. Hence the verse:

> A syllable that is short, when followed by *muta* and *liquida*,
> May become long, but a long one may never be shortened.[6]

However, in this sacrament a long syllable does become short, since a man of seven feet,[7] namely, Christ, is contained in a small piece of bread. Whence Isaiah 10[:23] says: "The Lord God of hosts shall make an abridgment in the midst of all the land." And likewise in Romans 9[:28]: "A short word shall the Lord make upon the earth." That came to be when "the word was made flesh" [John 1:14] or when Christ, God and man, is contained in this sacrament. Second, rhetoric is mistaken with regard to this sacrament. Its office is to produce many elegant and colorful words, which cannot really change their object; they usually have a lot of flowers but little fruit, as can be seen in the sayings of the poets and of the other sciences, which are spoken very rhetorically. But in this sacrament are few words, not elegant or colorful; they change their object, and they have few flowers but much fruit. Luke 1[:42]: "Blessed is the fruit of your womb." Thus in the Sequence:

---

5. In the late Middle Ages, "collation" could refer to several different kinds of preaching, ranging from a short monastic address through an afternoon sermon to a sermon in general. See *Collections*, 14–18, 41, 67, 127, 148, 262.

6. A basic rule of Latin pronunciation and prosody, referring to a syllable consisting of a short vowel followed by a plosive consonant (p, b, t, d, c, g) plus l, m, n, or r.

7. "Seven feet"—that is, *septipedalis;* the Jesus College manuscript reads *sextipedalis,* "of six feet."

> Blessed be that fruit also,
> Fruit of joy and not of woe, etc.

Benedictus, blessed, as if to say *bene auctus,* well brought forth. Third, dialectic or philosophy is mistaken about this sacrament because natural philosophy teaches that when food is ingested it is changed into the nature of whom it nourishes, the eater, and not the other way around. But here the eater is changed into the nature of the food he ingests, not the reverse. Whence, speaking in the person of Christ, Augustine says: "You eat me, but will not change me into yourself, but you yourself will be changed into me."[8] Fourth, arithmetic, which is concerned with numbers, is also mistaken here. Isidore, in the third book of his *Etymologies,* has a chapter on infinite numbers.[9] But for Christ, who is in this sacrament, there is no infinite number. Matthew 10[:30] and Luke 12[:7] declare: "The hairs of your head are all numbered." Fifth, geometry, which is concerned with figures, is mistaken here because it teaches that a circle covers the greatest area, while a triangle covers the smallest, and further, that a larger figure covers a greater area than a smaller one. But here, the triangle covers as much as the circle, because the triangular piece of the host after it has been broken contains as much as the whole host.[10] Likewise, the smaller part contains as much as the larger one or even the whole host. Whence it is said in the Sequence:

> Nor a single doubt retain,
> When they break the Host in twain,
> But that in each part remains, etc.
> [i.e., What was in the whole before].

Sixth, music is mistaken here because it states that every melody comes from a physical instrument. But here the greatest melody arises without any physical instrument, when the angels minister and sing to Christ. Isaiah 6[:3] describes how the angels cried out and sang,

8. Augustine, *Confessiones* 7.10.

9. Isidore, *Etymologiae* 3.9.

10. After consecration and before communion, the (round) host is broken by the priest into three pieces, at least two of which would be roughly triangular.

saying "Holy, holy, holy," etc. And in Tobit 13[:22]: "Alleluia shall be sung in all the streets of Jerusalem." Further, Revelation 14[:3] says of the song in heaven: "And they sang as it were a new song before the throne of God." From these passages it is plain beyond doubt that the angels who minister to Christ present in this sacrament sing a most sweet song not heard by mortal ears. Seventh, astronomy, too, is mistaken here. It teaches that heavenly bodies are brighter and more excellent than earthly ones, and that the former rule the latter and are not ruled by them. But here is a body that is brighter and more excellent than any body in the lower or the higher heavens, and which rules them all and is not ruled by them. Whence the church chants of Christ who is bodily present in this sacrament: "He rules heavens and earth forever and ever."[11] But: theology and canon law are not mistaken about this sacrament, as, God willing, I shall explain later.

Notice that the host of Christ['s body] has seven qualities, by which we must cast out from us the seven deadly sins.[12] The first is that it is small, against pride. Philippians 2[:7]: "He emptied himself, taking the form of a servant." Also Sirach 3[:20]: "The greater you are, the more humble yourself," etc. Second, it is smooth, against the roughness of anger. Matthew 11[:29]: "Learn of me, because I am meek and humble of heart." Third, it is without the sourness of leaven, against envy. Exodus 12 [39]: "Unleavened loaves," etc. Also 1 Corinthians 5[:8]: "Not with the old leaven," etc. And Proverbs 14[:30] says that "Envy is the rottenness of the bones," on which the Interlinear Gloss comments: "Through envy our virtues grow weak and die before God, just as through rottenness flesh goes to ruin before our eyes." Fourth, it must not be mixed with any other grain, against cupidity, which always collects more. Isaiah 5[:8]: "Woe to you who join house to house and lay field to field." Fifth, it is thin, against gluttony. Job 19[:20]: "The flesh being consumed, my bone hath cleaved to my skin." Sixth, it is round and can roll, against sloth.[13] Matthew 26[:41]:

11. From the introit for masses in honor of the Blessed Virgin beginning, "Salve, sancta parens"; cf. *Sarum Missal*, 389.

12. For the commonplace of the qualities of the host, see Wenzel, *Verses in Sermons: "Fasciculus Morum" and Its Middle English Poems* (Cambridge, Mass.: Medieval Academy of America, 1978), 182–83, and *Fasciculus Morum* V.2.

13. "Roll" in the sense of "move, be in motion or action."

"The spirit indeed is willing, but the flesh weak." And seventh, it is pure and white, against lechery. Wisdom 7[:26]: "For it is the brightness of eternal light, and the unspotted mirror of God's majesty." Therefore, **he who eats this bread,** etc.

[2]

In the second place, we should know how all of man's senses are mistaken about the sacrament, all except hearing. Some cleric tells the following allegory[14] about the soul as if it were a noble lady: A lady[15] who was the noblest of all creatures of this world was once sick unto death because she did not find food fit for her in the creatures of the world. A friend of hers brought her this sacrament and said: "Take this food. It will drive out your pain, heal you, comfort you, and keep you for eternal life."[16] Since this food was unknown to her, the soul called her messengers together and first sent one whom she considered worthy, namely, Sight, to go around the earth and bring her the truth about this food. When he came back to her, he told her that it was material bread. Then the lady said: "Alas that I sent you, you bring me bad news. For if it is so, I will not eat this food but give it to my servant, my flesh." Next she sent out her Sense of Smell, and when he came back, he spoke just as the first had done. Third she sent out Taste, and he said the same as the others. In the fourth place she sent out Touch, and when he came back, he confirmed with an oath what his companions had said before. Then the lady, at death's door, said with great weeping: "You are sad counselors. Is there none to console me? Who from among all that are dear to me shall bring me relief?" At that, the fifth messenger, Hearing, sprang up and said: "I will, send me forth." The lady replied: "Go, and the Lord be with you, and his angel be your companion on the way you are going to bring me back the truth." He came back soon and said: "I bring you the best message. What my companions have said is false. But in that food is the true body of the Lord." Then the soul said, as if she were waking up from a deep sleep: "It is enough for me to eat this food before I die. For I believe that

14. *Narracionem ymaginariam.*
15. The Jesus College manuscript here reads *anima,* "the soul."
16. "Hunc cibum ... eterne vite conseruatiuum."

it brings eternal life. And may you be blessed among all my messengers, for through you I first became Christ's spouse—Romans 10[:17], 'Faith comes from hearing'—and now I have become his nursling, fed by him. And I will say this: I will not believe the other messengers except insofar as they agree with you." A biblical figure for this tale you can find in Genesis 27, where we read that all of Isaac's senses were deceived except his hearing when he thought Jacob was Esau. It is said there that "his eyes were dim," that is, Isaac's, "and he could not see." This is the first messenger. Further, "as he smelled the fragrant smell of his garments," etc., the second messenger. Then, "Bring me," he said, "the meats of your hunting," etc., the third messenger. Further, "when he had felt him," etc., then follows, "the hands are those of Esau," the fourth messenger, and Isaac was deceived. But what did his hearing tell him? "The voice indeed is the voice of Jacob." And that was the truth, etc. For this entire development see Alanus in his *Anticlaudianus*, about Lady Nature who wanted to have a pure soul.[17]

Notice that if someone is served some unknown food, he could without shame send to the kitchen and find out what that food and its nature was. So also to our purpose. One can truly find out about this food [of the sacrament] from its cook, that is, Christ, who says: "This is my body," Matthew 26[:26], Mark 14[:22], and Luke 22[:9]. Likewise from the father of the cook, namely, God the Father, who says: "This is my son," in Matthew 3[:17] and 17[:5], and in Mark 9[:6] and Luke 9[:35]. Further, from the fellow cook, that is, the Holy Spirit, who may be called Christ's fellow because of the equality between them. He can say: "He was conceived by me," as is said in the Apostles' Creed: "Who was conceived by the Holy Spirit." In addition, one can find this out from the cook's wife, that is, holy church, who says: "We faithfully confess that before consecration it is bread and wine that nature produced, but after consecration it is the flesh and blood of Christ, which

---

17. The allegorical poem *Anticlaudianus* by the French theologian Alanus or Alan of Lille (d. 1203) narrates how Nature, dismayed at the immoral behavior of humankind, wants to create a new man. With the help of her powers, she can create a new human body, but then must send Prudence to heaven to fetch a new soul. The five senses are the horses that draw her chariot to heaven (4.95–212); they falter at 5.39–82 (ed. R. Bossuat, Paris, 1955).

the blessing has consecrated." Thus Augustine, and his words are put in the *Decretum, On Consecration,* distinction 2, "But we."[18] And in addition, we can find this out from the mother of the cook as well as the kitchen, that is, Blessed Mary, who is called "mother of the cook" because she was the mother of Christ, and can be called "kitchen" because this food was made in her. She can say: "This now is bone of my bones, and flesh of my flesh," Genesis 2[:23]. And she can similarly say the same that the cook's father says, "He is my son." With all these agree the waiters, that is, true Catholics.[19] Therefore, eat without doubt and fear, for **he who eats this bread,** etc.

[3]
In the third place, we should know that the miraculous and supernatural change can be somewhat illustrated with examples from nature, the crafts, biblical figures, and stories. First from nature. Natural philosophers say that when bread is eaten, it is changed into flesh and blood. And this change is said to be natural or formal, because in nature's operation, the original matter remains and its form changes. Since nature is thus powerful and effective, what shall we say of the Word of God which established the heavens? The Psalmist declares: "By the word of God the heavens were established" [Psalm 32:6]; and likewise, "The Lord has done all things whatsoever he wanted" [Psalm 113:11]. Second, in the crafts. From vile ashes a clear and noble material is formed, namely, glass, and from it one makes a mirror or lens, which greatly helps our bodily sight. So, what wonder is it if the word of the Lord, when it is pronounced by the priest, makes from good bread a body of the greatest purity that comforts our spiritual sight? Third, in scripture. Loth's wife "was turned into a statue of salt," Genesis 19[:26]. Also, Moses' staff was turned into a serpent, Exodus 4[:3] and 7[:9], and in the same chapter, the waters of Egypt were turned into blood [7:19–20]. Further, in John 2 we find that Christ changed water into wine, and our scholars say it was the best of wines. As a bibli-

---

18. *Decretum,* De consecratione, d. 2, c. 41 (Friedberg, *Corpus iuris canonici,* 1:1328).

19. This and the other texts here translated were written before the Protestant Reformation. "Catholics" thus means Christians, or at least Christians in union with the (Western) church (i.e., not heretics or schismatics).

cal figure of this bread we find the paschal lamb in Exodus 12,[20] with many details which, spiritually understood, are necessary in receiving the Eucharist. There is further the manna of Exodus 16, which "became fluid in the heat of the sun" but hardened in the heat of fire, as a sign that for those who have the love of God, the Eucharist becomes something good, just as food, after it is eaten, in the stomach at once becomes fluid for man's health; but in people who have the fire of lust or hate their brethren, it turns into something evil, just as food that after eating hardens in the stomach becomes harmful and deadly for a person.

But here one may ask the question how one and the same thing can be different and have contrary effects for different people. This can be answered with examples from nature, the crafts, and scripture. First, from nature. Natural philosophers say that almonds are harmful and deadly for foxes, but very beneficial for humans. Second, in the crafts. Through experience we know that the same food that is harmful or deadly to people in sickness is useful and natural to those in health. Also, wine, which for people who have a fever is almost a poison, is useful and pleasant for those who are well. Third, in holy scripture. In Numbers 21 we read of the brazen serpent that was a great help for the people wandering through the desert, but in 2 Kings 18[:4] Ezechias broke it to pieces because it was most harmful for idolaters. Further, Christ is good to the good, but not so to the evil; whence the Psalmist says of him: "With the holy you will be holy," and after that: "With the perverse you will be perverted" [Psalm 17:25, 26]. And some teacher says: "As one is toward God, so will God be toward him." And thus the Sequence speaks about the Eucharist:

> Death to the evil but life to the good, etc.

Fourth, the same is shown in a story. A Jew is reported to have come to a Christian church to hear Mass. Right after the words of the sacrament were pronounced, he saw as it were a most beautiful child in the hands of the priest and took great joy in this vision. For that reason, he came to church many times, and every time he saw the same.

---

20. In MS Bodley 187, the remainder of this sentence is replaced with a reference: "see above, selection 6.b."

At last he went to the bishop and told him what he had seen. And the bishop baptized him. But after that he could no longer see what he had seen before. And he went to the bishop again grieving and weeping and said he would rather see that child than have many possessions. And the bishop said to him: "This is happening for your own benefit, for as Gregory says, 'Faith has no merit where human reason offers proof by experience.'"[21] A similar tale is reported about another Jew. He attended Mass with a Christian companion in a Christian church. After Mass, the Christian said he was very hungry. And the Jew said: "If I had eaten as much as you did, I don't think I would be hungry for many days!" The Christian said: "Truly, I haven't eaten anything today." And the Jew replied: "I saw you eat a most beautiful child that the priest elevated at the altar, and afterward he ate this child. And a beautiful man came with many children in his lap and gave one such child as the priest had eaten to each of you." And the Christian said: "Since the Lord has shown you this, he wanted you to become a Christian." And this happened.[22] This shows us that anyone in the state of charity, when he attends Mass, communicates [spiritually]. Hence the priest says at the end of Mass, "We have received, Lord," etc.[23] Notice, therefore, that there are two ways of receiving the Eucharist, sacramental and spiritual. Some people receive the sacrament only in the first way, namely, those in the state of mortal sin. Hence 1 Corinthians 11[:29]: "He who eats unworthily, eats judgment to himself," to which Ambrose adds: "as if he were killing Christ."

And so we have some illustration of the truth concerning this miraculous transubstantiation or supernatural change of bread into the body of Christ. Therefore, Christ says in John 6[:52]: "If anyone eats of this bread," add: worthily, "he shall live forever," namely, in this world in a life of grace, and after this life in heaven, in a life of glory. Which he may grant us who lives and reigns without end, etc.

21. Cf. Tubach, no. 2689c. The Gregory quotation is from his *Homiliae in evangelia* 2.26.

22. The second eucharistic miracle story is not in the Jesus College manuscript. It is another variant of Tubach, no. 2689c. Both stories occur together in the anonymous *exempla* collection in London, British Library, MS Harley 1288.

23. The beginning of the prayer after Holy Communion (*Postcommunio*); cf. *Sarum Missal*, 167n5; 194, 326.

13

SIXTH SUNDAY AFTER EASTER
(A WYCLIFFITE PREACHER)

THE FOLLOWING SERMON has been preserved in an anonymous collection of sermons, extant in several manuscripts, which now and then voice views characteristically held by Wyclif and the Lollards. In this piece, the preacher speaks of the persecution that preachers of the truth suffer at the hands of disciples of Antichrist—in his view, bishops, priests, and false religious who call for their excommunication. This accusation is sounded several times elsewhere in the collection, together with critiques of the prohibition against reading the Bible in English and of the practices of pilgrimages and image worship. But here such criticism is relatively moderate. In fact, in one sermon the anonymous author takes a fairly positive stand on image worship, while elsewhere another major point of Wycliffite teaching, denying the need of auricular confession to a priest, is treated without the acerbity that is typical of the later Wyclif.

The structure that is found here appears consistently throughout the collection: in the first section of the sermon the preacher comments discursively on the entire lection in the manner of a homily, after which he selects one verse from it, offers a division, and develops its parts, as was standard procedure in the scholastic sermon.

SOURCE:
Oxford, Bodleian Library, MS Laud misc. 200, fols. 139v–142 (L-38).

144

LITERATURE:

Wenzel, *Collections*, 91–94.

Christina Von Nolcken, "An Unremarked Group of Wycliffite Sermons in Latin," *Modern Philology* 83 (1986): 233–49.

⮑

When the Paraclete comes, whom I will send you from the Father, the Spirit of truth, who proceeds from the Father, etc., John 15 [26–16:4].

In this gospel Christ informs his apostles of the sending of the Holy Spirit. There is no doubt that the Holy Spirit, who is the third person in God, proceeds from the Father as well as the Son, and he is sent from the Father and the Son, because Father and Son are one and the same principle that breathes forth the Holy Spirit. Thus Christ affirms that he himself sends the Holy Spirit from the Father. And no doubt it follows that Christ sends the Holy Spirit, therefore the Holy Spirit proceeds from Christ. And the text continues: the Holy Spirit proceeds from the Father; therefore, the Father sends the Holy Spirit. And since the Holy Spirit, who is the Paraclete, that is, our advocate and comforter who thrusts into us both fear and love—fear as he is our advocate, and love as he is our comforter—comes to fill men's hearts and consciences with his spirit, he will give testimony in our heart of Christ, that he is true God and true man. For he is the Spirit of truth coming from the Father and the Son, and not a spirit of untruth in the mouth of false prophets who comes from the devil, as the spirit that deceived Achab, the king of Israel, as we read in 1 Kings 22[:20–23]. But the Holy Spirit moves our intellect to belief, and the affect of our heart to love, and our memory to constant hope in God, and consequently with the Holy Spirit to give outward testimony in our voice, deed, and example. And thus Christ says, **You shall give testimony, because you are with me from the beginning.**

The Holy Spirit gives testimony in our heart, hence the Psalmist says: "I will hear what the Lord God will speak in me, for he will speak peace unto his people, and unto his saints, and unto those who are converted to the heart" [Psalm 84:9]. And Christ says rightly that through the inspiration of the Holy Spirit his disciples will give testimony about him because they **were with him from the beginning** of his preaching to its end. And therefore they could the better report the truth, because "we speak what we know, and we testify what we have seen" John 3[:11]. But the enemies of Christ and of the truth, who hear the word of God with scorn for the truth, report the words of a true preacher very badly. But Christ forewarned his disciples in this way so that they **would not be scandalized** later on and retreat from truth through either fear or folly. For it is a scandal to stumble and come to ruin. Spiritual ruin for a man occurs when the affects of his soul make him stagger and hurt his feet on a rock, namely, Christ, by fearing what is not to be feared, or grieving at what is not to be grieved at, or hoping for what is not to be hoped for, or rejoicing in what is not to be rejoiced in. And that the disciples should not thus be scandalized while he was away from them in his human nature, Christ warned them in advance through his promise of the Holy Spirit, not by threatening them or giving them fear, as do those who forewarn others to frighten them instead of consoling them. And Christ mentions persecution by evil people against his preachers when he says, **They will put you out of the synagogues,** as if to say: "Even if kings and princes, bishops and prelates, priests and religious throw you out of their synagogues and churches and excommunicate you on account of preaching the truth, do not fear them, for 'Blessed are you when men revile you, and persecute you, and speak all that is evil against you, untruly, for my sake' [Matthew 5:11]." And that they should not be afraid of death, which is the greatest of fearful things, he said: **The hour comes that whosoever kills you will think that he does a service to God.** Indeed, such disciples of the Antichrist will be wondrously blinded by their malice when they deem they are serving God by persecuting and killing you preachers. For in our days bishops, priests, and false religious say they would want to kill with their own hands such a preacher of the gospel, and at once go to say Mass without confession. **And these things they will do to you because they have not known the Father or me.** The reason why such men ignore God, certainly, is that they ignore holy scripture and despise it. Hence Jerome says, in distinction 38: "Since according to the Apostle Paul Christ is the wisdom of God and the power of God, not knowing the scripture is not knowing Christ."[1]

---

1. *Decretum*, distinctio 38, c. 9 (Friedberg, *Corpus iuris canonici*, 1:142), quoting Jerome's commentary on Isaiah, prologue (PL 24:17).

To such people one can therefore apply the words of Matthew 22[:29]: "You err, not knowing the scriptures or the power of God." And finally in the gospel follows: **But these things I have told you, that when the hour comes,** that is, of tyrannous persecutors, **you may remember** and be comforted by the visit of the Holy Spirit, knowing **that I** who cannot lie **told you of them beforehand** to confirm your faith.

You shall give testimony, because you are with me from the beginning.

These words were said to Christ's disciples because they should be faithful witnesses to testify to Christ's life and the articles of faith through their true preaching. Whence in Acts 1[:8] it is said: "You shall receive the power of the Holy Spirit coming upon you, and you shall be witnesses unto me in Jerusalem, and in all Judea, and Samaria, and even to the uttermost part of the earth." And so Paul preached to the wise and the foolish, to the Jews, who were under the Law, and to those without the Law, to lay folk and to the weak, that he would lead all to salvation in as much as in him lay [cf. 1 Corinthians 9:22]. And thus Christ had twelve chief witnesses, that is, the twelve apostles. For when Judas had killed himself, after Christ's resurrection Peter and the other apostles elected Matthias in the place of Judas, that he would be a witness to Christ's resurrection, as is shown in Acts 1[:15–26]. And Peter affirmed that he and the other apostles were witnesses to Christ's resurrection when he said, in Acts 3[:15]: "But you killed the author of life, whom God has raised from the dead, of which we are witnesses."

The testimony we must give is fivefold, namely:

the testimony of our conscience,
the testimony of our speech,
the testimony of our good reputation,
the testimony of scripture,
and the testimony of a good life.

[1]
On the first, 2 Corinthians 1[:12] says: "For our glory is this, the testimony of our conscience." This testimony of conscience gladdens a man and comforts him in faith, hope, and love, and brings quiet

to his soul in many ways, and gives him some certainty of his salvation—not the certainty of knowledge but of hope and confidence in
his salvation. Three things help this conscience "which give testimony
on earth: the spirit, the water, and the blood" [1 John 5:8]. The spirit of Christ when it was separated from the body in death, the water
from his side, and the blood of his Passion give testimony in our conscience that Christ died for us, and that any sinner, however grievously
he may have sinned, if he amends himself through contrition, confession, and satisfaction, will be saved through Christ's death. Furthermore, through the testimony of their conscience men know when they
have done evil, as their conscience gives testimony and accuses them
of their failure and stirs them to amend themselves. Romans 2[:14–15]:
"For when the Gentiles, who do not have the Law, do by nature those
things that are of the Law, these not having the Law are a law to
themselves. Who show the work of the Law written in their hearts,
their conscience bearing witness to them, and their thoughts between
themselves accusing or defending." Much more so are we Christians,
who have the law of the gospel written and preached and believed
in, obliged to have a good conscience to accuse us of our sins and to
defend the gospel truth and its virtues to the death. But in Romans
9[:1–3] the Apostle Paul, by the testimony of his conscience, confesses that he had sinned grievously in persecuting [Christians], saying:
"I speak the truth in Christ, I do not lie, my conscience bearing me
witness in the Holy Spirit: that I have great sadness and continual
sorrow in my heart, for I wished to be an anathema from Christ for
my brethren," that is, for love of the Jews, because he persecuted the
apostles out of love for the Old Law and the Jews, who were his relatives according to the flesh. The conscience that gives witness in a man
will be good with respect to God, just with respect to one's neighbor, and pure with respect to oneself. On the first, Paul says in Acts
23[:1]: "Men, brethren, I have lived with all good conscience before
God until this present day." To the second one may apply the words
of Sirach 13[:31]: "Riches are good to him who has no sin in his conscience." But with respect to the riches of this world, man is held to
acquire goods rightly, keep them honestly, and spend them justly and
piously—justly in regard to what he owes, and piously in regard to the
works of mercy. On the third kind of conscience, a pure one, 1 Tim-

othy 3[:9] says: "Holding the mystery of faith in a pure conscience." This conscience must be purified through the Passion of Christ; Hebrews 9[:14]: "The blood of Christ, who by the Holy Spirit offered himself unspotted unto God, shall cleanse our conscience from dead works, to serve the living God." And Hebrews 10[:2]: "The worshippers once cleansed should have no conscience of sin any longer."

[2]

After the testimony of our conscience, it is necessary to have the testimony of a good reputation; 1 Timothy 3[:7]: "He must have a good testimony of them who are without, lest he fall into reproach and the snare of the devil." Though a good reputation is necessary to all men, it is supremely necessary to priests and clerics and especially to teachers. Whence Augustine says, in *On Christian Teaching:* "Let a teacher choose a good life so that he does not neglect his good reputation."[2] Augustine further says in his common sermon for the clergy: "You need to have two things, [a good] conscience and reputation— conscience for yourself, and reputation for your neighbor. A person who relies on his conscience but neglects his reputation is cruel."[3] And he puts it well when he says that "he is cruel," for on account of his negligence he gives occasion that his name is killed and the word of God that he preaches and teaches is blasphemed, and thereby God is scorned. This good reputation is not the same as a vainglorious name, but a good name founded in God and the virtues. Of it Sirach 41[:15–16] says: "Take care of a good name, for this shall continue with you more than a thousand precious and great treasures. A good life has its number of days, but a good name shall continue forever." Such a name is not founded on the vain praises of men but on the true praise of Christ, who has written it in the book of life. And of it one can greatly rejoice; Luke 10[:20]: "Rejoice, for your names are written in heaven."

[3]

After the testimony of a good reputation we need the true testimony of speech. Of it is said in John 18[:37]: "For this I was born and

---

2. Augustine, *De doctrina christiana* 4.28.
3. Augustine, *Sermo 355.*

came into the world, that I should give testimony to the truth." Likewise, all human beings were born into the world for the same purpose, that when they speak, they should speak the truth; 1 Peter 4[:11]: "If any man speak, let him speak as if the words of God," and elsewhere, in Zechariah 8[:16]: "Speak the truth, every one to his neighbor." For someone to speak a true testimony it is necessary that he knows or sees what he speaks or testifies; John 3[:11]: "We speak what we know, and we testify what we have seen, and you do not receive our testimony." A person who gives false testimony in his speech runs into a manifold danger. First, he sins against the precept that God gave in Exodus 20[:16]: "You shall not bear false witness against your neighbor," and in Exodus 23[:1]: "You shall not receive the voice of a lie, neither shall you join your hand to bear false witness for a wicked person." Second, he does much harm to others. Whence Isidore says in book 3 of *The Highest Good:* "A false witness does harm to three persons: first to God, whom he scorns in his perjury; second to the judge, whom he deceives with his lie; and third to the innocent, whom he hurts through his false testimony."[4] Third, he will incur God's hatred and curse; whence in Proverbs 6[:16–19] a false witness who utters lies is one of the six things that God hates, and in Proverbs 12[:22]: "Lying lips are an abomination to the Lord." Fourth, he is the cause and occasion for many dangers to others; Proverbs 25[:18]: "A man who bears false witness against his neighbor is like a dart and a sword and a sharp arrow." He is like a sword that kills those present, like a dart that digs into close friends, and like a sharp arrow that wounds people at a distance. Fifth, a false witness incurs the danger of temporal and eternal punishment; Proverbs 19[:5]: "A false witness shall not go unpunished, and he who speaks lies shall not escape." Whence in the Old Testament a false witness would receive the same punishment as a person who, if accused of a crime, were to be found guilty, as can be seen in Deuteronomy 19[:16–21] and in Psalm [5:7]: "You will destroy all who speak a lie," add: unless they recover their senses; Proverbs 21[:28]: "A lying witness shall perish"; and at the end of Revelation [22:15]: "Without" heaven "will be everyone who loves and makes a lie."

4. Isidore, *Sententiae* 3.55 (PL 83:727).

[4]

After the testimony of speech we need the testimony of scripture, to confirm all the others. For this testimony has the greatest authority before God. If we must needs accept any conclusion that has been proved with the testimony of Aristotle, Augustine, or any other expositors, so much more must we accept a truth proved with the testimony of holy scripture. Of this testimony Christ says, in John 5[:39]: "Search the scriptures, for you think in them to have life everlasting; and the same are they that give testimony of me." And that testimony is most true, even though the disciples of Antichrist say that holy scripture is false. Whence the Psalmist says: "The testimony of the Lord is faithful, giving wisdom to little ones," that is, the humble [Psalm 18:8]; and elsewhere: "[I will keep] my testimony faithful to him," that is, the just king [Psalm 88:29]. And in this way God's law is faithful to good commoners, good knights, and good clergymen. The articles of faith are God's "wonderful testimonies, and therefore my soul has sought them," as the Psalmist says [118:129]. The Ten Commandments are God's testimonies that we are held to keep; Deuteronomy 6[:17]: "Keep the precepts of the Lord your God, and the testimonies and ceremonies which he has commanded you." Whence the Psalmist says: "You have commanded justice, your testimonies, and your truth exceedingly" [Psalm 118:138]. The Old Testament can be understood to be represented in the tabernacle of the testimony, described in Exodus 30, but the New Testament in the ark of the testimony, for just as the ark was kept inside the tabernacle, so is the New Testament contained in the Old. But the gathering of the articles of faith, of the commandments, and of the petitions in the Lord's Prayer can be seen in the heap of Genesis 31[:51]: "Behold, this heap and the stone which I have set up between me and you shall be a witness." This heap, I say, and the stone are to be as a testimony, and thus is the whole gathering of the articles of the creed and the commandments of God a testimony between us and God, that we should serve him faithfully all our life. In this way people "overcome" the devil "by the blood of the Lamb and by the word of his testimony" [Revelation 12:11].

[5]

And finally we must speak of the testimony of a good life. This thrives mostly in good works. On them, John 10[:25]: "The works that I do in the name of my Father, they give testimony of me"; and afterward [37–38]: "If I do not do the works of my Father, do not believe me. But if I do, and you will not believe me, believe the works." In three situations do we require witnesses: in a deposition against delinquents, in purging people falsely accused, and in letting true heirs come into their heritage. The same is true spiritually. Works of penance show a person to be a sinner and punish him for his sins. So every sinner is held to submit himself humbly to works of penance because they give testimony of his accusation and punishment. Therefore a sinner must assent to them, even if these works and witnesses are adverse to his flesh. Matthew 5[:25]: "Be at agreement with your adversary quickly, while you are in the way with him, lest perhaps the adversary," that is, temporal punishment, "deliver you to the judge," Christ, "and you be cast into prison" because you do not patiently undergo penance in this life. Next, works of justice, such as the works of the commandments, repaying what is owed, and a pure life, are as it were witnesses that cleanse a person, both with respect to his guilt and with respect to his good name. Such works each one of us must bring before the highest judge, and before men as well, to give testimony of his good life; Matthew 5[:16]: "So let your light shine before men, that they may see your good works," that is, works that testify to your good life, "and may glorify your Father who is in heaven." And in 1 Peter 2[:12] it is said: "Let them by the good works they shall behold in you glorify God in the day of visitation." Finally, the works of mercy, both bodily and spiritual, are men's witnesses and testimonies that lead them to eternal life, which is the inheritance of the elect. Thus it is necessary that men have these works ready before Christ on the day of judgment, just as people who try before an earthly judge to recover their inheritance wish to have twelve witnesses who through their true testimony allow them to enter their inheritance. And as such a person works without ceasing for his earthly inheritance, that he may have enough witnesses in his favor for earthly gain, so should a man work even harder that he may have works of mercy that go with him to the highest judge, to gain eternal life; Revelation [14:13]: "For their works follow them." And in truth, since works of mercy above all lead a man to his eternal salvation, on judgment day our Savior will rehearse these works and reward the laborers who carry such witnesses with them. Hence the gospel says: "Call the laborers and pay them their hire" [Matthew 20:8]. And then Christ will render, as the Psalmist says, "to every man according to his works" [Psalm 61:13]. For those who work badly he will finally punish with eternal pain, and those who work well he will reward with a heavenly and eternal inheritance. To which may the Holy Spirit lead us.

14

FIRST SUNDAY AFTER TRINITY
(JOHN WYCLIF)

JOHN WYCLIF (c. 1330–84), philosopher and theologian at Oxford, where he developed a series of positions that were declared heretical, also wrote a number of sermons on the gospels and epistles for Sundays and saints' feasts, which he later in his life collected into regular cycles. In them he normally follows the structure illustrated here. He first goes through and comments on the entire lection, like an ancient homily. Then he puts a question *(dubium* or *dubitatio)* derived from the lection, which he answers and develops argumentatively at length. In the present case he attacks the friars' claim that their poverty and begging represents a higher degree of perfection—a pet target of Wyclif's criticism. In their written form, the sermons lack such standard sermon features as address, invitation to pray, main division, principals, and closing formula. Instead their tone is very academic and sometimes hard to follow, not only for the modern reader but apparently also for the medieval scribe, as is revealed by textual corruptions. To ease understanding my translation here is somewhat freer than of other sermons in this book.

On the basis of these Latin sermons, one or more writers created the *Wycliffite Sermons* in English, likewise in several sets. For comparison with the present Latin sermon, see Anne Hudson and Pamela O. Gradon, *English Wycliffite Sermons,* 1:223–26. The Middle English sermon lacks the attack on the mendicants.

SOURCE:

Johann Loserth, ed., *Iohannis Wyclif Sermones,* 4 vols. (London: Wyclif Society, 1887–90), 1:223–28.

LITERATURE:

Penn R. Szittya, *The Antifraternal Tradition in Medieval Literature* (Princeton: Princeton University Press, 1986), chapter 4 and passim, on Wyclif's opposition to the mendicants and its background.

Anne Hudson and Pamela O. Gradon, eds., *English Wycliffite Sermons,* 5 vols. (Oxford: Clarendon Press, 1983–1996), 4:134–45, on antifraternalism in Wyclif and in the English Wycliffite sermons.

⁓

There was a certain rich man, Luke 16:19[–31].

This gospel parable clearly reproves the rich who are made foolish by the world, and commends the poor who are humble before the world. This **rich man** transgressed the right order[1] in two ways. First, **he was** superfluously **clothed in purple and fine linen,** so as to lure his subjects into giving him worldly honors, through both their fear and their adulation. Second, **he feasted sumptuously every day,** so as to richly feed, in his continuous worldly lavishness, both his high rank and his carnal desires. **But a beggar, named Lazarus, lay at his gate, full of sores, while he desired to be filled with the crumbs of that rich man.** But the rich man's contemptuous greed denied him this. **But the dogs,** that is, the rich man's low servants, **came and licked the poor man's sores:** in their natural compassion they had pity on his misery and expressed it in their voice. However, often having a good will alone is not very useful unless the power to act goes with it. Thus, in John 6 Christ raised his body and his eyes high to a mountainous place and showed that he had pity on the hungry and at the same time could reveal in himself divine acts. The same is true of a person who is powerful in the world as well as merciful, a follower of Christ. Con-

---

1. "Right order": in medieval thought, the Latin word *ratio,* "reason," has a wide range of meaning, from the human faculty to the God-given order of society and of the universe.

versely, mere feigned compassion from a person who has the power to act is like the licking of a dog. But at the end of Revelation [22:15] is said: "Out with the dogs!" Thus this gospel tells us openly, not that the virtuous use of clothing and food is to be condemned (if this were possible), but that the faithful must avoid the proud, superfluous, and greedy misuse of such things. At the same time, begging or the lack of worldly things, as was the case with Lazarus, is not in itself praiseworthy. Rather, it is virtuous when God sends it and the needy person humbly accepts it. In this sense this gospel commends Lazarus's begging and reproves the rich man's superfluity. It calls the former by name but passes over the latter's name, thereby indicating that people who are virtuously needy are known to God for blessedness, while those powerful in the world like the rich man are unknown to God for blessedness.[2]

And it came to pass that the beggar died, and his spirit was carried into Abraham's bosom, which means the limbo of the fathers, where the predestined as to their souls rested before the Incarnation. **But the rich man also died and was buried in hell,** because his soul was set in perpetual pain. The poor man's servants are indicated to be the **angels,** whereas the rich man's servants did not care for him. He, being condemned, by God's miracle and for the later instruction of the church, **lifting up his eyes when he was in torments, saw Abraham afar off, and this Lazarus.** He made known his wretchedness, and since he was a Jew, he called Abraham his father and prayed for some relief from Lazarus, that he would dip the tip of his finger in water and refresh the rich man's tongue, who was tormented in his damnation. As the damned are destitute of reason and break forth into wild raging words, it is no wonder that the rich man thus erroneously wanted to be relieved, whether he believed Lazarus to be alive or dead. But if this rich man understood that Lazarus was dead in body and happy in limbo—which seems more likely from the gospel account—we may understand this in a spiritual sense, that the rich man's soul asked Abraham that Lazarus's soul (which is the same person with him, according to its faculty to act) bring him some bodi-

2. "Known" and "unknown" (*noti* and *incogniti*): in Wyclif's theology these two terms nearly correspond to "predestined" and its opposite.

ly water to refresh the power of the rich man's tongue who was thus damned. The ignorance of the damned cannot be totally excused, nor can any long-lasting or subtle gloss be added to their words any more. Yet it seems probable that the souls of the damned are tormented, by some corporeal elements, in the faculties they earlier had in their bodily organs. Since then this rich man had sinned in his tongue, through pompous speech as well as exceedingly voluptuous taste, the gospel indicates meaningfully how he is tormented in the faculty of the tongue. This torment can come about when this faculty is involuntarily joined to material fire that burns spiritually and torments accidentally. For according to Augustine, people are tormented in this way in their dreams.[3] But Abraham, although he was merciful, was at that point unable to do anything against the right order; therefore, he replies to being called "father" by calling the rich man "son." **Son,** he says, **remember that you received good things**—sensible delight, but undeservedly—**in your lifetime, and** that this **Lazarus** received in his body **evil things** that afflicted him, but in contrary fashion to yourself, for he took them patiently and meritoriously. And therefore in God's right judgment he has now gained consolation, and in the same right judgment you have gained torment. Nor can the soul of Lazarus now be touched by such wretchedness, since for all who live in purgatory and are condemned and buried in hell a great chasm is set, that is, a great distance in space, in which their black bodies are confounded, so that the predestined souls, even if they wanted to pass across to the damned, or vice versa, have no power to do so.

As the rich man, then, is shut off from this relief, he turns to something else that he believes is possible for him. **Then, father, I beseech you,** he says, **that you would send Lazarus to my father's house, for I have five brethren, that he may testify to them** of the retribution of torment and of eternal reward, **lest they also come into this place of torments.** But Abraham denied this petition and declared it to be as unreasonable as the former one. **They have,** he says, **Moses and the prophets; let them hear those.** For God, who put all things in a measured order, ordained that the living members of a particular group should give counsel to the living. Since Christ is both God

---

3. Augustine, *Sermo 328, in natali martyrum* 6 (PL 38:1454).

and man, whose word was set forth in the Old Testament, if the living are not converted by his words, they will not be converted by either the words of angels or those of the dead. Thus all the sin of the church comes from the fact that people faithlessly do not believe the words of Christ. The rich man did not make this prayer out of charity for his living brothers, but because he would be punished more severely if they were to be damned, since he concurred with them in sin. The condemned have this spark of reason, that they hate those the more who have done them some spiritual evil. For this reason they hate God the more, together with the multitude of the condemned, who out of his immense justice inflicts on them the punishment for their sin.

Concerning this gospel one may raise the question[4] whether begging is praiseworthy in itself, and being rich to be condemned, as this gospel seems to suggest. This is certainly not so, because this beggar, who is uniquely praised in scripture, is received into Abraham's bosom, and consequently into the bosom of one who is even further praised, for it is certain that Abraham like Job and other patriarchs was rich. But let us talk about clamorous and importunate begging, not about the quiet begging [of our prayers] before God, as each one is bound to beg. Then it is clear that the former amounts to sin, for otherwise it would not have been commanded in God's law that "there shall be no beggar among" the Jews, as is said in Deuteronomy 15[:4]. Further, the Wise Man prays that God give him "neither riches nor beggary," in Proverbs 30[:8]. And further, such begging seems to be against the law of the gospel and of nature. For the apostles lived on the labor of their hands, as is said of the "vessel of election" [Acts 9:15] in Acts 20:34. The same is manifest in the private rules of religious orders, which prescribe work.[5] And even further, according to civil laws, healthy beggars are to be punished for their begging.[6]

Regarding the law of nature: It is certain that anything that is su-

---

4. The beginning of the sermon's second part: "Circa hoc evangelium dubitatur."

5. Referring to the manual labor decreed, for example, in the *Rule of St. Benedict* and others. "Private" rule or religion, in Wyclif's vocabulary, refers to the religious orders.

6. Cf. Justinian, *Codex* 11.25 (Justinian, *Corpus iuris civilis Iustinianei*, 5:148–49).

perfluous in nature is against its law. Lawful begging, then, implies the need of the beggar and the time he spends in begging without receiving equivalent recompense. Hence the Apostle commands that he who does not labor should not eat [cf. 1 Thessalonians 3:10]. Hence, if we consider the sumptuous and superfluous works of art among the friars and other mendicants, it seems that their begging is more culpable than theft. Thus the use of the time in which they thus beg is made a loss. And this is confirmed by what has been said elsewhere, that their community life, for whose sake they beg thus eagerly, is superfluous and unjustifiable. For if every one of them were to be scattered among the people like rain, they would do more good and would tolerate their food more easily. Christ and his apostles never hinted at their own need, except in so far as it was necessary for those who supported them to give them more helpful alms. Therefore the obligation to beg in this fashion forever is absolutely detestable, both because such begging is often a matter of guilt both to the beggars and in view of the poor people who are being thus robbed, and because of the truants for whom such begging is done. Thus, that rule of an order by which a brother is bound to beg in this fashion forever is blind.

Clearly, then, when friars praise their [own] voluntary begging while they criticize the necessary begging [of others] that is ordained by God, they accuse themselves, especially since they ought to exemplify Christ's need. This way they loudly extort the good of the needy and, as much as it lies in their power, give scandal to God. But Christ says in Matthew 11:6: "Blessed is he that shall not be scandalized in me." If in respect to their need they stand in Christ's stead, they should not [display it] excessively but rather, like others, share more widely in Christ's suffering and [gain his forgiveness while they, with other wise people, despise temporal gain].[7] But these men, to achieve the same end, simulate their need and truly enhance their theft. The remedy against such men, who beg against the right order, would be for a lay person not to give them anything, simply because they belong to such a private order. Rather, they should help with food and clothing those more needy than they are, since it would be more fit-

7. The words in square brackets are a suggestion to make sense of the otherwise corrupt text.

ting that persons who have greater means in earthly things and who should be more merciful, should help the more needy ones. Since [the mendicants] pretend that to possess temporal goods in this fashion is for them perfection, it would be a much greater perfection for a lay person who is not obligated in this way to any mendicity. It seems against the law of nature to accept the perfection of one's fellow human being and to diminish one's own.

Nor do they bring any proof in favor of such open mendicity, except a sophistical one which they deceitfully beg from scripture.[8] For they say that in John 4[:7], when Christ ordered the Samaritan woman "to give him to drink," he *begged* for a cup of water. Now, some maintain logically that in the same act the whole Trinity begged that the commandments be observed, while Christ's human nature begged for what he was asking, for himself and all his members. And therefore, they say, he ordered that drink as lord, or asked for it from the Samaritan woman as a friend and acquaintance; on the same evidence would not only a friend beg something from a friend, but a lord something from his servant. For Christ showed his lordship there, as with his prophetic spirit he told that woman of her past. And thus it seems, according to the gospel, that he spoke mystically to the apostles when they came and exhorted him to eat: "I have food to eat that you do not know" [John 4:32]. Just as doing his Father's will was Christ's spiritual food, so also was the drink which the woman gave him on that occasion, which she offered to him both in her own person and as a figure of the church of the Gentiles. Wherein Christ worked miraculously, doing the will of God his Father.

These beggars, therefore, should open up the description of [such] begging, but [instead] they hide it, as they do elsewhere, so that their poison may be more skillfully hidden and the schooling of the devil less clearly shown. And although all these things have been considered of little importance, they yet foreshadow a greater evil. For first, the Christian religion begs [*read* begged?] as it should, according to its legitimate need; second, the sects have been begging rapaciously according to their monstrous pride; and third, it is to be feared that thieves

---

8. Notice Wyclif's punning: "Quam mendicant mendaciter ex scriptura."

might rise openly who in their begging depopulate the poor Christian religion. For because of the flaw in the ways to receive alms, Antichrist has gradually become strong, so that thieves today can say the words of Proverbs 1:14: "Let us all have one purse." Therefore it is necessary that the people stay within the limits[9] of the Christian order.

9. Possibly a pun on the geographical "limits" within which friars were allowed, or sent, to beg.

PART III

SAINTS' FEASTS

Sermons delivered on the feast days of saints use the same variety of structural patterns observed in *de tempore* sermons. In their development they tend to combine eulogy of the saint and his or her virtues with applying those virtues to the audience's spiritual and moral life. For their rhetorical development they often employ the florid style of monastic preaching (selection 16, for example). Specific devices that are characteristic of such panegyric rhetoric are addresses to the saint (18), outdoing (18, beginning and passim), name etymology (20, 24, 25), and others. For closer analysis of saints' sermons and their rhetoric, see Siegfried Wenzel, "Preaching the Saints in Chaucer's England," in *Earthly Love, Spiritual Love, Love of the Saints*, ed. Susan J. Ridyard, Sewanee Medieval Studies 8 (Sewanee: University of the South Press, 1999), 45–68, and "Saints and the Language of Praise," ibid., 69–87.

15

THE ANNUNCIATION OF THE BLESSED VIRGIN MARY (JOHN DYGON)

AFTER STUDYING AT OXFORD and obtaining a degree in both civil and canon law, John Dygon served at various churches in the south of England, including St. Andrew's, Holborn (London). Then he became a recluse at the recently founded Carthusian priory at Sheen in Surrey, where he lived from 1435 until at least 1449 and possibly 1456–58. He owned a number of books, many of which he compiled and wrote himself. Among them is a collection of sermons for saints' feasts and several feasts in the temporal cycle, from which the following piece is taken.

The sermon for the Annunciation (March 25) shows various features that are characteristic of the entire collection, including Dygon's eagerness to quote authorities and to copy longer excerpts for the catena-like development of his main points; his attention to his possible audience; and his occasional sympathies with the moral seriousness (but not doctrinal positions) we tend to associate with the Lollards. The sermon also demonstrates the structure of the ancient homily, in which—after an introductory section that leads to the request for prayer—a literal exposition of the entire gospel reading is followed by its moral or "mystical" application. Here Dygon suggests two different applications, for different audiences, and develops the second, which deals with the duties of noble lords in following the great example set by Mary.

SOURCE:
Oxford, Magdalen College, MS 79, fols. 1–4v (DY-1).

LITERATURE:
Wenzel, *Collections*, 100–115.
Ralph Hanna, "John Dygon, Fifth Recluse of Sheen: His Career, Books,
    and Acquaintance," in *Imagining the Book*, ed. Stephen Kelly and John J.
    Thompson (Turnhout: Brepols, 2005), 126–41.

❧

**Behold the handmaid of the Lord; be it done to me according to
your word, Luke 1:38.**

As the Blessed Virgin Mary, the mother of God, has five feasts
that are approved in the church, so she has five corresponding virtues, namely, faith, hope, love, humility, and chastity. The feast of her
Conception corresponds to her faith; the feast of her Nativity, to her
hope; the feast of the Lord's Annunciation, to her love; the feast of
her Purification, to her humility; and the feast of her Assumption, to
her chastity. Through faith the Blessed Virgin conceived the Son of
God; through hope she nursed him with her milk and motherly care;
through love she was pleasing to the Highest One and stood by her
son in his works of the gospel and in the hard suffering of his death;
through humility she deemed herself the lowest among all servants of
the Lord, crediting God's grace with all that was worthy of praise in
her; and through chastity of mind and body she merited to dwell in
heaven with the angels, where she will rejoice without end, praising
the Trinity and taking delight with her own, most beloved son, our
Lord Jesus Christ.

In these five virtues the Blessed Virgin, mother of Christ, holds
the first place among all women and among all pilgrims, after Christ,
her blessed son. For in faith and humility she conceived the Son of
God when she said, "Behold the handmaid of the Lord," etc. She also
showed strong faith in the prophets and in the angel's visit, that a pure
virgin would conceive the Son of God without male seed, and would
remain a wholly untouched virgin in his conception, in his birth, and
after his birth. In the three days of Christ's death also she had the

strongest faith in the resurrection of her son and his divinity, whereas the apostles and disciples of Christ all abandoned Christ and denied their faith because of the danger of death they were in and because of the horrible Passion of their Lord Jesus Christ. For this reason the church has dedicated the Saturday especially to the service of the glorious Virgin Mary. Further, she had the firm hope of reaching beatitude on the grounds of her son's grace and the good works she had done in this life. In this hope she stood close by her son in his many labors and immense dangers. She had an excelling love, in loving God above all things and her neighbor perfectly and, by her compassion, giving the suffering her timely help. For as is said in Luke 2[:51] and elsewhere, "Mary kept in her heart" the words of the prophets and of the angel, the events involving the kings from the East and the shepherds, and the words of Christ and his actions in his childhood and later until his glorious death. And she shared these events and words with the apostles and other disciples of Christ. She further had a very great humility, calling herself "the handmaid of the Lord" when she was chosen by the whole Trinity to be the mother of the Son of God and a queen, whom all generations would bless forever, according to the words of Luke 2[:46ff.]: "My soul does magnify the Lord," etc., "because he has regarded the humility of his handmaid, for behold, from henceforth all generations shall call me blessed, because he has done great things to me," etc. And Mary was chaste beyond all women, as she resolved, without any commandment or example, to remain a virgin in body and mind. She possessed such chastity and grace that, although she was most beautiful and of a most noble ancestry, she stirred all who looked at her to chastity, humility, contempt of the world, and the other virtues. Hold these virtues firmly, and you will be well oriented. Venerate this lady, this glorious virgin. That we may be worthy to imitate this virgin in her great virtues, and fruitfully hear about the conception of the Son of God, let everyone say with devout mind an Our Father and Hail Mary.

Behold the handmaid of the Lord, etc. To see how the Blessed Virgin Mary gracefully spoke these words at which she conceived the Son of God, we shall follow the gospel text step by step with a short commentary. **In the sixth month,** says the evangelist, **the angel was sent,**

and so on. Here is first of all declared that, just as man was created on the sixth day, so "in the sixth month"[1] the Son of God was conceived of the Virgin Mary, to redeem mankind from sin and slavery to the devil. An angel is sent from God—not some lower angel but the archangel Gabriel, who is called "the strength of God" because he came to announce him, the Son of God, who is the wisdom and strength of the Father. He had come into the world to fight the powers of the air, and he is "the Lord strong and mighty in battle," and "the king of glory," and "the Lord of hosts" according to the prophet's prediction in Psalm 23[:8–10]. Next: **to a virgin espoused,** etc. This virgin was espoused before she conceived the Son of God for many reasons, according to Jerome and other doctors of the church. First, in order to commend physical marriage, which at the end of the world heretics want to condemn, as Paul testifies in 1 Timothy 4[:3]. Second, so that the Jews would not in justice reject Christ for being illegitimate if he had been born out of wedlock. Third, so that Mary's descent would derive from the pedigree of Joseph, who was of the house or family or lineage of David; because the divine scriptures customarily do not give the pedigrees of women. For Mary was of the lineage of King David, and thus the earthly reign belonged to Christ by this blood relation on his mother's side, according to the bishop of Armagh.[2] But because of the perfection of his priesthood he did not claim or accept such a reign, even when it was freely offered him by the people, as is shown in John 6[:15], where it is said: "But Jesus, when he knew that they would come to take him by force and make him king, fled into the mountain, himself alone." Fourth, so that when Mary fled to Egypt with her child because of Herod's persecution and returned from there (Matthew 2), she would have a man's help and her husband as her protector, and comfort, and true witness to her unblemished virginity. Fifth, that the virginal birth would be hidden from the devil, who knew from prophecies that the Son of God would become flesh and destroy his power over many, according to John 12[:31]: "The prince of this world shall be cast out," and John 16[:11]: "The

1. That is, of Elizabeth's pregnancy; see Luke 1:26.

2. Richard FitzRalph, archbishop of Armagh (1347–60). But the reading is not entirely certain: "secundum ardima'um."

prince of this world is already judged." And further lest, if Satan in his envy knew Christ to be born of a virgin, he should fear to procure Christ's death, through which mankind was to be saved. Sixth, that the evil Jews should not defame the mother of Christ, which would make shameless virgins audacious.

And the virgin's name was Mary. "Mary" means enlightened, or bringing light, or bitter sea, or mistress. She was enlightened by the Holy Spirit beyond any other woman to understand the mysteries of holy scripture and to love God above all. She was also bringing light to other faithful people by her word and example in the way of virtues. She was a bitter sea because of her sorrow in the Passion of her son, and because of her compassion with sinners, with the weak, and with the miseries of the needy. And she was mistress of the world because she bore the lord of all creatures and savior of the world. **And the angel being come in, said unto her: Hail, full of grace,** etc. Where we should notice that the angel found this gentle virgin of thirteen years,[3] not in a tavern or a theater, not gossiping with immodest youths, but in her praying chamber, devoutly praying for God's grace and the redemption of mankind. Imitate this virgin in such works, and you shall merit God's help, and the visitation or consolation of an angel, and preservation from errors and sins! The first woman, Eve, our mother, brought sin, death, and damnation to mankind, as stated in Genesis 2 and 3. But Mary brought us grace, joy, and glory through the mediation of her blessed son. And so Eve's name was changed into Ave, for Mary was far from that "Vae" or woe that Eve brought to this world.[4] Eve was full of deadly poison and misery, but Mary was "full of grace" and of the saving help for our human nature. According to Acts 6[:8], Stephen was "full of grace and fortitude," in a fullness that was fitting for a martyr and defender of the gospel. Mary was full of that grace which was fitting for the mother of God. Christ was "full of grace and truth" [John 1:14], in the fullness that was fitting for the Son of God made flesh, "of whose full-

---

3. Medieval legends held that at the Annunciation Mary was in her fourteenth year; for example, *Legenda aurea*, 217.

4. The common pun on the Latin names: *Eva* was turned into *Ave*, meaning *a ve*, that is *sine ve*, "without woe."

ness we all have received" [John 1:16]. Truly, Mary was full of grace, who merited to carry the lord of grace and savior of the world and to be the bride and mother of Christ, our mother, the mother of God, and a perpetual virgin and placed above the angels in power and glory. Rightly then is she **blessed among women,** and beyond all women and beyond all the angels in heaven, for through her the dishonor of women has been taken away, mankind saved, sin and the devil's power destroyed, and every heresy repelled, according to the words: "Rejoice, Mary, virgin mother of Christ. You alone destroyed all heresies when you bore God and man as a virgin and after his birth remained an unstained virgin."[5]

Who having heard, was troubled at his saying, and thought with herself what manner of salutation this should be. Troubled not so as to suffer harm in her virtue, for such trouble does not befall a wise or constant person, according to what philosophers teach; but troubled in her admiration and reverence because of the newness of such an unusual thing that had never been heard of before. Since this devout and pure virgin was troubled in the presence of an angel, weak virgins should be troubled and tremble at the visits, talk, kisses, or touches of unchaste or lecherous youths, who are sent by the devil to poison souls who have been consecrated in baptism to be Christ's spouses. **And the angel said to her: Fear not, Mary, for you have found grace with God.** A good angel's function is to comfort the fainthearted, just as an evil angel's function is to trouble them and through terror lead them into error or rage. That the Virgin should not fear is shown in her name, for virginity is a close relative to the angels,[6] and the holy angels are friends or guardians of devout virgins. "You have found grace with God," of which we have already spoken.

In the next words the angel is more specific, where it is written: **Be-**

---

5. A Marian antiphon listed in R. J. Hesbert, *Corpus antiphonalium officii,* vol. 3 (Rome: Herder, 1968), No. 2925 (p. 234), for the Assumption. A similar but shorter form (No. 2924) was used in Advent; see *Sarum Missal,* 496; and *Breviarium ad usum insignis ecclesiae Sarum,* ed. Francis Procter and Christopher Wordsworth, 3 vols. (Cambridge: Cambridge University Press, 1882–86), 1:xxxiv and lxxiii, and 2.286.

6. *Angelis cognata est virginitas:* a commonplace found in Jerome *(Epistula 9 ad Paulam et Eustochium),* Peter Chrysologus *(Sermo 143),* etc.

hold you shall conceive in your womb, and shall bring forth a son; and you shall call his name Jesus. "For he shall save his people from their sins," Matthew 1[:21]. "Nor is there any other name under heaven given to men whereby those who believe must be saved," Acts 4[:12]. Of this name it is said in Philippians 2[:9–10]: "God has exalted him," that is, the Father has exalted the Son, "and has given him a name which is above all names, that in the name of Jesus every knee should bend," etc. Thus, blessed be he who is the Son of God from all eternity, and the son of Mary by grace and in the fullness of time, through whom all those who are chosen are saved and the ruin of the angels is restored. He shall be great, etc. For he is "a great king over all the gods" [Psalm 94:3], that is, the angels and blessed humans. He is also "king of king and lord of lords," Revelation 19[:16]. And further, he is "the prince of the kings of the earth," and "Alpha and Omega," "the First and the Last," Revelations 1[:5, 8, 17]. And he shall be called the Son of the Most High and will be truly and naturally the Son of God, eternally equal with the Father and the Holy Spirit in omnipotence, omniscience, and omnivolence,[7] patience, mercy, and love. And he has the power to judge the living and the dead, John 5[:22]. And the Lord God shall give unto him the throne of David his father; and he shall reign in the house of Jacob forever, and of his kingdom there shall be no end. The "throne of David" is the Jewish people, over whom Christ ruled spiritually in faith and the virtues. Just as David ruled them in time defending them from their enemies with his strong hand,[8] so Christ, from the omnipotence and strength of his godhead, which is unlimited, defends those that adhere to him in faith, hope, love, and lasting perseverance, and defends them from the demons and their helpers, who are powerful in their subtlety and malice and practiced from of old in their enmity and evil cruelty. The angel did not say that he would rule in everyone by grace, but meaningfully "in the house of David," that is, in those who fight strenuously against the devil and manfully overcome all his temptations—in true Catholics,[9] who are the house of David. He will reign in the church,

7. *Omnivolencia*, the quality of willing everything.
8. The name "David" is normally thought to mean "strong hand."
9. See selection 12, note 19.

that is, in the Church Militant through his grace, and in the Church Triumphant forever through his glory, where he will be seen brighter than light. The archangel does not speak of a temporal reign or of worldly dominion, for neither of these is eternal but of necessity comes to an end. Hence Christ says plainly, in John 18[:36], that "my kingdom is not of this world." And John 6[:15]: "Jesus therefore, when he knew that they would come to take him by force and make him king, fled again into the mountain, himself alone." Matthew 8[:20]: "The Son of Man has nowhere to lay his head." Let all the proud blush, the greedy, and those who go to war for land, for Christ was supremely humble, voluntarily poor, the prince of peace, and detached from the world. He spent the night in praying to God and was solicitously busy in preaching the word of God, dying in peace for his enemies, so that he might gain the kingdom of God forever, as can be seen everywhere in the gospels of Luke, Matthew, and John.

But Mary said to the angel: How shall this be done, because I know not man? From this we see that Mary did not doubt God's promise made by the angel, as Zechariah doubted, in Luke 1[:18–22], for which he was punished and lost his speech. Rather, Mary prudently asked about the way the Son of God was to be conceived and incarnated. This also shows, according to Augustine, that blessed Mary intended firmly in her mind to preserve her virginity, whence she said, "I know not man," that is, I have vowed never to know a man but to keep my virginity for the Lord forever.[10] But in the end she submitted to God's will, and this obedience is praiseworthy and approved by the Lord. **And the angel, answering, said to her: The Holy Ghost shall come upon you, and the power of the Most High shall overshadow you,** etc. Here the archangel bows before such a lofty mystery and confesses that he is powerless to explain the details of such a sublime mystery, namely, the incarnation of the Son of God in an untouched virgin. He refers her to the unique teaching of the Holy Spirit, who teaches all truth and knows the secrets of the godhead. Through surpassing grace the Holy Spirit came upon Mary and made her will, faith, and obedience ready to give full assent to the divine mysteries.

10. Perhaps Augustine, *Sermo 195* (PL 39:2108).

And so "the power of the Most High overshadowed" Mary, protecting her mind against inordinate concupiscence and against sinful hesitation, that through faith and humility and the working of the Holy Spirit she might conceive the Son of God without human seed and without stain to her virginity, which she had consecrated to God. **And therefore that holy one,** unique and miraculous, **which shall be born of you shall be called the Son of God**—[unique and miraculous] in nature, [just as when God] made a man from dust without a human father and mother, and a woman from the man's rib without the normal way of human procreation.[11] **And behold Elizabeth,** etc., as if the angel were saying: Just as Elizabeth, who was aged and sterile, conceived a son in her old age out of faith and grace alone against the normal course of nature, so likewise could an untouched virgin conceive and give birth to the son of the Most High and God blessed above all. **And this is the sixth month** from the conception of the Lord's precursor **with her who is called barren,** that is, the aged and sterile Elizabeth, who through faith and obedience overcame [the limitations of] woman's nature. And this conception of the Son of God by an untouched virgin is an easy work to the Holy Spirit, **because no word shall be impossible with God,** for with God nothing is impossible, but whatever he has wanted to do, he has done in heaven and on earth. **And Mary said: Behold the handmaid of the Lord; be it done to me according to your word.** Behold the surpassing humility of the glorious Virgin: when she was chosen to be the mother of God and queen of heaven, she humbled herself to the lowest level of Christian service, according to the words of Sirach 3[:20]: "The greater you are, the more humble yourself in all things, and you shall find grace before God." And in grace and her humility she assented to God in conceiving the son of the Most High.

These things have been briefly said about the text of the gospel, where the Annunciation of the Lord and his incarnation and concep-

---

11. Reference to the four ways a human being may be created: from a man and a woman (everybody), without a man and a woman (Adam), from a man without a woman (Eve), and from a woman without a man (Christ). See, for instance, Geoffrey of Bath, *Ad fratres in eremo* 28 (PL 40:1285, often ascribed to Augustine) and also above, selection 7 (p. 73).

tion in the womb of the glorious Virgin are treated. For the moral instruction of the common people, develop the five virtues that were
mentioned in the beginning, if your audience can understand them.
But if lords are present, you could continue speaking about their estate, praise justice and just judgment and condemn pride, avarice, robbery, and lionlike tyranny.

For that, we should notice that lords ought to precede all others in
virtue as they precede them in their rank, and particularly so

in the study of holy scripture,[12]

in mercy,

and in justice toward their subjects, especially those in misery and
need.

For at the end of Deuteronomy 17[:18–19] the Lord commands: "After he is raised to the throne of his kingdom, he shall copy out to
himself the Deuteronomy of this law in a volume, taking the copy of
the priests of the Levitical tribe, and he shall have it with him, and
shall read it all the days of his life, that he may learn to fear the Lord
his God and keep his words and ceremonies that are commanded in
the law." And in Joshua 1[:8] the Lord commands Joshua, who led his
people directly under God: "Let not the book of this law depart from
your mouth, but you shall meditate on it day and night, that you may
observe and do all the things that are written in it. Then shall you
direct your way and understand it." Whence in Psalm 2[:10] the Almighty commands: "And now, O you kings, understand: receive instruction, you who judge the earth." And in Proverbs 14[:35]: "A wise
servant is acceptable to the king; he that is good for nothing shall feel
his anger"—"good for nothing," that is, unwise, according to the Paris master.[13] And in Psalm 77[:70–71]: "And he chose his servant David," etc., "to feed Jacob his servant," etc.

12. The suggestion that (temporal) lords should study scripture has a Wycliffite
ring to it, a feature that appears elsewhere in this otherwise clearly orthodox sermon
cycle; see *Collections*, 107–10. For the Lollard urging that lay lords should study scripture, see *English Wycliffite Sermons* (cited above, p. 154), 5:77 and 157.

13. *Secundum Parisiensem*. Elsewhere Dygon quotes as "Parisiensis" both William
Peraldus (*Summa de vitiis and de virtutibus*) and William of Auvergne (*De sacramentis*).

About the mercy of lords Job 31[:18] says: "From my infancy mercy grew up with me, and it came out with me from my mother's womb." And Proverbs 3[:3]: "Let not mercy and truth leave you." And in 20[:28]: "Mercy and truth preserve the king, and his throne is strengthened by clemency." Luke 6[:36]: "Be merciful, as your Father also is merciful." And in Psalm 24[:10]: "All the ways of the Lord are mercy and truth." Thus all the works of lords will be mercy and truth if they are "ministers of his kingdom," Wisdom 6[:5] and Romans 13[:6].

About the justice of lords Exodus 23[:2] says plainly: "You shall not follow the multitude to do evil, neither shall you, in judgment, yield to the opinion of the majority, to stray from the truth." Later it says to the judges [Deuteronomy 1:16–17]: "Hear them," namely, the children of Israel, "and judge that which is just, whether he is one of your country or a stranger. There shall be no difference of persons, you shall hear the little as well as the great. Neither shall you respect any man's person, because it is the judgment of God." And in 2 Chronicles 19[:6–7] King Josaphat said to the judges: "Take heed what you do, for you exercise not the judgment of man but of the Lord, and whatsoever you judge, it shall redound to you. Let the fear of the Lord be with you and do all things with diligence; for there is no iniquity with the Lord our God, nor respect of persons, nor desire of gifts." So, since their judgment is God's judgment, if they give an unjust judgment, they impute it to God and thus blaspheme him. Hence Exodus 18[:21]: "Provide out of all the people able men, such as fear God, in whom there is truth, and who hate avarice." And in Deuteronomy 1[:13] Moses said to the children of Israel: "Let me have from among you wise and understanding men," that is, prudent ones, "and such whose way of life is approved among your tribes, that I may appoint them as your rulers." And for their justice and conformity with God, such judges are called gods, in Exodus 22[:8]: "If he is not known," that is, the thief, "the master of the house shall be brought to the gods," that is, to the judges, as the text there makes clear. And in Exodus 23[:8] the Lord says: "Neither shall you take bribes, which even blind the wise, and pervert the words of the just." And Sirach 20[:31]: "Presents and gifts blind the eyes of judges and make them dumb in the mouth, so that they cannot correct." Proverbs 17[:23]: "[The wicked man] takes gifts out of his bosom, that he may pervert the paths of judgment." And Job 15[:34]: "Fire shall devour the tabernacles of those who love to take bribes."

Further about the humility and mercy of lords: Since Christ, the almighty God, is surpassingly humble and the teacher of humility, how detestable is the pride of lords who are his servants and vicars of his mercy! Since the almighty king is so humble, "Why are earth and ashes so proud?" [Sirach 10:9]. Hence in Deuteronomy 17[:20] the Lord says of the king: "Let not his heart be lifted up with pride over his brethren." Therefore the bishop of Lincoln, in his sermon *A Rod Shall Come Forth* [Isaiah 11:1], writes that in Christ's genealogy appears Jesse, who was humble and mild, for according to Chrysostom, "the glory of great people lies in their ability to humble themselves, nor can high standing be more gloriously praised than when it is shown to freely accept humility." Anyone who considers the forefathers of the Lord and his mother should lay aside his pride and not take glory in the high standing of his own parents, for he should take glory in the virtues, not of himself, but of God alone, putting his hope in nothing else than God's mercy, in holiness of his life. For if he stems from parents of high rank and himself lacks noble manners, he shames his parents. And if he is like them, he does not borrow glory from others, for in this case he would be nourishing the vice of vainglory. And Jerome says: "No one can flatter himself of his noble descent if hatred rules in him, or envy, avarice, wrath, or any other vice. For it is much more unworthy to be a slave with one's mind than with one's body."[14] And Jerome again: "I shall not take pride in noble descent, that is, in goods that belong to others, since Abraham and Isaac, both holy men, sired sinners like Ishmael and Esau; while Jephthah, who is numbered by the Apostle's voice among the just, was born of a prostitute."[15] Further, this Virgin Mary is set higher than God her son, according to Bernard, on the words "And he was subject unto them."[16] Why, then, do temporal lords, who are filled with wretchedness, swell with pride in their name of dominion, while blessed Mary, mother

---

14. Pelagius, *Epistula ad Demetriadem* 22 (PL 30:36–37).

15. Jerome, *Epistula 60*, 8. For the reference to Jephthah, see Hebrews 11:32 and Judges 11:1.

16. Cf. Bernard, *Super Missus est angelus,* hom. 1.7.

and princess of the prince of princes, humbles herself to the state of a handmaiden? So far the bishop of Lincoln.[17] When, therefore, Lucifer, the highest angel and brighter than all the others, was so severely punished for his pride, what will happen to earthly lords, who are very poor in comparison with him, in their knowledge, power, and nimbleness? Is not pride more tolerable in a wealthy and famous person than in one who is poor and like a worm? Whence it is said in Sirach 25[:3–4]: "Three sorts my soul hates, and I am greatly grieved at their life: a poor man who is proud, a rich man who is a liar, an old man who is a fool and doting." Since the apostles could not enter the kingdom of heaven unless they were truly humble, as Christ says in Matthew 18[:3], it is impossible for earthly lords to possess the kingdom of heaven or enter it with their pride. Rather, with Satan, who is king over all children of pride, Job 41[:25], they will descend to hell like lead in troubled waters. And so King David says to God in Psalm 131[:1]: "O Lord, remember David and all his meekness." And in Psalm 130[:1]: "Lord, my heart is not exalted," etc.; "if I was not humbly minded," etc; "as a child that is weaned is toward his mother." Therefore the bishop of Lincoln writes in his sermon *As Oil Poured Out* [cf. Canticles 1:2] as follows: "True governance is to rule those who have submitted themselves to us with firmness and power. Lords must also rule their servants with reason in the way of good behavior and compel them toward honorable things, not push them cruelly into misery but mercifully lift them out of it and love them as equals by nature, for it was not nature (which made all men equals) that made them servants, but error and vice. Take error and vice away, and there will no longer be a place for dominance. But dominion has been established by God's ordinance of necessity in order to correct and to ward these off, that is, errors and vices. God also says in Genesis [1:28]: 'Rule over the fowls and the fishes,' that is, over desires that are

17. I.e., Robert Grosseteste, bishop of Lincoln 1235–53. This passages reproduces selections from his *Sermon 3 ("Egredietur virga de radice Iesse")*; cf. Oxford, Bodleian Library, MS Bodley 830, fols. 140va–143ra. Dygon follows Grosseteste's thought and quotes his quotations from Chrysostomus, Jerome, and Bernard verbatim. Grosseteste's works have been transcribed from this manuscript by Joseph Goering et al. and can be found at http://www.grosseteste.com.

fleshly, proud, and too eager. Therefore, the true rule of one man over another is the rational and firm control of these irrational motions, and calling them back to rational ones. When someone is established as lord among men, it is for him an occasion of grief rather than joy. If he is wise, he will not rejoice in his temporary preponderance but will be inconsolably sad that men are subjected because of their errors and vices. Further, proud lords are servants of servants, not lords, for according to Augustine, that is true dominion which is useful, not to the lord but to the servant, which does not need the service of a servant but rather the servant needs that lordship. In this way, God alone is a true lord. Moreover, everyone who gives, insofar as he is the giver, is greater than the recipient. Therefore, if a lord receives from his servant what is useful to him, he is of lesser status than his servant. Therefore, a lord must know, from the word and its meaning,[18] that he ought to share his goods with his servants by supplying their needs, correcting their errors, freeing them their vices, and teaching them moral behavior." So far the bishop of Lincoln.[19]

Therefore, secular lords must fear pride and carry out justice, especially for the poor, after the example of Job 29[:11–17], who says: "The ear that heard me blessed me, and the eye that saw me gave witness to me. Because I had delivered the poor man that cried out, and the fatherless that had no helper. The blessing of him that was about to perish came upon me, and I comforted the heart of the widow. I was clad with justice, and I clothed myself with my judgment, as with a robe and a diadem. I was an eye to the blind and a foot to the lame. I was the father of the poor, and the cause which I knew not, I searched out most diligently. I broke the jaws of the wicked man, and out of his teeth I took away the prey." Here Christian lords, instructed in the law of Moses and the prophets and above all in the law of the gospel, must see how much justice and mercy flourished in a knight of noble descent who was instructed by the natural law,

18. Grosseteste seems to have the etymology of *dans munus*, "giving a gift," for *dominus*, "lord," in mind. See also selection 25, p. 304.

19. Verbatim extracts from Grosseteste, *Sermon 4* *("Unguentum effusum");* in MS Bodley 830, fols. 145vb–146va. Augustine's teaching on (God's) dominion occurs in *De Genesi ad litteram* 8.11 (PL 34:382). See also the preceding note.

and they should imitate him in this respect, so that they themselves may not be harshly judged in the Last Judgment for transgressing the laws of nature, of Moses, and of the gospel, with its eminently plain example of the Lord Jesus Christ. Also, in Isaiah 1[:17] the Lord says to temporal lords and their deputies: "Seek judgment, relieve the oppressed, judge for the fatherless, defend the widow." And in Jeremiah 7[:3]: "Hear the word of the Lord, all you men of Juda. Make your ways and your doings good, and I will dwell with you in this place. Trust not in lying words, saying: 'The temple of the Lord, the temple of the Lord, it is the temple of the Lord.' For if you will order well your ways and your doings, if you will execute judgment between a man and his neighbor, if you do not oppress the stranger, the fatherless, and the widow, and do not shed innocent blood in this place, and do not walk after strange gods to your own hurt, I will dwell with you in this place, in the land which I gave to your fathers from the beginning and forevermore." And in chapter 22[:3] the Lords speaks thus: "Execute judgment and justice, and deliver him that is oppressed out of the hand of the oppressor: and do not afflict the stranger, the fatherless, or the widow, nor oppress them unjustly; and do not shed innocent blood in this place." And shortly afterward [:5]: "But if you will not hearken to these words, I swear by myself, says the Lord, that this house shall become a desolation."

Behold, the office of lords and their punishment if they do not fittingly and justly carry it out as it has been ordained by the Lord, for in that case they are no true lords but tyrants. Whence Augustine says in book 4 of *The City of God*, at the beginning of chapter 8: "Justice being taken away, what are kingdoms but great robberies?"[20] And Gregory says, in book 5 of the *Register*, about the middle of chapter 33: "Evil and rapacious judges do more harm to the people than the sword of its enemies. Therefore they are to be justly punished by the Lord who are set by him as defenders of the people and harm it more by their tyranny, extortion, or robbery than enemies would do in open battle."[21] And in the book on *Twelve Abuses*, under the ninth, Augustine says: "Let the king know that, as he was set as the first in rul-

---

20. Augustine, *De civitate Dei* 4.4.
21. Not identified.

ing over men, so he will also have the first place in punishment if he does not execute justice. All the sinners he had underneath him in the present, he will have implacably above him in his future torment."[22] The same is said implicitly by Chrysostom in homily 51 of his *Imperfect Work*. Whence the Lord, speaking to kings and judges of the earth, says in Wisdom 6[:4–9]: "For power is given you by the Lord, and strength by the Most High, who will examine your works, and search out your thoughts. Because being ministers of his kingdom, you have not judged rightly, nor kept the law of justice, nor walked according to the will of God. Horribly and speedily will he appear to you, for a most severe judgment shall be for them that bear rule. For to him who is little, mercy is granted, but the mighty shall be mightily tormented. For God will not except any man's person, neither will he stand in awe of any man's greatness: for he made the little and the great, and he has equally care of all. But a greater punishment is ready for the more mighty." In contrast, good lords and just judges are very often praised by the Lord, for they are servants of God and carry out his desire. Their office is to bring peace to the common weal, or to bring it back and preserve it in the community of the peoples. Of them Christ says in Matthew 5[:9, 6]: "Blessed are the peacemakers, they shall be children of God," and "Blessed are they who hunger and thirst for justice, for they shall have their fill." And in Psalm 105[:3]: "Blessed are they who keep judgment and do justice at all times." And in Romans 13[:3–4]: "Princes are not a terror to the good work, but to the evil. Will you then not be afraid of the power? Do what is good: and you shall have praise from the same. For he is God's minister to you for good. But if you do what is evil, fear, for he does not bear the sword in vain. For he is God's minister, an avenger to execute wrath upon him who does evil." And in [1] Peter 2[:13–14]: "Be you subject therefore to every human creature for God's sake, whether it is to the king as excelling, or to governors as sent by him for the punishment of evildoers, and for the praise of the good."

Therefore, just as almighty God is full of justice, mercy, and piety, secular lords shall follow him in these virtues as much as they can. By

---

22. *De duodecim abusivis* 9 (PL 40:1086). The treatise is of uncertain authorship and was attributed to various medieval authors.

this they will be the house of Jacob in their manly resistance against the temptations of the devil, the flesh, and the world, and in their rational bridling of the evils in their people, and by preserving justice, peace, and the other virtues in God's people and the Militant Church. In this way they will be followers of the humility of the Glorious Virgin, humbling themselves before God and attributing to their Creator all the good that God's grace is working in them, so that in all things God may be glorified and they may praise him in this life and the next. May Christ Jesus multiply such humility, justice, mercy, peace, and charity in every estate of Christians, that we can become sharers in his eternal glory. Amen.

16

THE ASSUMPTION OF THE
BLESSED VIRGIN MARY

EVEN THOUGH THE DOGMA that after her death the Blessed Virgin Mary was taken up to heaven in body and soul was not officially defined until 1950, in the later Middle Ages the feast of her Assumption (August 15) was the most celebrated of the five feasts mentioned in the preceding selection, as is shown by the large number of surviving sermons for this feast from late-medieval England. The following piece demonstrates the florid style customary in panegyric preaching by Benedictine monks; it has been preserved in two manuscripts associated with that order (see above, selections 5 and 9).

SOURCE:
Oxford, Bodleian Library, MS Laud misc. 706, fols. 27–30 (R-5); also in Worcester Cathedral, MS F.10, fol. 17r-v (W-4).

LITERATURE:
Wenzel, *Collections,* 88–90 and 151–58.

❧

Daybreak has arisen, daybreak has arisen, Genesis 32[:26]
Reverend fathers in Christ and lords, the most pious ruler of the heavenly empire, seeing that human nature which, with the lamp of its reason as it were extinguished, was foully blackened with the stain of manifold sin, was, in the Egypt of our wretched habitation, fre-

quently wandering from the straight path of truth off through the desert and trackless regions of heresies and errors—like a good shepherd planned to bring back his sheep that he had redeemed to the fold of the Catholic truth. And so that on the way of our pilgrimage the confusion of paths and the blindness of ignorance should not make us despair of reaching the prize of our labors, having first destroyed Pharaoh, the prince of darkness, he gave us here on our way such a guide as he had no hesitation to take up with him into his precious home. Oh, great love of our Redeemer! Oh, immense affection of divine charity toward us, which wished on the solemn day of this feast to call, not Moses his servant as once in the Old Testament, but his most pious mother, call her to the mountain of radiant Olympus, the mountain of God, Horeb, where she, completely illumined with splendor and most worthily exalted above all the choirs of angels, is contemplating God face to face forever. And whenever she sees that some trouble of violent affliction or some danger of tribulation is threatening her people, the Israelites, who had been faithfully signed with the sign of faith, she at once, revealing her breasts of maternal care,[1] through her pious prayer obtains from her sweet child a happy antidote of consolation.

This is that cloud, most bright and with its light shining more clearly than the dawn, which once led the chosen people of God through Egypt to the Promised Land. This is that solar star which, in rising to the apogee of its orb, puts the head of the poisonous dragon under her foot. This is she who, clothed in the shining tunic of the sun, now sits in the temple of the true Solomon crowned with an eternal diadem. Of her, John the Evangelist, that most luminous visionary of heavenly secrets, writes thus: "A great sign appeared in heaven: a woman clothed with the sun, and the moon under her feet, and on her head a crown of twelve stars," Revelation 12[:1]. Oh, with how great and devout celebration of our praises must this glorious Virgin be extolled! Oh, with how devout praises must she be recalled to mind! Indeed, if I had received the keys of worldly knowledge with Paul, if I had learned all kinds of languages to the point that, with Mercury, I would surpass the florid

1. For the motif of the Virgin pleading for mercy by showing her breast(s), see above, selection 10 (p. 122).

eloquence of the language of Cicero's throat in the sweetness of a honeyed voice, I would still not only be found insufficient for the praise of our advocate, but would appear before all to be stupid and ignorant, and likewise mute and without tongue. Thus, halting of tongue and uncircumcised in my lips, I who have hardly passed the crossroads of the Pythagorean letter[2] in the schools of the grammarians, am afraid to say anything about the excellence of this great Virgin before such a venerable audience. No wonder that it would be much more fitting for me to be taught by the rod than to teach, especially because, as I believe it is no secret to your reverences, I have been recently asked by our brothers, or rather compelled by our father's request (as they say, "When leaders ask it is a kind of violent command")[3] to take on this task—may it be fruitful!—which is a burden far beyond my own strength. I would rather that the compassionate hearts of your discretion would uphold my insufficiency with its burden than that I should in any way, with an undisciplined mind, go against my father's desires. What then shall I say? I shall say with the prophet: "I cannot speak, for I am a child," Jeremiah 1[:6]. The silver of rhetoric eludes me and thus "I cannot speak," and the gold of wisdom I lack because "I am a child." Let us, then, follow in the footsteps of our intercessor who, as often as she might help in our needs, "went up into a mountain to pray," Luke 9[:28]. She "went up into a mountain" so that she might avoid the uncertain bridge of this world's fragility; but she "went up into a mountain to pray" so that she could more easily implore help for her followers.[4] Let us therefore with one mind go up into the mountain of devotion and call upon the fountain of wisdom and knowledge with sweet prayers, so that he may instill plentiful drops of his grace

2. The "Pythagorean letter" is the letter Y, symbolizing a crossroads, where the wayfarer has a choice of roads to follow. Here the image is probably used to mark the end of undergraduate studies (the arts) and the choice between different graduate careers (theology, law, etc.).

3. Peter of Blois, *Epistula 1* (PL 207:1), who attributes the saying to his teacher; cf. Walther, *Proverbia* 7758.

4. The quoted biblical verse refers to Christ's going up into the mountain (for the Transfiguration), but the sermon passage speaks clearly of *mediatrix nostra*. The (young) monk preacher seems to have confused Jesus' *ascendit in montem ut oraret* with Mary's *abiit in montana* (Luke 1:39).

into the dry well of my mind and kindle the light of my intellect, and guide my mute tongue to speak the praise of his mother. Commending in our prayers all whom we here are accustomed to fittingly commend, let each one of you pray for the grace that is necessary to you and to me in this work with the usual petition: Our Father.

Daybreak has arisen, as above. Reverend fathers and lords. The dawn of the eternal light and ineclipsable splendor of the palace of heaven, after[5] he rose in body from the wretched hovel of this world to the right hand of his Father in his miraculous Ascension, endowed his glorious mother with such constancy in the four cardinal virtues that she, standing on these as if on four columns and armed with the protective shield of the theological virtues—that is, faith, hope, and love—and enlightened by the rays of the other virtues, might drive off the poisonous audacity of the raging tyrant, and brighten more brilliantly with the most clear light of her radiance those whom the malice of faithlessness had made blind or had thrust into the dark prison of sins. The virtuous purity of our *mediatrix* shone with all the virtues like the morning star in the midst of a cloud. Strengthened on all sides by the unshaken pillars of her virtues against the arrows of the devil's deceit and the fawning world, she fought in the black darkness of the world's night with perseverance like another angel with Jacob, until she felt the dissolution of her body approach. Then, that she might not withhold her own soul any longer from the horizon of eternity, she addressed the world with the angel's words and said without delay: "Let me go, for it is the break of day" [Genesis 32:26]. Thus, then, **Daybreak has arisen.**

In these words I consider two things that are especially to be offered to our attention in praise of the devout mother Mary and the merits of her bright soul:

First, choosing the sweetness of the contemplative life, which we enjoy through the **rising;** and second, moderating the busyness of the active life, which is born with **daybreak.**

The busyness of daybreak, which is to be moderated, ends the night of our vices, but the sweetness of the rising that is to be chosen en-

---

5. *Priusquam* ("before") in R-5, *postquam* ("after") in W-4.

lightens the day of our joys. If we then combine the single terms in a fitting bond, the following two branches will spread out from the infertile stem of our thema:

The sweetness of contemplation that is to be chosen, which we enjoy through the rising, gives to those who love God perfectly unobstructed light;
but the busyness of the active life, which begins with daybreak, ends at once the vicious weariness of the night.

For both these statements together it is written, in the form of a question, in Canticles 6[:9]: "Who is she that comes forth as the daybreak rising, fair as the moon," which indicates the busyness of life that is to be moderated; and second, "choice as the sun," which indicates the sweetness of the contemplative life which is to be chosen. For, first, the most pious mother of Christ, who was a fair daybreak from the very beginnings of her youth, showed forth the necessary moderation of an active life by her resplendent example, like the moon; and "choice as the sun" aflame with the blazing light of contemplation she rose as her merits demanded to the realm of heaven. Of her I can rightly say, in a metaphor, that now **daybreak has arisen.**

[1]

In my first main part I say that to those who love God perfectly the sweetness of contemplation that is to be chosen, which we enjoy through the rising, gives unobstructed light. The white-haired knowledge of some ancient philosophers, as is shown in the book of their sayings and deeds,[6] openly scorned the changeable wealth of temporal affluence and bridled the uncontrolled attacks of their rebellious flesh, so that by cultivating the moral virtues they might more easily raise their minds to the quiet practice of contemplation—this however not for God's sake but for the temporal tranquillity of their bodies and to spread the reputation of their name and to acquire the glory of a very vain praise. And since the trumpet of blessed Gregory sounds

---

6. "In libello de dictis et moribus eorundem" seems to refer to an actual book title, which could be the work of Valerius Maximus, or John of Salisbury's *Policraticus,* or Walter Burleigh, or a similar collection of sayings and deeds of philosophers.

in his *Moral Commentary:* "No one can acquire true tranquillity or reach the peak of quiet contemplation most perfectly unless he will first in humility scorn lower things for the love of his Creator and apply himself to practicing the work of virtues for God's sake,"[7] the lamentable blindness of these same philosophers, being denied the splendor of the higher light, rightly failed to enjoy the true delights of contemplation in everlasting tranquillity. Oh, blind faith of philosophers and damnable presumption of their false belief, which presumed to assert that the highest tranquillity of our mind lay in contemplating creatures, not in the love of their Creator! Oh, holy piety of our *mediatrix,* Oh, sincere and fervent devotion to God, which for the love of eternal happiness attended the honorable school of the virtues, and thus in the fullness of virtues obediently entered the cloister of devotion and thereby raised her mind higher than any other creature to the high endeavor of perfect contemplation! It is no wonder that the Blessed Virgin transcended other creatures in her endeavor of contemplation. For as is proven in the experience of many, when an eggshell is gently filled with rainwater and placed on the ground, as the sun's heat arrives, the fuller of rainwater it was, the higher it is said to gradually rise. In like fashion, the most devout Virgin Mary, filled with all kinds of virtues and the rainwater of grace, through the heat of the eternal sun rose up on high to the uppermost level of love and the summit of the most devout contemplation. Of her, the devout Jerome writes, as he is quoted in *The Mirror of the Blessed Virgin:* "Such gifts it was fitting for the Virgin to receive as pledges that she should be full of grace, so that in ascending the mountain of the contemplative life she brought glory to heaven, God and peace to earth, faith to the nations, an end to vices, order to life, and discipline to our morals."[8] From this authority it is sufficiently plain that our Blessed Virgin especially exemplified the devout life of monks.

But all faithful members of holy religion must mourn that the renowned life of the religious, which once shone brightly in the cloister, is now darkened through a dishonorable way of life and insolence

---

7. Gregory, *Moralia* 3.23.

8. Paschasius Radbertus, *De Assumpcione sanctae Mariae Virginis,* also known as Jerome's Epistle to Paula and Eustochium on the Assumption (CCCM 56C, 120).

of the young and is lamentably being brought to an eclipse through the dense clouds of carnal desires. For modern monks have no taste for the sweetness of holy reading; their eagerness for devout prayers is languishing; and dedication to holy contemplation is now becoming tedious. Where, I ask, does the ready obedience of our holy fathers dwell? Where is that perfect love or unfeigned humility that at one time flourished in the holy school of honorable living, namely, the paradisial cloister of the monks? Certainly, if I must speak the truth, obedience is now dying out, humility is banished, and love fades away, and the reverent honor that senior monks of mature age should receive from the young is very often, by youthful disrespect, turned into derision. Nowadays sobriety does not respect the boundaries of modesty, the integrity of holy fasting is violated, and the tongues of many monks, who should devote themselves to holy reading and eagerly keep a devout silence, are unleashed with frivolous and vain talk in the shrine of the cloister. In this way they frequently seem to use the school of virtues not for the pious practice of contemplation but rather for contentious strife. Let it not be thus, most beloved brethren, not thus, but according to the prophetic counsel of Isaiah, "Come, let us go up to the mountain of the Lord, and he will teach us his ways," Isaiah 2[:3]. "Come, let us go up to the mountain of the Lord" that through the love of God we may be joined to his eternal light. "He will teach us his ways" that we may receive surety about the reward of our virtuous work. In order that our mind may be thus illuminated by the divine light, in our going up to the mountain of the Lord, and that it may be instructed in its virtuous work by God's teaching, I can fittingly say the words I chose for my thema, namely, that **Daybreak has arisen.**

[2]

For my second and now the final part I said that the busyness of the active life, which begins with daybreak, ends at once the vicious weariness of the night. The monks' lawgiver, our most holy father Benedict, in considering the nature of human frailty and that the devout practice of contemplation cannot be maintained for long without the help of the active life, ordained as it were by a general decree that some monks should devote themselves constantly to the divine office and thereby taste the sweet honeycombs of meditation; others should carry out works of moderate busyness in the faithful governing of the monastery and exert themselves in pious labors for the profit of the church and the relief and help of cloistered monks, so that, whenever the need of their dependent brethren demanded it, they would come to their aid with fraternal piety and no contradiction or murmuring. Of these things the most blessed teacher Gregory writes in his *Moral Commentary* as follows: "There are many in the Church Militant who see others aspire to heavenly things and despise earthly ones. And although they themselves labor hard in the tasks of this world, they bring help from what has been delegated to their governance in this life to those whom they perceive to aspire to heavenly things, and thereby freely support those who tend heavenwards in contemplation."[9] Thus Gregory. This shows plainly that the active life is firmly linked with the contemplative life, in a mutual bond of need. But whoever you are, assigned to the governance of worldly things, see to it that you so attend to the laborious task that is given to you with Martha that you prefer the eternal sweetness of a better life with Mary. Do not lower your sight so deeply in the giddying pit of earthly work that you can in no way raise your eye of contemplation to God, but rather do after the counsel of the gospel: "If your eye scandalizes you, pluck it out and cast it from you. For it is better for you to enter glory with one eye than to be cast into hell with two" [Matthew 5:29]. If this kind of work is undertaken to God's honor and for the help of cloistered monks, it is approved by our holy fathers as not only necessary but meritorious. So, when you go to the restless tasks of your work, let the prudence of bees teach you. In his book *On the Nature of Things* Alexander reports that when bees fly from their hives to gather honey, as it is their nature, they carry with them small pebbles in their feet, and with the help of these keep their course and easily evade the dangers of the winds.[10] In this way, my beloved fellow brethren, whenever tasks outside the monastery call you to go out on worldly business, I ask you to take the firm pebbles of your virtues

9. Gregory, *Moralia* 16.45.

10. Alexander Nequam, *De naturis rerum* 163; in Alexander Neckam, *De naturis rerum*, ed. Thomas Wright, Rolls Series 34 (London: Longman, Green, 1863), 271.

and the unbroken stones of constancy with you, so that in this way you may temper the stormy cares of the active life with this balance and be able to return, through the dark corners of vices and stormy winds of sins, with unhurt feet to the paradise of the cloister. Then what is written in [2] Samuel 23[:4] will apply to each one of you: "As the light of the morning, when the sun rises, shines without clouds." Devotion in the mind expels the shadows of vices "as the light of the morning when the sun rises"; and by virtuous labors it gleams with virtues, for the morning "shines without clouds." Therefore, to begin the works of virtue happily with a clear intention of our minds in the morning of this passing life, and to love God perfectly through our fervent contemplation rising at midday, so that we may deserve to be awarded the sweetness of eternal happiness at last after the evening of this life, may he grant us who crowned the glorious Virgin in eternity. Thanks be to God. Amen.

17

KATHERINE 1
(RICHARD FITZRALPH)

RICHARD FITZRALPH was born in Ireland at the beginning of the fourteenth century. After earning a doctorate in theology and serving as chancellor of Oxford University, he was appointed dean of Lichfield Cathedral (1335) and subsequently archbishop of Armagh, Ireland (1347). He spent four extended periods of his life at the papal curia in Avignon, where he died in 1360. FitzRalph left a collection of his sermons that are supplied with precise indications of the occasion, year, and audience of their delivery, and hence form a diary of his preaching activity. Many of them are merely reports of what he said, as this following item, while others record his preaching more completely, as does selection 18.

As its rubric states, this sermon was preached in the church of Lichfield, on the feast of St. Katherine (November 25) in 1345. St. Katherine of Alexandria, who supposedly died in the fourth century under Emperor Maxentius, enjoyed a very great popularity in medieval England, as witnessed by the number of churches dedicated to her, her appearances in Middle English literature, and the number of surviving sermons in her honor, including four by FitzRalph. Although FitzRalph himself says he preached this sermon "in the vernacular" (presumably English), he reported it in Latin, giving only the gist of what he spoke and punctuating it with such reporting comments as "it was shown [*ostensum fuit*]" or "it was urged [*suasum fuit*]," etc. In translating the Latin text, I have rendered these passive constructions with corresponding active phrases, such as "I showed," "I urged," and so on.

SOURCE:

Bodleian Library, MS Bodley 144, fol. 2r-v (FI-3).

LITERATURE:

Katherine Walsh, *A Fourteenth-Century Scholar and Primate, Richard Fitzralph in Oxford, Avignon, and Armagh* (Oxford: Clarendon Press, 1981).
Wenzel, *Collections*, 31–35.

～

Behold there were four wheels beside the Cherubim, Ezekiel 10[:9]

First a prayer was spoken. After repeating the thema in the vernacular, I showed that the **Cherubim** could be manifestly understood as blessed Katherine, because of the character of that order [of angels] and the meaning of its name. Because of the character of that order: it is nearly the highest, namely, the second in the hierarchy of heaven,[1] and Katherine was the second in the hierarchy of the church, namely, first after the Virgin Mary, the mother of God. Further because of the meaning of its name: "Cherubim" means fullness of knowledge[2] or knowledge increased,[3] and she was the fullest [of knowledge] among women. To prove these things, I told her entire life story,[4] and from this story culled her ten prerogatives, which existed in her together at the same time, as in no other woman after Mary. These are shown on the second folio below.[5] But her tenth prerogative comes from the eminence of her place of burial, more eminent than the place of any other man or woman, for it was closer to that of the Virgin Mary,[6]

1. According to medieval biblical exegesis, the second order in the hierarchy of heaven are the cherubim.

2. *Plenitudo scientiae*, often in Augustine.

3. *Scientia multiplicata*, Jerome, *Liber interpretationis hebraicorum nominum.*

4. *Historia.* Katherine's (legendary) biography can be found in the *Legenda aurea*, 789–797.

5. This must refer to another sermon on St. Katherine (FI-5), *O mulier, magna est fides tua, fiat tibi sicut vis* (Matthew 15:28), and in this manuscript the nine prerogatives appear on fol. 3.

6. According to the legend, after her decapitation angels carried her body to

so that from this fact it is manifest that she is closer to Mary in rank. Her increased knowledge I showed in her being brought to the emperor, her refuting the philosophers, her instructing the empress and Porphyrius, and her manifold wise answers to the emperor. After repeating her life story with the four wheels among which she was to be torn apart, I concluded from these things that this thema can be understood more fittingly about her than about any other creature.

But the prophet seemingly wanted to refer to different **four wheels** in his thema that were **beside** Katherine filled with knowledge, not above her or below:

> well-being in her and in her loved ones,
> means in earthly wealth,
> pleasures in bodily desires,
> and high rank in worldly honors.

In our lives, these four constantly turn like wheels. In Ezekiel 10[:13] it is said: "And these wheels he called 'spinning' in my hearing," and in chapter 1[:18, etc.] he says they were "dreadful to see," and in chapter 10[:9] that "the appearance of the wheels was to the sight like the chrysolite stone." Therefore, I made my sermon about these four, how they had stood beside Katherine and were put aside by her, like the other wheels [of her torture].

The first [wheel, i.e., her well-being] she put aside when, as the emperor proposed that she either leave the worship of God and sacrifice to the demons, or else suffer unthinkable pains of whatever kind, she scorned the pains and freely accepted to die for Christ, just as he had offered himself to die for her sake. At that point I urged that people should not fear bodily sicknesses, which come to them for many good purposes, such as, to complete penance not previously done, or that a person may be more readily converted through sufferings, or that a great virtue may be instilled in him. These I verified through rational arguments and through scripture, in referring to Paul and to Job. And I concluded that people should attentively reflect on this wheel that stood "beside the Cherubim," that is, beside Katherine full of knowl-

---

Mount Sinai. The Blessed Virgin died in her house near Mount Sinai (*Legenda aurea*, 504).

edge, according to the words of the thema, and imitate her as much as it lay in their power. The second wheel beside her, she put aside through the fullness of her knowledge, when she left her possessions so that she might recall the emperor and the people from worshipping idols. And I urged that men and women should imitate her, if not by leaving everything behind, at least by giving what is superfluous to the poor, for it is not good to retain unnecessary temporal goods until death, since after death these cannot help people in heaven. They can go before man but not follow him, as blessed Thomas the apostle said to the king of India and his mother.[7] The third wheel, fleshly desires, she put aside when, although she was a queen, a most beautiful girl of eighteen years, whose voice the royal household obeyed, she kept her virginity. Whence no woman can legitimately excuse herself that she is unable to keep herself chaste, even if very few men or women may be chaste. The fourth wheel she put aside when, as the emperor offered to make a statue for her, etc., she confidently asserted she would consider this a crime. And that men and women might imitate her, because these wheels were "spinning" I urged them to place the wheels besides themselves, not above or beneath, that the wheels might not tear them apart. And thus, in these words three things were proposed to our attention:

> the manifold prudence of this virgin, in the word **Cherubim;**
> the restless movement of all worldly things, in the **wheels;**
> and the usefulness for us all, in the word **behold,** that is, "see."

And I made an end speaking about the rewards of Katherine that, in the end of her life story, are promised to all that follow her footsteps, however moderately, as this was promised by our Lord Jesus Christ, who is true God on high, blessed, world without end. Amen.

7. Ibid., 36.

18

KATHERINE 2
(RICHARD FITZRALPH)

ON FITZRALPH, see the headnote to the previous selection. In contrast to the preceding brief report, in the following piece Fitz-Ralph writes out a complete and carefully wrought sermon in honor of the same saint held in 1338 before the Franciscans at Avignon, the papal residence, where he spent many years. The rhetorical structure is a sophisticated tour de force. After a hyperbolic introduction, in which FitzRalph praises St. Katherine as superior in her faith to many biblical heroes, he combines four "etymologies" of the Latin word for "woman" with four main aspects of faith and shows, with details taken from her legend, that Katherine, by nature a frail woman, was strong in spirit through her faith. All this yields a complex division into four parts, which are then developed at length and lead the theologian in FitzRalph to deal, in question-and-answer form, with several major aspects of faith. His several references to the Tatars and Saracens, and to trustworthy reports about them, reflect the missionary efforts of the Franciscans at this time, as well as Fitz-Ralph's own interest in bringing about a reunion of the Eastern and Latin churches.

SOURCE:
Oxford, Bodleian Library, MS Bodley 144, fols. 179v–187 (FI-78).

LITERATURE:

Katherine Walsh, *A Fourteenth-Century Scholar and Primate: Richard FitzRalph in Oxford, Avignon, and Armagh* (Oxford: Clarendon Press, 1981), 196–98, 217.

~

O woman, your faith is great, Matthew 15[:28].

Reverend fathers and my lords. In Hebrews 11[:32–34] the Apostle exclaims in a great celebration of the prophets and patriarchs: "The time would fail me to tell of Gideon, Barak, Samson, Jephthah, David, Samuel, and the prophets, who by faith conquered kingdoms, wrought justice, obtained promises, stopped the mouths of lions, quenched the violence of fire, escaped the edge of the sword, recovered strength from weakness, became valiant in battle." But I confidently say that for the praise of the virgin Katherine not only would time fail me but also my tongue to enumerate the marvelous works of her faith. Those men by their faith conquered kingdoms; this one much more gloriously overcame Maxentius, the emperor over all kingdoms.[1] Those by faith wrought justice, though only few to the shedding of their blood; this one by her faith wrought justice to the death of her body. Those by faith obtained promises, though promises of an earthly possession; this one by her faith more gloriously obtained the promise of dwelling in heaven. Those by faith stopped the mouths of lions, that is, of raging men, one against one; this one by her faith stopped more marvelously the mouths of fifty rhetoricians that roared like lions. Those by faith quenched the violence of fire to save the just; this one by her faith more marvelously kindled it to burn the impious. Those by faith escaped the edge of a human sword, namely, that it might not kill the just; this one by her faith more marvelously brought a two-edged sword to slaughter the impious.[2] Those by faith recovered strength from their weakness, that is, their bodily weakness; this one by faith more gloriously healed many from their spiritual languor. Those by faith became

---

1. For the biographical details in this paragraph, see the *Golden Legend's* section on St. Katherine: *Legenda aurea,* 789–97.

2. Apparently a reference to the two-edged sword of the word of God, Hebrews 4:12. The dependent clause clearly reads "ne impios trucidaret," probably a scribal error.

valiant in battle, to bodily overcome evil people; this one by her faith in the Lord became more acceptably valiant in battle to rouse evil people in their spirit. In the quoted passage Paul says that "by faith Abel offered to God a sacrifice exceeding that of Cain" [Hebrews 11:4], when he only offered "of the fruits of the earth" [Genesis 4:3]. And I say that by her faith Katherine brought a more praiseworthy sacrifice of her own blood. Paul exclaims that "by faith Enoch was translated, that he should not see death" [Hebrews 11:5], and I say that by faith Katherine was as marvelously translated by angels to Mount Sinai after her death. Paul says that "By faith Noah, having received an answer concerning those things which as yet were not seen, moved with fear and framed the ark for the saving of his house" [Hebrews 11:7], and I say that Katherine, after she had received a message from an angel that she would suffer martyrdom, did not fear but with an even greater faith in the Lord died and persuaded her whole household to suffer death for the Lord. Paul says that "By faith Abraham offered" his son [Hebrews 11:17], and I say that by her faith Katherine much more acceptably offered God her own body. Paul says that "By faith Jacob dying blessed each of the sons of Joseph" [Hebrews 11:21], and I say that by her faith Katherine, in much greater holiness, blessed the empress of the whole world, Duke Porphyrius, and two hundred soldiers and led them to heaven. Paul says that "By faith Joseph, when he was dying, made mention of the going out of the children of Israel" [Hebrews 11:22], but of their going out into the land of people bound to die, and I say that by her faith Katherine, when she was dying, in much greater holiness made mention of the going out of all Christians into the land of the living. Paul says that "By faith Moses left Egypt" [11:27], but he had been a foreigner there, and I say that in much greater holiness Katherine left Egypt where she had been ruler and queen. Paul says that Moses and the Israelites "by faith passed through the Red Sea" [Hebrews 11:29], and I say by Katherine's faith the bodies and clothes of fifty rhetoricians remained unburned and unharmed in the midst of a most fierce fire. Paul says that by Joshua's "faith the walls of Jericho fell down" [Hebrews 11:30], and I say that by Katherine's faith angels ruined that immense machinery of the wheels. What more? What to other saints was given in part, by merit of their faith, is found all together in you, most holy Katherine, by virtue of your faith.

O woman, your faith is great. Not only on this account but even more so on a different one can the cited words be most fittingly be applied to you, Katherine, because of the power of your faith. Because the word *mulier*, "woman," according to definitions by various authors, derives from *mollis* or *molleo*, "soft" or "to be soft"; or else from *mulgeo*, "to milk"; or else from *molo*, "to grind"; or else from *mulceo* or *mulceor*, "to stroke" or "to be stroked."

If this word is derived from *molleo* or *mollis*, it is clear that in the noun is shown the weakness of a woman's nature.

If it comes from *mulgeo*, which means "to draw milk from the breast," what else does it show but the dullness or ignorance of nature in need?

If it is understood to come from *molo*, which means "to turn a grinding stone," in such servile work the inferiority and humbleness of woman's nature is indicated.

But if it is derived from *mulceo* or *mulceor*, no doubt the weakness of woman's nature is expressed, as if it is to be stroked by a man.

And thus, wherever this word comes from, it denotes or conveys the softness and inferiority of [a woman's] natural disposition. But it cannot be hidden to any reasonable person that the weaker or more infirm the owner of some virtuous quality is, the higher is the value of that quality. This truth is manifested in nature, manmade objects exemplify it, scripture declares it, and biblical figures make it plain. And to use the words of Augustine: this the poets used to sing in the theaters, the schoolmasters teach in their schools, shepherds say in the field, and learned as much as unlearned men affirm.[3] For who is in doubt that speed, gait, and the strength to carry are more praiseworthy in a small horse than in a large one? Thus, firmness or unbreakability are considered more precious in a vessel of glass than in one of silver or gold. Thus a sweet smell is thought to be more outstanding in the blossom than in the gross root. In this way, then, nature manifests this truth. Art or manmade objects, too, exemplify it. For when a thin garment protects against cold equally well as a thick one,

---

3. Augustine, *De duabus animabus contra Manichaeos* 11.15 (PL 42:105).

it is praised much more than the thick one. And a tent that shelters against rain as effectively as a house is thought of much more highly than the house. Thus, if a wooden shield protects fighters and soldiers as sufficiently as one of iron, it is preferred to the iron one. Therefore, manmade objects exemplify this truth. Scripture, too, says the same. For from God's mouth Paul received the words: "My grace is sufficient for you, Paul, for power is made perfect in infirmity." And Paul at once added: "I please myself in my infirmities, for when I am weak, then am I powerful," 2 Corinthians 12 [9–10]. Thus, then, scripture says the same. Finally, a biblical figure makes this truth plain. For the widow Judith, after she had cut off the head of Holofernes, who was the leader of the army of the king of the Assyrians, was so much praised by the people and accepted by God that in memory of her strength an entire book about her deed was put in the canon of scripture. Thus you see that in all things the glory of their virtues is so much greater as their natural disposition is weaker. Therefore, without doubt a virtue is much more praiseworthy in a woman than in a man. Hence scripture says not without reason: "A holy and shamefaced woman is grace upon grace," Sirach 26[:19], as if to say more plainly: in a man, because of his natural strength, the grace of virtue is, as it were, simple; but in a woman, because of the softness of her nature, a single virtue is rightly counted double. Therefore, you, Katherine, virgin most sweet, by whose natural weakness not only your female gender but your tender age, a pleasant upbringing, being used to living in the home of your father the king, and being accustomed to baths and anointings show in a marvelous and as it were contrary way that, the weaker and frailer you are found to be in your womanly nature, the more glorious you are proven by the virtue of your faith, so that in admiring and praising you and your faith, as was mentioned before, we can say to you also on this account: **O woman, your faith is great,** as above.

In these words, O admirable virgin, you are described in your praise as frail and stable, dull and discreet, humble and sublime, tender and robust. For by the nature of your flesh, O woman, you are frail, but in the disposition of your mind very stable, for your faith is great. By the limitation of your sex, O woman, you are very dull, but from the enlightening of your spirit you are very discreet, for your faith is great. On the ground of your origin, O woman, you are humble, but through the uplifting of your virtues you are very sublime, for your faith is great. From your bodily constitution, O woman, you are quite weak, but from divine support you are very robust, for your faith is great. What an admirable combination! There frailty of the flesh, here sturdiness of mind. There dullness of the body, here sharpness of spirit. There bodily lack, here mental perfection. There languor of the flesh, here vigor of the spirit. Thus, O chaste virgin, thus we see in you—

how weak your natural inheritance was, O *mulier* from *mollis* or *molleo*, and how strong your spiritual birth, for **your faith is great;**

how small was what you took from the progenitor of your body, O *mulier* from *mulgeo*, and how rich what you had from the maker of your spirit, for **your faith is great;**

how much nature humbled you, O *mulier* from *molo*, and how much grace exalted you, for **your faith is great;**

and how defective the nature of your body is, O *mulier* from *mulceor*, and how much grace makes it perfect, for **your faith is great.**

In this way, "good is set against evil, and life against death: one against one, and two against two," Sirach 33[:15]. For to you can be applied what is written in Deuteronomy 28[:56]: "The tender and delicate woman, who could not go upon the ground, nor set down her foot for overmuch softness and tenderness." And on the other hand the Lord also says of you through his prophet: "They are new every morning, but your faithfulness is great." Lamentations 3[:23]. **O woman, your faith is great!**

To explain these things and develop them more clearly, we should notice that in book 6 of *On the Trinity*, chapter 8, Augustine says: "In those things which are not great in bulk, to be greater is to be better."[4] But in every sort of being, that one is better and more perfect which can carry out its proper actions better and more ably. Thus a horse is the better the faster it can run and carry its rider. And a knife is the better the more easily it can cut or chop. And so with all other things. Whence it is clear that faith is better or more perfect, and con-

---

4. Augustine, *De Trinitate* 6.8.

sequently greater, the more perfectly it can carry out the actions proper to it. Now, it seems to me that the action of faith consists in four things, namely, in:

consent of the mind,
confession of the voice,
accumulation of merits,
and working of miracles.

Of the first and second, speaking about faith the Apostle says in Romans 10[:10]: "With the heart we believe unto justice; but with the mouth confession is made unto salvation." Regarding the accumulation of merits, it is said in James 2[:22]: "By works faith was made perfect." Regarding the working of miracles, Matthew 17[:19]: "For, Amen, I say to you, if you have faith as a grain of mustard seed, you shall say to this mountain, Remove from hence hither, and it shall remove; and nothing shall be impossible to you." Therefore, faith is truly great when it operates perfectly in these four kinds of actions. But:

with regard to the first action, namely, assent of the heart, faith is weak and infirm without tenacious adherence of the will;
with regard to the second, namely, profession by mouth, it is difficult and obscure without the full knowledge of scripture;
with regard to the third, namely, the accumulation of merits, it is feeble and lukewarm without fervent love;
and with regard to the fourth, namely, the working of miracles, it is useless and inept without a strong hope.

Therefore let us say that, on the contrary, that faith is truly great

which is firmly glued or rooted through adherence of the will;
which is brightly illumined through full knowledge;
which is eagerly quickened or stirred through fervent love;
and which is prudently applied through strong hope.

These four stand against the four weaknesses of a woman's nature of which I spoke in my introduction, and they agree with the members of the main division in the thema.

[1]

First I say, with respect to the first action of faith, namely, consent of the heart, that without tenacious adherence of the will, faith is weak and infirm. In order for faith to be truly great with regard to this action, it must necessarily be glued firmly through adherence of the will. It seems to me that this adherence of the will by which the mind wants to adhere to faith is like a glue or cement that binds faith together. And no wonder, for Augustine says on the Gospel of John, homily 26: "One can enter a church unwillingly, one can approach the altar unwillingly, but believe one cannot except willingly."[5] And the Apostle, in Romans 1 and in the last chapter, urges to obey faith, which he would do in vain unless faith is accepted willingly and freely.[6] And it seems to me that as faith is accepted willingly and freely, so it is strengthened by adherence of the will, so that it may be stable without change. This tenacious adherence of the will by which the will wants to adhere to faith unchangingly, I believe is called "root" by Our Lord in Luke 8[:13], where in his exposition of the seed that fell on the rock he says: "These are they who, when they hear, receive the word," that is, of faith, "with joy; and these have no roots; for they believe for a while, and in time of temptation, they fall away." Whence trustworthy people report that they saw some Christians who by the Saracens were turned away from the law and faith of Christ. Which they would not have done if they had had this root, that is, the tenacious adherence of the will. This adherence of the will is rightly called "root" because it begins the faith, as I said before, and after beginning it, it firms it up and sustains or cements it.

But now you will perhaps say: "How can the will thus freely accept faith? If an unbeliever can with free will believe that God is threefold and yet of one simple substance; that the Son of God, the most simple being there is or can be, is a human being composed of body and soul; and that the entire body of Christ is under the species of bread on the altar; and other articles of this kind which contradict his natural judgment: if he can believe this, he can with even greater reason believe anything else that is false and impossible, which to his judg-

5. Augustine, *In Iohannis evangelium* 26.2.
6. Cf. Romans 1:5 and 16:19.

ment appears less false, as for instance that the sun will not rise to-morrow, that the moon will not suffer an eclipse within a year, and similar things that to him appear less impossible than the quoted articles. But if you were to say that he can freely believe these and similar things, your conscience condemns you, because you yourself cannot believe them in any way, even if you wanted to. Therefore, the will does not do anything to accept faith or strengthen it, as you say."

I answer that this acceptance of faith is not from its beginning as free as you suppose. For the Apostle says in Romans 10[:17]: "Faith comes from hearing, and hearing from the word of God." Therefore, no one receives faith initially in the common way of understanding but is first persuaded by scripture or the word [of the preacher]. If I were to say to a heathen, "Believe that God is threefold in person, or that the Son of God took flesh, or that Christ's whole body is under the species of bread on the altar," he could quite rightly laugh at me and say, "All this seems to be impossible, and therefore I cannot believe any of it." But if I were to argue against this as follows: God is omnipotent and thus is able to do many things that your reason does not comprehend. Therefore, you do not know whether the matters I have mentioned are true. Further, Christ as a true prophet, which you and all saints maintain he is, has said that he is God's only natural son and of one substance with God the Father, and saying this, he not only healed the sick, cleansed the lepers, cast out demons, and did other miracles by himself, but in addition his apostles and disciples sometimes did the same in his name and said so. He therefore was not a liar. Why, then, do you not believe such a teacher, by whom without doubt the unbeliever was persuaded to adhere with free will to these and similar articles, as for instance Dionysius the Areopagite, a philosopher in Athens, believed Paul after hearing him frequently, even though the Athenians afterward called Paul "a setter forth of new gods," as is reported in Acts 17[:18]? But if the natural argument against these things became weakened, the same probable argument cannot be applied to other impossible things with which you have objected, and therefore he cannot believe the latter as he can believe the former. In addition, the holy life of the teacher helps toward this most forcefully, because one believes such a man more easily than any other.

But you say: "Why should a Saracen or Tatar believe me more than I him? For he will commend his religion and its author as much as I commend mine. If in this case he will not believe me or receive my faith, why is he who does not accept my religion going to be damned, rather than I who do not wish to receive his?" I answer: As far as I can see, in this case he is not going to be damned for not believing you, just as you will not be damned for not believing him, because in this case it will not be better or worse for him on your account, that is, if he cannot believe you against his natural reason. But he will be damned because he does not have the ground for salvation, namely, faith and baptism. As it is said: "He who believes and is baptized, shall be saved, but he who does not believe shall be condemned," at the end of Mark [16:16]; and in John 3[:5]: "Unless a man is born again of water and the Holy Spirit, he cannot enter into the kingdom of God." But you say: "This damnation seems to be unjust, namely, that God condemns a person who did not do what he could not do. For if an unbeliever does not believe the articles of Christian faith because he cannot believe them against his judgment, as we have assumed, his condemnation seems to be unjust. For Augustine says, in his book *On Free Will,* that no one commits a sin in what he cannot avoid.[7] Therefore, he who remains an unbeliever because he cannot believe commits no sin." I answer: He does not commit a sin properly speaking, that is, which deserves bodily punishment. But if he follows his natural reason in all things, he will only be punished as an infant [who dies] without baptism is punished, that is, with the pain of damnation, which is but the lack of divine vision or of true beatitude. Nor is this unjust. For he is not owed beatitude, because "life eternal is God's grace," Romans 6[:23]. It is not unjust if God does not grant him beatitude. For if your father were to lose his heritage, would it not be an injury for you, even if he had never given it to you? Thus it is no injury to an infant or an unbeliever if they do not receive the beatitude that their forefather lost in paradise. But you say: "In Romans 14[:23] the Apostle says that 'all that is not of faith is sin.' On which the saints comment that the entire life of unbelievers is sin." I answer: By "sin" I mean, as philosophers have it, evil of nature, er-

---

7. Augustine, *De libero arbitrio* 3.18.

ror and deformity, not guilt in the proper sense, as the Apostle says in Romans 7[:14ff.] that sin lives in the flesh, that is, deformity and the lack of good. In this sense every act of an unbeliever is sin, that is, a deformed act, because it lacks that grace that would inform it. Far be it from us to say that every act of an unbeliever is sin in the proper sense [i.e., of guilt], so that he deserves eternal bodily punishment. For Augustine says in book 5 of *The City of God* that God rewarded the ancient Romans, who out of their moral virtue built up their commonwealth and ruled it, with a temporal reward, as he did not want to give them true beatitude. Thus, such deeds are in no way sins in the proper sense, since God rewards them, for one cannot say that the supremely just God rewards one and the same deed in time and punishes it in eternity.

Thus it is true what I have said: that in order to be great with regard to the first act, namely, consent of the heart, faith must be firmly glued or cemented through adherence of the will. In you, most holy Katherine, this adherence of the will was certainly very frail and weak from your physical condition, because your nature, O woman—*mulier*, from *mollis*—was soft and frail. This the serpent, who was "more subtle than any of the beasts of the earth," showed by his action when he tempted your first mother, Eve, in paradise as being weaker than her husband, as we read in Genesis 3. But on the contrary, you did have this very firm adherence of the will to faith by the disposition of your mind, and thus with respect to this action your faith is indeed great. For neither flattery nor adversity could draw you from this greatness of faith, this firm adherence. I notice that the emperor urged your frail nature: "O noble virgin, have regard for your youth and you shall be called second to the queen in my palace, and when your statue is built in the middle of the city, you shall be adored by all as a goddess." And I see in you the totally firm adherence of your faith in which you believed that only God is to be worshipped and that friendship of the flesh is to be scorned, when you answered against him: "Leave off urging such things, Emperor, which it is a crime even to think. I have given myself to Christ as his bride. He is my glory, he is my love, he my sweetness and delight."[8] I further notice how the

---

8. *Legenda aurea*, 792.

emperor's power threatened your frailty to choose one of two things: either to sacrifice to the gods that you might live, or to suffer choice torments that you might die. And I hear you adhere to faith in Christ and answer against the emperor: "Whatever torments you can think up, do not delay, for I desire to offer my flesh and blood to Christ, as he offered himself for me."[9] And so you remained unmovable in the faith of Christ through this adherence of the will, for you had learned from Tobit that "we look for that life which God will give to those that never change their faith from him," Tobit 2[:18]. **O woman, your faith is great!**

[2]

In the second place, with respect to the second action of faith, namely, confession or profession by mouth, I say that without a full understanding of scripture faith is difficult and obscure. Therefore, in order that faith be truly great with regard to this action, it is necessary that it be brightly illumined through a full understanding of holy scripture. Whence it is said in 1 Peter 3[:15]: "Sanctify the Lord Jesus Christ in your hearts, being ready always to satisfy every one that asks you for a reason of that hope which is in you." But no one would be ready to satisfy anyone who asks about the faith unless he is well informed in holy scripture. No doubt about it, since Augustine says in book 14 of *The City of God*, chapter 1: "Through this knowledge a most wholesome faith is generated, nourished, defended, and strengthened."[10] Look, my brothers and lords, how elegantly the apostle Peter invites us to have the fruit [of this knowledge]: "Sanctify," he says, "the Lord Jesus Christ in your hearts" [1 Peter 3:15]. And then he describes the principal effect of this fruit for us: "Ready always," and so on, as if to say more plainly: if you have the knowledge of scripture so that you may be always ready to satisfy anyone who asks for the reason of your faith, then you will sanctify the Lord Jesus Christ in your hearts. Nor do I think the words "Ready always" are to be passed by lightly. For it seems to me that holy scripture urges us to four things about knowledge, that is, of faith. When it says "be-

---

9. *Legenda aurea*, 793.
10. Augustine, *De civitate Dei* 14.1.

ing ready," it wants doctrine to be ready in us, speaking against negligent and lukewarm people who have the cure of souls and seldom or never instruct or inform them in the faith. When it says "always," it urges solicitous attention, speaking against people devoted to other fields who have a large number of books on law or medicine in their chambers and not a single small Bible which they could look into at the end of the day, so as to lead the palate of their heart that has been blunted all day long back to something savory. When it says "to satisfy," it urges deep understanding, speaking against presumptuous men who, when they know in general a few authorities of scripture that are contained in law decrees, think they overflow with the knowledge of the scriptures and yet are found ignorant of the greater part of scripture. And when it says "everyone who asks for a reason," it urges the fullness of knowledge, speaking against pure historians who ignore the difficult questions of divine scripture.

But you will say to me (and in this you are wiser than necessary), if men were to pay attention only to theology and nobody were to study law, no one could pass just judgment between one brother and another. O exceedingly unwise man who says this! You reckon that the law of nature is insufficient to provide a tranquil life and thereby contend against God's disposition, and you do not consider how much tranquillity there was among men before this age of laws, or how much there is in the country among people who do not know these laws. For there has never been such an epidemic of law cases in the world as there is among us Christians. I do not know any other cause for this than the great number of laws, for where there are many laws, there have to be many tricks and oppositions which render clear cases obscure and muck up the entire business of the world. Further, you who say so do not consider how reasonable the justice established through the law of the Old Testament was and how tranquil the rule in the whole Jewish people. For then one man ruled in quietness thousands of people, as we read in Exodus 18. I ask you, brother, read what Paul writes to Timothy about the doctrine of our faith, in 2 Timothy 3[:16]: "All doctrine inspired of God is profitable to teach, to reprove, to correct, to instruct in justice, that the man of God may be perfect, furnished to every good work." Note well that he says, "the man of God, furnished to every good work." Either such judgments about transitory goods are not good works, or the man of God is sufficiently instructed from this divinely inspired scripture to make them, since Paul says that through it "the man of God" is "perfect, furnished to every good work." I am telling you all these things, brothers, not in order to despise any field of knowledge, for all are useful to those who use them well, but in order to urge you to study the doctrine of this faith, in which there is salvation and health of the soul, without admixture of any other field of knowledge except what the wretchedness of our life requires, since perhaps it was such admixture on whose account it was said, "A little leaven corrupts the whole lump," Galatians 5[:9]. Regarding such admixture I have no doubt that "dying flies spoil the sweetness of the ointment," Ecclesiastes 10[:1]. You can be sure that reading and studying and taking delight in the things contained in these human laws, like flies stings the mind that is at rest through the understanding of this doctrine of the faith in Christ by means of studying holy scripture. They suck at it and finally draw forth blood, that is, some wrong desire. And if they do not inject anything evil, at least they diminish or totally corrupt the delight in holy scripture by which you would be sanctified in your heart. Whence the Philosopher says elegantly in book 10 of his *Ethics* that external pleasures as much as one's own pains cause the delight that follows the exercise of any intellectual field to be corrupted.[11] Therefore, after the counsel of Peter, always attend to the doctrine of this faith that you may fully and perfectly sanctify Jesus Christ in your heart. Without this doctrine, as I have said, faith is difficult and obscure. And therefore, so that faith may be truly great with respect to the second action, that is, confession, it is necessary that it be brightly illumined through a full understanding of holy scripture.

You, Katherine, from the lesser power of your senses had this obscurity or ignorance with respect to showing or professing the faith, O woman—*mulier* from *mulgeo*—who of her nature needs to be nourished by a man with the milk of knowledge. As the Apostle says in 1 Corinthians 14[:34–35]: "Let women keep silence in the churches, for it is not permitted them to speak, but to be subject, as also the Law says. But if they would learn any thing, let them ask their husbands at

11. Aristotle, *Nicomachean Ethics* 10.5.

home." But in contrast, through the illumination of your spirit, you, lady, had a full understanding of holy scripture, and thus with respect to this action your faith is great. For as the renowned hermit Antony, as Augustine says in book 1 of *On Christian Doctrine,* had understanding of holy scripture through the revelation of the Holy Spirit,[12] so you also, most learned one, received it, as I believe. For I do not doubt that at your tender age of eighteen years you could not have had such a great understanding of holy scripture from a human source. I read of you, O most saintly teacher and most well-taught saint, that you demonstrated to fifty rhetoricians irrefutably that God could become man and had to suffer in his assumed body. And in addition you disputed many parts of your faith and its different articles most subtly, namely, that God is the creator, ruler, and rewarder of all things, and that deaf and mute idols are not to be worshipped by anyone. In the greatness of your faith, that is, the clear understanding of holy scripture, you confirmed this with various arguments, allegorically, metaphorically, logically, and mystically.[13] And so it became splendidly manifest in you that "Faith is the substance of things to be hoped for, the evidence of things that appear not," Hebrews 11[:1]. **O woman, your faith is great!**

[3]
In the third place I say that with regard to the third action, namely, the accumulation of merits, faith without fervent love is feeble or frail and lukewarm; and that in order for faith to be truly great with regard to this action, it must be eagerly quickened or stirred through fervent love. Whence the Apostle says fittingly in Galatians 5[:6]: "In Christ Jesus neither true circumcision avails anything, nor uncircumcision, but faith that works by charity" (or affection *[dilectio],* in another translation). My brothers and lords, although love or affection is the form[14] of faith, without which faith is utterly formless, according to 1 Corinthians 13[:2]: "If I should have prophecy and all knowl-

---

12. Augustine's point in *De doctrina christiana,* prooemium, is different.

13. Cf. *Legenda aurea,* 790.

14. "Form" here in the technical Scholastic sense of "the essential determinant principle of a thing; that which makes anything (matter) a determinate species or kind of being; the essential creative quality" (OED).

edge and all faith, but have not charity, I am nothing"—yet the act of love or affection in every meritorious work of faith is the instrument of faith, just as a knife is the instrument of the worker, according to these words of the Apostle: "Faith that works by charity." For faith is not the direct principle of an external good action or motion of our members to an act, for nothing moves directly our members to an action except an act of love, just as in animals the direct principle of physical motion is their appetite or desire, as worldly science teaches in book 3 of *On the Soul*, at the end.[15] For even if you *believe* that God rewards a good deed, you are not yet performing a meritorious deed for that reason, for you are as yet not sufficiently motivated to the deed, because neither men nor demons, neither the good nor the bad, neither the ready nor the lazy have any doubt about it [i.e., that God rewards a good deed], but the ones are ready because they *love*, the others remain idle. Therefore it is clear that with regard to the accumulation of rewards, faith without love is frail and lukewarm.

Reverend lords, it seems to me better to lack faith altogether than to have a faith that is thus asleep. For in Revelation 3[:14–16] it is said: "These things says the Amen, the faithful and true witness, who is the beginning of the creation of God: I know your works, that you are neither cold nor hot. I would you were cold or hot. But because you are lukewarm, and neither cold nor hot, I will begin to vomit you out of my mouth." This word of John I understand, not about one who has a little love, but about one who has faith without works, that is, without the love that stirs his faith to action. (For to be lukewarm is better than to be cold, and no one who has love, however little, is to be vomited out of God's mouth, nor would what follows be fittingly said of him: "You do not know that you are wretched, and miserable, and poor, and blind, and naked" [17], for no one who has love is naked, blind, and poor.) Attend therefore, whoever you are, who are inactive in good works, that it would be better for you to lack faith altogether than to be thus "lukewarm" that your faith is not quickened or stirred through love to a good deed. "For it had been better for them," says Peter, "not to have known the way of justice than, after they have known it, to turn back," 2 Peter 2[:1].

15. Aristotle, *De anima* 3.10.

In case you do not know yourself, I will show you to yourself. You have a treasure of money, either from some gain or perhaps from the goods of the church, deposited in your moneybox. Perhaps it is rusting away, and every night it makes you restless and anxious lest you lose it in some way. And you do not help people in need, who die in nakedness and hunger? Truly, you are lukewarm. You have a case to deal with in the palace from early morning till noon. You are very eager to hear Mass or say it, or the canonical hours, or devout prayers and holy meditations, so you deal [with the case] little or not all? You are lukewarm. You are a learned advocate, a discreet procurator, you see a poor man in a lawsuit who has no protector and lacks help. Though his cause is most just, you do not defend him because he has no money to give to you? You are lukewarm. What more? If you are more solicitous about temporal things than about spiritual ones in your heart and in your deed, I say you are lukewarm, and you will be punished more harshly than an unbeliever. It were better for you to lack faith, unless you do penance. Listen to "the beginning of the creation of God" [Revelation 3:14]: "I would you were cold or hot. But because you are lukewarm, I will begin to vomit you out of my mouth," you, that is, who have faith without works, faith that does not stir you through love. "For faith without works is dead," James 2[:20]. So then, that faith may be truly great with regard to this action [i.e., the accumulation of merits], it must be eagerly quickened or stirred through fervent love.

Of this fervent love, you, Katherine, received little[16] from your natural disposition, O woman—from *molo*—because being of a lesser natural disposition, you were less fit for noble deeds. For this reason scripture says: "Better is the iniquity of a man than a woman doing a good turn," Sirach 32[:14]. This I understand as follows: a man who sometimes commits a sin and then repents is better than a woman who always does good, because a man is fit for a more fervent love than a woman, and thus he pursues deeds of greater love, even if he may sometimes fail. But in truth, however much your nature lowers you and weakens you, O woman, so much does grace lift you up

16. In the Latin text, apparently a word like "little" is missing: "Huius dileccionis feruide tu, Katerina, ex institucione originis accepisti."

and raise you to love. And therefore in this respect your faith is great, that is, eagerly quickened or stirred through fervent love. Proof is on hand, because for the love of Christ, your spouse, you gave up your inherited worldly kingdom. When you were put in a painful jail, you did not cease from the office of preaching. You publicly convicted the emperor Maxentius of idolatry. You comforted the rhetoricians who had been converted by you, as well as the queen and the soldiers in spite of the emperor's warnings, so that they should not grow weak in their torments. You showed yourself ready for every kind of torment publicly in word and in deed. And at last you accepted capital punishment for the sake of Christ. Thus, that your faith in Christ might not grow lukewarm or weaken in you, you quickened it with the most fervent love, so that the Lord said in your praise and to our shame: "I have not found such great faith in Israel" [Matthew 8:10], that is, in the congregation of the clergy who see God. **O woman, your faith is great!**

But now you [the audience] say to me: "If the Lord had given *me* such faith with so great a love, I would be ready to do similar things. Therefore it is not my fault that I do not do such deeds or equally great ones; I have never received the necessary wherewithal to do them." Against this I say openly that you are wrong. For any degree of faith and of love is sufficient for this. Do you want to know how? Behold, people from any group of unbelievers, who we think lack charity altogether, are ready to suffer not only pains but also death in defense of their religion. This you can see every day in the Jews. Moreover, trustworthy people report that among the Tatars worshippers of certain idols cut their members with extremely sharp knives and throw them in the face of their idol, and at last they pierce themselves with a knife. Reporters say they have seen that themselves. Do you say that those men have the disposition for such deeds more fully than you? If you were to say this, it is to be feared that you may in part be speaking the truth, for you do perhaps not have the love and faith that in your presumption you think you have. But now you say: "If those people show such deeds in defense of their law—since they love God whom they worship more than their law, for they observe the law in this way for his love—I do not doubt that they love God more than themselves, that is, above all things, and thereby they fulfill the whole law, after the words of the Apostle in Romans 13[:10]: 'Love therefore is the fulfilling of the law.'" To this I reply that those people love neither God nor the law primarily, but themselves, and thus they do these things not out of charity nor out of love of God or the law, but because, being deceived by devils, they hope that for these acts they will later be happy; therefore, they do them primarily of out self-love, not out of love of God. In contrast, Christians suffer such torments primarily for the love of Christ, their Redeemer. The words of the most saintly Katherine show this plainly: "He," she says, "is my love, he my sweetness, he my glory."[17] Therefore, be assured that this is the difference between people who have love and those who do not, that, although both can do similar things in external deeds, those who lack love can never suffer so greatly primarily for the love of God as they who have love, for in the former rules cupidity. Augustine says in his *Handbook:* "Fleshly cupidity rules where there is no charity,"[18] calling "cupidity" the self-love by which one desires to do good to oneself. This rules in all who are not Christians, so that, whatever they do, they do primarily for their own good, not primarily for the love of God, which is called "charity," by which God is loved above all things. That love is the fulfilling of the law, and all who are not truly Christians lack it.

[4]

In the fourth place, I say that with respect to the fourth action, namely, the working of miracles, faith is useless and inept without a strong hope. So that faith may be truly great with respect to this action, it is necessary to apply it prudently through strong hope. On this, listen to the teaching of the Savior in Mark 11[:21–24], where it is written: "And Peter, remembering, said to him: Rabbi, behold the fig tree which you cursed is withered away. And Jesus, answering, says to them: Have the faith of God. Amen I say to you, whosoever shall say to this mountain, Be removed and cast into the sea, and does not stagger in his heart but believes that whatsoever he says shall be done, it shall be done to him. Therefore I say to you, all things whatsoever you

---

17. *Legenda aurea*, 792.
18. Augustine, *Enchiridion de fide, spe, et caritate* 31.

ask when you pray, believe that you shall receive; and they shall come to you." A similar teaching we have in Matthew 21[:21–22]: "And Jesus answering, said to them: Amen, I say to you, if you have faith and stagger not, not only of the fig tree shall you do this, but also if you shall say to this mountain, Take up and cast yourself into the sea, it shall be done. And all things whatsoever you shall ask in prayer, believing, you shall receive." Behold how our Savior shows that such miraculous works can be done without hesitation, so that man may safely believe that he will obtain what he intends to ask for in faith: "and does not stagger in his heart," he says, "but believes that whatsoever he says shall be done, it shall be done to him." And he added as a rule: "Therefore I say to you, all things whatsoever you ask when you pray, believe that you shall receive; and they shall come to you." And according to Matthew he says: "All things whatsoever you shall ask in prayer, believing, you shall receive." Such faithful trust or hope to obtain what one asks for applies the faith one has about God's omnipotence to the working of a miracle. The lack of such hope, namely, to obtain what one asks for, I believe the Lord himself calls "incredulity," not lack of faith. When a lunatic had been healed by him and his disciples asked him privately, "Why could we not cast that demon out?" Jesus answered, "On account of your incredulity," Matthew 17[:18–19], calling "incredulity" the lack of hope and that aforementioned certainty, not the lack of faith, which he knew they doubtless had, through which they were earlier healing the sick, cleansing the lepers, and casting out devils. But as they were hesitant in healing this lunatic specifically, he said, "on account of your incredulity." James, who had heard this teaching from his master's mouth, as a true disciple agrees with his master and expresses it more fully: "If any of you lacks wisdom, let him ask of God, who gives to all men abundantly and does not upbraid, and it shall be given him. But let him ask in faith, nothing wavering. For he that wavers is like a wave of the sea, which is moved and carried about by the wind. Therefore, let not that man think that he shall receive anything of the Lord" [James 1:5–7]. Behold here expressly that such strong hope applies faith so that a man will obtain what he asks for. Otherwise, if one hesitates, one must not think to receive anything from God.

But you say: "How can I be sure and have hope to obtain this?

I would like to do so but cannot. For first it seems to me that this teaching was given only to Christ's disciples. Second,[19] I begin to hesitate very much when I consider that I am a sinner, for we all know that God does not hear the sinner, as the blind man said who had gained his sight, in John 9[:31]. Third, Christ asked conditionally when he said, 'Father, if it be possible, let this chalice pass from me' [Matthew 26:39], and I should imitate this action. But if I pray conditionally, I seem to hesitate in my heart about receiving what I am praying for. And fourth, I do not see how in praying that a miracle may happen I can be certain that God will hear me, that is, that my prayer is reasonable, because one that is not reasonable cannot be heard. But of this I cannot be certain unless I know God's mind, as it seems. Therefore, I am forced to hesitate about receiving what I pray for." To this I respond: Be assured that in this case you can be certain, for otherwise the supreme Wisdom would not have urged this, nor James, who wrote this to the twelve tribes in the Diaspora. Also, Christ's words apply to all. When he said: "Whosoever shall say to this mountain, Be removed," and so on, he did not say, "Whoever among you," etc. Further, in the end of his gospel Matthew says [28:19]: "Teach all nations; baptizing them in the name of the Father, and of the Son, and of the Holy Spirit, Amen, teaching them to observe all the things that I have commanded you." From which it is clear that Christ wanted them to hand this lesson and every one that he had given them on to others. And so you should not doubt that that teaching about the way to pray that miracles may happen applies to you. But what you object [in the second place] should not move you if you are clean of mortal sin and penitent according to the teaching of faith, for that quotation should be understood as concerning a sinner who is in mortal sin. Otherwise God would not hear anyone, "for there is no just man upon earth, that does good, and does not sin," Ecclesiastes 7[:21]. And "if we say that we have no sin, we deceive ourselves, and the truth is not in us" [1 John 1:8]. But your [third] objection that Christ prayed conditionally does not prove that there is hesitation in the heart of the praying person, just as Christ did not hesitate, but rather that there is rever-

19. I have rendered the Latin text's "item" with ordinal numbers to facilitate the reading.

ence, as in a son who is certain of his father's care for him. He can
say, "Father, give me a robe for the winter if you please" and not intend anything else by this added condition than reverence and obedience to his father, whether he grants his wish or not. Further, the
example of Christ is a model for a correct petition, and he who imi-
tates it does not err; but it is not a model that must necessarily be followed, because it was given not because of its necessity but because
of its fittingness. In the Lord's Prayer Christ teaches you to ask without condition for your daily bread, for the forgiveness of sins, and for
preservation from temptation, and thus it pleases him when you ask
him with or without condition, as long as you are ready to obey him
always. Therefore, Christ's example is no objection that a man can be
certain in sometimes praying that a miracle may happen.

Your fourth[20] objection [i.e., that your prayer may not be reason-
able] should not deter you, because there is no doubt that you know
God's mind as long as, according to the teaching of your faith, you
believe firmly that your petition is reasonable, and you can be certain
in your conscience that God will grant you what you are asking for.
And it seems to me that in order to be certain that your petition is
reasonable, you must have a legitimate reason and the right intention.
Your reason is legitimate when the specific occasion requires a miracle, and your intention is right when you primarily seek God's glory.
Concerning the first, James says [1:5]: "If any of you lacks wisdom,"
etc. This is a legitimate reason: he does not say, "if any of you *wants
to have* wisdom, let him ask God," etc., but rather, "if any of you *lacks*
wisdom." When difficult matters against the faith are raised up against
you by unbelievers which you do not know how to solve, you lack
wisdom. When you need to inform the pope about something that
you do not know how to communicate, you lack wisdom.[21] When
you work to convert unbelievers and you have some doubt about the
teaching you intend to present, you lack wisdom. And so in similar
cases, and when you are in sudden danger or your neighbor is in danger of either water or fire or evil persons, you need divine help, for

20. The manuscript gives "tercium."
21. This sentence is written in the margin and only partially preserved. I have tried
to make some sense of it.

human help is impotent in such cases. There are infinite similar cases, which I cannot nor know how to list at present. In these and similar cases there is a legitimate reason to pray for a miracle. In addition, you must see to it that you have the right intention, namely, that you pray for a miracle primarily for God's praise and glory, after the words of our Savior, "Let your light shine before men, that they may see your good works and glorify your Father who is in heaven," Matthew 5[:16]. This must be observed in every good work, according to the Apostle in 1 Corinthians 10[:31]: "Whether you eat or drink, or whatsoever else you do, do all to the glory of God." But if you pray for a miracle for any other cause without the right intention, as for instance, when you pray for knowledge in order to make money, or for a benefice in order to be praised by the people or to be called "Master" by them, or for a similar cause, you are not seeking primarily God's glory. If however you want God to be glorified in what you pray, that you may finally obtain what you desire, that is the right intention. Whence it is said in James 4[:3–4]: "You ask and do not receive because you ask amiss, that you may consume it in your desires. Adulterers, do you not know that the friendship of this world is the enemy of God?" by which he means that a petition is wrong in its intention if anything transitory is primarily aimed at. The sons of Zebedee, through their mother, petitioned Christ that one of them might sit at his right hand in his reign and the other at his left, Matthew 20[:20–22]. And Christ answered them: "You do not know what you are asking." Paul said of himself: "Three times I besought the Lord that it might depart from me," speaking of the "thorn" in his flesh; and he received the answer, "Paul, my grace is sufficient for you," 2 Corinthians 12[:8–9]. Moses, who was most acceptable to God, prayed to the Lord, "Either forgive them this trespass," the people who were adoring the calf, "or strike me out of the book that you have written." And he received the answer: "He who has sinned against me, him will I strike out of my book," Exodus 32[:31–33]. David, of whom the Lord says, "I have found a man according to my own heart" [Acts 13:22], prayed to the Lord for the child he had begotten in adultery on the wife of Uriah, and, as scripture says, "David kept a fast"; and then "it came to pass on the seventh day that the child died" [2 Samuel 12:16–18]. Thus the mother of Christ asked him to give help when she said, "They have no wine," and had as an answer, "What is that to you and me, woman?" [John 2:3–4]. Further, Christ himself asked his Father that the cup of his Passion should pass by him, so that he should not drink it, and he did not obtain what he was praying for. This petition came from his natural love, just as the other petitions I have mentioned came from natural or from worldly love and therefore were not heard. Thus, when you pray for a miracle, keep these two in mind: a legitimate reason and the proper intention, and your prayer will be reasonable. Nor do I doubt that when you pray in this way, the Holy Spirit will for the most part make you certain in your prayer, and you will obtain it, even if mountains have to be moved. However, in our time, among Christians, people have this hope but rarely, even if they are saints, for there is no need for miracles among them. But among Saracens and Tatars, where miracles are needed, trustworthy people have told me that devout Christians commonly command demons and cast them out. The reason is that there they have a reasonable cause of such firm hope. And thus the Holy Spirit renders them certain in praying for miracles. Go there, and you will be able to be certain.

Thus it is true what I have said, that in order for faith to be ready for this action, that is, the working of miracles, it must be prudently applied through strong hope. From your frail physical makeup, Katherine, you lacked this greatness, O woman—from *mulceor.* Since by nature you were made to be stroked or fondled by a man, you could not attain such strong deeds. But I have no doubt that you did possess such greatness, namely, of a faith that was prudently applied through a strong hope for divine support, since I read that you prayed: "O hope and salvation of your faithful people, O ornament and glory of virgins, Jesus, good king, I beg that whoever will devoutly remember my Passion and invoke me, whether in the hour of his death or in any other need, may obtain the fruit of your atonement." And on the other side I hear that voice coming from heaven and saying to you: "Come, my chosen one, my spouse, the gate of heaven is open to you. For I promise protection from heaven also to those who honor your Passion."[22] Oh, happy and pleasing answer given to you and to us,

---

22. *Legenda aurea,* 794.

most holy patroness! Thus, thus has your faith brought salvation to you and your followers. **O woman, your faith is great!**

Through your merits, most pure patroness, may he open this gate for us and show us the fruit of his atonement, he, our Lord Jesus Christ, who with the Father and the Holy Spirit lives and reigns, God forever and ever. Amen.

19

JOHN THE BAPTIST (JOHN MIRK)

JOHN MIRK was an Augustinian canon of Lilleshall Abbey, Shropshire. He wrote several aids for preachers, in Latin and in English, including a collection of homilies in English prose called *Festial*, which was written before 1415 and perhaps as early as between 1382 and 1390. In it he covered selected Sundays, feast days, and saints' feasts in an order that echoes that of the *Golden Legend*. The latter is also the source of much of his material, though by no means the only one. The individual "sermons" are much concerned with the exposition of the particular day or feast for which they were written, and apparently the pieces for the saints' feasts were intended to be read or preached on the Sunday before the feast. They normally have no thema, but many use an address ("good men and women" or the like) as well as a division and subsequent development. Well known to modern students for their pious stories—and often reviled for them— their primary function was to furnish parish priests with material on the meaning of the respective liturgical occasion, as Mirk himself states in a short prologue to the cycle. As such they gained great popularity. The original cycle has been preserved complete in about half a dozen manuscripts; during the fifteenth century it was abridged, enlarged, rearranged, and used in vernacular sermon cycles; and between about 1483 and 1532 it was printed some twenty times.

SOURCE:

John Mirk, *Festial. A Collection of Homilies*, ed. Theodor Erbe, Early English
Text Society, Extra Series 96 (London: Kegan Paul, Trench, Trübner &
Co., 1905), no. 44, 182–86 (here modernized).

M. F. Wakelin, "An Edition of John Mirk's Festial as It Is Contained in the
Brotherton Collection Manuscript" (Ph.D. diss,, University of Leeds,
1960).

LITERATURE:

Wenzel, *Collections*, 58–65 (with recent studies and suggestions about the use
of these sermons in regular preaching).

H. Leith Spencer, *English Preaching in the Late Middle Ages* (Oxford: Clarendon
Press, 1993), 311–16, 182–83.

~

On the Feast of St. John the Baptist and his solemnity.

Christian men and women, on such-and-such a day[1] you will have
the day of St. John the Baptist, who is thus called because he baptized
Our Lord Jesus Christ in the water of the Jordan. Therefore, on that
day you shall come to church in worship of God and St. John, and
also you shall fast on the eve.[2] Then you must know that such eves
were established in olden times. In the beginning of holy church, men
and women came to church at night with candles and other lights,
and in their devotions held wakes in the church all night long. But afterward, in the course of time, people abandoned such devotions and
used songs and dances, and thus they fell into lechery and gluttony
and thereby turned good holy devotion into sin. For this reason, our
holy fathers ordained that people should abandon those wakes and
fast on the eve, and in this way wakes turned into fasts. But they have
still retained the name and are called "vigils" in Latin, that is, "waking" in English; and in English they are called "eves," because at the
eve people used to come to church, as I have told you.

---

1. Referring to the coming day of the week on which the feast would occur.

2. "Eve": liturgically the vigil of the feast (as in "Christmas Eve"). The following
explanation of vigils derives from John Beleth (twelfth century), *Rationale divinorum of-
ficiorum* 137 (PL 202:141–142).

But still people keep a wake in the evening in worship of St. John and make three kinds of fire:

one of clean bones and no wood, which is called a "bonfire";
another of clean wood and no bones, which is called "wakefire," because people sit by it and wake;
and the third of bones and wood, which is called "St. John's fire."

[1]

The first fire was made of bones, as John Beleth says,[3] for in that country[4] there is great heat, which causes dragons to come together and fly in the air and let their natural froth [i.e., sperm] fall down into the waters and so poison the waters that many people come to their death by it and to many other great sicknesses. Then there were many great scholars,[5] and they had read about King Alexander how, when he was about to have a battle with the king of India, and the king brought with him many elephants bearing wooden castles on their backs, as is their custom, and armed knights in the castles all arrayed for war. Then Alexander knew the nature of elephants, that they fear nothing as much as the grunting of pigs. So he let all the pigs that could be gotten be gathered together, and had them driven so close to the elephants that they should well hear their grunts. Then he made one pig cry out, and at once all together grunted so much that the elephants fled and cast off their castles. And they slew the knights that were in them, and thus Alexander had the victory. These wise scholars knew well that dragons hate nothing so much as burnt bones. Therefore, they taught the people to gather all the bones they could find and set them on fire. And so, with their stench, they drove the dragon away and thus were cured of their sicknesses.

---

3. See the previous note. Beleth is also cited in *Legenda aurea*, 363.

4. "In that country" seems to be a nonspecific reference to ancient times, as in Beleth and *Legenda aurea*.

5. For the intercalated story about Alexander, see Vincent of Beauvais, *Speculum historiale* 4.55, in Vincent of Beauvais, *Speculum quadruplex*, 4 vols. (Douais, 1624; repr., Graz: Akademische Druck- und Verlagsanstalt, 1964–65), 4:132.

[2]

The second fire was made of wood, to burn and bring light, for St. John was a torch that burned and gave light.[6] They also made blazes of fire to be seen from afar, because it is the nature of fire to be seen from afar at night. And St. John was of the same kind; for Jeremiah the prophet, many years before John was born, prophesied of him and thereby spoke with God's mouth and said: "Before I formed you in your mother's womb I knew you; and before you came out of her body I sanctified you and gave you as a prophet to the people" [Jeremiah 1:5]. Then, as St. John should be sanctified before he was born, God sent his angel Gabriel to Zechariah, St. John's father, as he was offering the sacrifice in the place of Abia the bishop in the temple and was eagerly praying to God to have a child, for both he and his wife, Elizabeth, were barren and old. Then this angel said to him thus: "Zechariah, God has heard your prayer and grants you a child, whom you shall call John; and he shall be filled with the Holy Spirit in his mother's womb, and many shall be glad on the day of his birth" [cf. Luke 2:13–14]. Then, as Zechariah was old, he asked the angel to have a token of this promise. Then the angel said that he should be mute until the child was born. And so he was. Then Elizabeth conceived; and when she was with child, Our Lady, also with child, came to speak with Elizabeth. And right as she was greeting Elizabeth, St. John leapt for joy in his mother's womb at Christ's presence whom he saw in Our Lady. Wherefore Our Lady was with Elizabeth till John was born and was her midwife and took him from the earth. And when the neighbors heard that Elizabeth had a son, they were glad and came, as was the custom at that time, to give the child his name, and called him Zechariah after his father. But Elizabeth asked to call him John. But as there was none in her family who was thus called, they asked Zechariah by signs what the child should be called. Then he wrote for them and asked them to call him John. And with that, God loosed Zechariah's tongue, and he spoke readily and blessed God aloud for all his ordinances. Thus was John sanctified before he was

6. One of the "etymologies" or meanings of the name John is *lucerna*, light or torch, as said in the beginning of his section in *Legenda aurea* (p. 356).

born. For which he would give everyone the light of a good example. Further, when he was of the proper age, he went into the desert and was there preaching and baptizing the people until Christ came to be baptized by him. Then John was clothed in camel hair, and girt with a belt of rough skin, and he ate some kind of worms that are nourished in that desert among herbs and are as thick as a man's finger but somewhat shorter, and they suck honey from the flowers and are "honeysuckles," which poor men gather and fry in oil for their food. St. John also ate leaves that are broad and round and white, which grow on trees also in that desert; and when they are rubbed between men's hands, they are sweet as honey and good to eat, and they are called "honey of the wood."[7] And he drank water from a well that is there. This was John's life in the desert till Our Lord Jesus Christ was thirty years old. And then he and John met at the water of the river Jordan. And there John told the people about Christ and showed him with his finger and said: "See, this is the lamb of God, this is he I have told you about. I have baptized you in water, but this one will baptize you in the Holy Spirit" [cf. John 1:29 and Luke 3]. Then John and Christ went into the water, and there John baptized Christ. And when he had been baptized, such a light came from heaven that John was abashed. Then he heard the Father in Heaven. Here John learned first to know the three persons of the Trinity. All this is the meaning of the second fire.

[3]

The third fire, of wood and bones, signifies John's martyrdom, for his bones were burned. Now you shall hear how. We read that King Herod had a brother who was called Philip. And as this Philip had a fair wife whom Herod liked, he took her and made her his wife. Of that St. John reproved him many times and said it was not lawful for him to have his brother's wife. For that, Herod had John put to prison and devised between himself and his wife how John might be done to death without disturbance of the people, for the people loved John. Then Herod planned to make a great feast of all the men of the

---

7. Both "honeysuckles" (for locusts) and "honey of the wood" are used in the contemporary Middle English translation of the Bible.

country, to keep with him if the people were to rise. And so, when the day of the feast came and all men were richly served, his wife, as was their agreement, sent her daughter into the hall to dance and tumble in front of the guests. And she pleased Herod so much that he asked her to ask of him whatever she would and she should have it, and he swore a great oath to it. Then the damsel asked for John the Baptist's head, as she had been taught. Then Herod feigned to be wroth, but [in reality] he was happy at it. But since he had made such an oath before so many men, he would not be false, but sent at once and had John's head struck off in prison without any other judgment. And it was brought to the damsel. And so her mother let the head be buried in a secret place as she had ordained, far from the body. So, the night after, John's disciples stole the body and buried it, and it was there until Julian the Apostate, emperor of Rome, came that way. He had the bones of John's body taken up and burned and afterward scattered in the wind, hoping that after that he would never rise to live again.

Thus, good men, you can understand how holy this man was, that an angel came from heaven to tell of his conception, and that the angel brought his name from heaven, and that in his birth Our Lady took him up from the ground, and that he was sanctified in his mother's womb, and that he afterward baptized Our Lord Jesus Christ.

You should also know that St. John *the Evangelist* died on the same day; but holy church makes no mention of it, for his day is sanctified at Christmas.[8] Then, as these two Johns are held to be the greatest saints in heaven, it happened that of two masters of divinity one loved this one, and the other the other John. And so each was busy to prove that his John was more worthy than the other, and a day was ordained to dispute this matter. But during the night before the day of disputation either John appeared to his devotee and bade him to leave their disputation, for they were in good accord in heaven. And so, in the morning, each told his vision to the people that had come to hear their disputation, and so all the people blessed God and both Johns.

8. The feast of St. John the Evangelist is December 27.

A Story

Likewise two lepers loved the two saints very much: one loved St. John the Baptist and the other St. John the Evangelist. And so it happened that in talking of them one said that his John was the greater, and the other said No. And so in their strife they started and would have fought. Then a voice came from heaven and said to them: "Let be your fighting on earth, for we are at great peace in heaven." And straightaway both were healed of their leprosy, so that on their whole bodies they became as clean as children. Then they kissed and were friends, and they thanked God and those holy saints, as they had much reason to do.[9]

Let us now pray these holy saints that they be our intercessors before Our Lord Jesus Christ, that we may so act here that we may have the bliss for which he redeemed us. Amen.

9. A variant of these two tales, deriving from Caesarius of Heisterbach, is listed in Tubach, no. 2829.

PART IV

SPECIAL OCCASIONS

Besides Sundays, feast days, and saints' feasts, other occasions also required or were graced with a sermon, such as meetings of the clergy in synods, visitations of parishes and religious institutions, funerals, ordinations and entrances into a religious order, the opening of Parliament, and even academic acts at the universities. In these cases late-medieval preachers again used the scholastic sermon form, often filled with particular personal details or references to contemporary events.

20

FUNERAL

FUNERAL SERMONS COULD HAVE BEEN GIVEN within or outside a Mass for the dead, and a preacher had greater freedom than usual to choose his thema from texts other than the prescribed lections. Consequently he often chose a biblical verse that had some relevance to the deceased. In the case of the present sermon, he even the changed the biblical wording, making its statement into a question.

The sermon, by an anonymous author, has been preserved in at least two manuscripts, one a Benedictine collection (W, where it is actually copied twice; see above, selection 9), the other a later fifteenth-century collection that contains several other sermons of some popularity.

In its structure this sermon faithfully follows the pattern of the scholastic sermon, with protheme, invitation to pray, introduction of the thema, division, and development of parts. But the introduction of the thema here is disproportionately long. In it, the anonymous preacher postpones the answer to his question about the fate of the person at whose burial the sermon was preached—evidently a nobleman named Simon—until nearly the end of the lengthy discourse, thus creating an unusual amount of rhetorical suspense. The eulogy itself, which one normally expects in a funeral sermon, is rather muted. Similarly muted is another characteristic element of funeral sermons, punning on the name of the dead. Here the preacher is content with the standard etymology of Simon as "obedient" and eschews the more fanciful etymologizing found in selection 24 and in many other funeral sermons (see for instance the sermons edited by Horner, indicated below).

SOURCE:

Worcester Cathedral, MS F.10, fols. 143va–145rb (W-83) and 174v–177 (W-92), and London, British Library, MS Harley 331, fols. 9v–13 (H-3).

LITERATURE:

Wenzel, *Collections*, 151–58, 193–96, and Index, "Funerals."

Patrick J. Horner, "John Paunteley's Sermon at the Funeral of Walter Froucester, Abbot of Gloucester (1412)," *American Benedictine Review* 28 (1977): 147–66.

————, "A Sermon on the Anniversary of the Death of Thomas Beauchamp, Earl of Warwick," *Traditio* 34 (1978): 381–401.

❧

Where has Simon gone? 1 Maccabees 5[:21].

My reverend sirs, speaking to his disciples in parables Christ, the Son of God, says in Luke 19[:12]: "A certain nobleman went into a far country, to receive for himself a kingdom," etc. According to its literal sense this parable refers to Christ, who came down from heaven into the wretchedness of this world as into a far country, where he, with the price of his blood, received the human race as a dear and precious kingdom, with which, after overcoming the prince of death, he rose gloriously up to heaven and will come again at the end of the world to judge the living and the dead. However, in moral terms the parable may be understood to be about the person for whom we have assembled together, who not undeservedly can be called noble, not only on grounds of his parental lineage but also because of the renown of his life and behavior, for nobility and the worthiness of one's parents are worth little or nothing without the nobility and worthiness of one's behavior. And yet, grievous to say, people nowadays rejoice more in the nobility of their family than in that of their behavior and holy way of life. They do so foolishly, as can be proven by holy scripture as well as by natural reason. This is also shown by Chrysostom in his *Imperfect Work on Matthew*, homily 3, when he says: "What use is a famous descent to him who is stained by his way of life, or what harm is a vile descent to him who is adorned by his morals? He who takes glory in his forefathers shows himself empty before good men. For what did it help Cain's reputation that he was the son of Adam? Did he not become a murderer of his brother and was banished from the face of God? Or what did it help Cham that he was the son of Noah? Was he not separated from his brothers and sons although according to the flesh he was born their brother, but according to his soul became a slave? Of him is said in Genesis [9:25]: 'Cursed be Cham; a servant of servants shall he be to his brothers.' And what did it help Esau that he was the son of Isaac the patriarch and brother of Jacob, of whom God, speaking through the mouth of the prophet Malachi [1:2–3], said: 'I have loved Jacob but have hated Esau'? Or what did it help Judas the traitor that he was an apostle and disciple of Christ—did he not sell his master and, driven by remorse, went and hanged himself and spilled all his intestines? Or what harm did it do to Abraham that he had a father who worshipped at an altar of gods of clay? Was he not selected out of his kin and made the head of the faithful, so that he is no longer called the son of sinners but the father of saints, nor could his father's errors stain his own glory? For gold is born from dirt but is not the same as dirt, and gold is chosen, but dirt is scorned. Likewise dross[1] comes out of silver but is not the same as silver, and the filtrated silver is kept while the dross is thrown away. Therefore it is better to become renowned after issuing from a contemptible lineage than to issue contemptible from a renowned lineage." So far Chrysostom.[2] But this nobleman here was born renowned from a renowned family and distinguished by the integrity of his moral behavior and the holiness of his life, as the entire course of his life shows brilliantly. To receive the price of life he has left this valley of tears and is now gone into a far country. But since I am not sure where he has gone, I ask of you now, **Where has Simon gone?** of whose death I have already spoken. Let us therefore say for his soul an Our Father and Hail Mary.

Where has Simon gone? as before. My reverend sirs, we see with our own eyes, and daily experience tells us, that about something that

1. The text speaks of *stagnum*, "tin."
2. Pseudo-Chrysostom, *Opus imperfectum in Matthaeum*, homily 3 (PG 56:651).

is hidden, doubtful, or unknown we ask what it is and how it may be known; and about something absent and distant, we ask where it is and how it can be found. In this way the disciples, when they heard their master, Christ, telling them, "A little while, and you shall not see me; and again," and so on, they said to one another: "What is this that he says to us: 'A little while,' etc., we do not know what he is saying," John 16 [16–18]. Likewise the Magi, when they were seeking Christ in order to adore him, said: "Where is he who is born," etc., Matthew 2[:2]. And in a similar way the prophet Baruch, chapter 3[:16–19], asks about those who have left this world: "Where are the princes of the nations who rule over the beasts that are upon the earth? Who take their diversion with the birds of the air? Who hoard up silver and gold, wherein men trust, and there is no end of their getting? Who work in silver and are solicitous, and their works are unsearchable? And yet they are cut off, and others are risen up in their place." Since therefore this man has been cut off by death, I now ask about him, **Where has Simon gone?**

In a treatise on the pain of the damned and the joy of the elect, Augustine says that the king of kings and lord of lords has, within the wide space of his kingdom, three cities or dwelling places: one on high, another in the middle, and a third on low, that is to say, heaven, the world, and hell. The first city is that of the blessed and the angels, the third that of the devils and the damned, and the one in the middle that of humans on their way.[3] The two cities on either end are in every respect opposed to each other and do not share in any fellowship, according to the Apostle in 2 Corinthians 6[:14–15], where he asks: "What fellowship has light with darkness? What concord has Christ with Belial? Or what part has the faithful with the unbeliever?" as if to say, None. But the one in the middle shares the features of either extreme. But since there is naturally no other way out of the middle except to one of the extremes, and since the man for whose burial we have come together has now left the city in the middle, and I am not certain to which extreme he has gone, I now ask, **Where has Simon gone?**

3. In medieval sermons, human beings in this life are commonly called *viatores* or *in via*, on their way to their heavenly home *(patria)*.

Job asked a similar question in chapter 14[:7–10], about man when he leaves the city in the middle: "A tree," he says, "has hope: if it is cut, it grows green again, and its boughs sprout. If its root grows old in the earth, and its stock is dead in the dust, at the scent of water it will sprout and bring forth leaves, as when it was first planted. But when man is dead and consumed, where I ask is he?" Since this man here is now dead, where I ask is he and where has he gone? Solomon answers this question as follows, in Ecclesiastes 11[:3]: "If a tree falls to the south or to the north, in whatever place it falls, there it shall be." On this verse Gregory writes, in his *Moral Commentary*, book 12: "In the day of his death, the just man falls to the south, the sinner to the north, because the just man is led by the heat of the spirit to joy, but the sinner is condemned in his cold heart with the apostate angel who said in his heart, 'I will sit in the mountain of the covenant, in the sides of the north' [Isaiah 14:13]."[4] Let then everyone see which way the tree of human life will fall before it falls, for once it has fallen, it will not stand up again. And since the apostle[5] says in Matthew 3[:10], "Now the axe is laid to the root of the tree, and everyone who does not yield good fruit, will be cut down and cast into the fire," let everyone consider diligently where he will fall before he falls, because he cannot fall to the east or the west but has to fall either to the south or to the north, that is, to one of the two cities at either end, either heaven or hell. But what else is south or north but the full light at noon or the deepest darkness at midnight? Happy the man who shall fall to that south where he whom the devout soul loves "feeds and lies at midday" [Canticles 1:6]. That midday will be that repletion that lacks no good whatsoever, which "eye has not seen, nor ear heard, neither has it entered into the heart of man," 1 Corinthians 2[:9]. In that midday, I hope, rests and feeds now the man of whom the question has been asked, **Where has Simon gone?**

But you might want to know which way, whether to the south or the north, that is, to punishment or to glory, any tree of the human race will fall—or where this Simon has now gone. Look at its branches, consider well where they are in greater plenty and of heavier weight,

4. Gregory, *Moralia* 12.4.
5. Referring to John the Baptist.

and no doubt if the tree were cut down or overthrown by a whirlwind or some other cause, it will fall that way. Our branches are our desires, affections, and works that stretch out and incline toward the south. So is it spiritually, if all things are done with a view toward and for the sake of God. All true love and affection draws and inclines us toward the object we love, and it not only draws but even makes us the same, as Augustine says in treatise 4 on the Epistle of John: "Everyone is like his love. Do you love the earth?" he says. "Then you are earth. What shall I say? You love God? Then you are god. And this I dare not say from myself, but let us listen to scripture: 'I have said: You are gods and all of you the sons of the Most High' [Psalm 81:6]."[6] Thus Augustine. But if our desires, affections, and works are fleshly, they stretch out to the north and incline that way. This means that, if our desires stretch out to the flesh and fleshly things, and to the world and worldly things, and our works are done for that reason, all our branches stretch out to the north and bend the tree in that direction, and it will fall that way, unless someone will bring some remedy before the axe is laid to the root of the tree. Let then everyone examine before he falls in what direction his branches stretch out, and he will know what way he will fall, unless someone brings some remedy.

But there are people nowadays who, although they see that their branches stretch to the north, yet think and hope that their tree will fall to the south, either by some trick or by some skill, as it happens with a tree that from the weight of its branches bends to the north, but with the help of a prop or a rope is turned into a different direction: when it is cut down, it is pushed or drawn in a different direction, namely, to the south or east. In this way, many people today whose branches bend and stretch to the north intend and think to make a general confession at the end of their lives, or to give many alms to the needy from all their temporal goods they have at some time acquired, and in this way to be pulled in the opposite direction through the poor people's prayers, namely, to the south, where the sun of justice, Christ, dwells in the midday of eternity.

But indeed, even if this may perchance happen, it is very dangerous to put too much trust in this remedy. For we often see that people

---

6. Augustine, *In Epistolam Iohannis ad Parthos* 2.2.

who try to pull a tree in an opposite direction from where it bends are thwarted in their attempt by three causes, and the tree falls exactly the way in which it had been first bent. The first cause is that the tree takes the course of its fall before they start pulling. The second is that those who pull it are not strong enough. And the third cause is that the rope is split or broken or else is tied to a different tree. Thus, ill-disposed people, whose branches bend to the north, are sometimes taken from life without confession and without giving their temporal belongings away, and thus fall to the north, that is, to the punishment of eternal damnation, before anyone pulls them the other way. For that reason it is said in Ecclesiastes 7[:18]: "Do not act wickedly and be not foolish, lest you die before your time," that is, before you fall, or fall differently from what you have believed. And in this regard notice the parable of the rich man in Luke 12[:16–20], of whom Christ said to his disciples as follows: "The land of a certain rich man brought forth plenty of fruits. And he thought within himself, saying: What shall I do, because I have no room where to gather my fruits? And he said: This I will do: I will pull down my barns, and will build greater ones; and into them I will gather all things that are grown to me, and my goods. And I will say to my soul: Soul, you have many goods laid up for many years. Take your rest; eat, drink, make good cheer. But God said to him: You fool," etc. "Whose will those things be which you have provided?" as if to say, Not yours but someone else's. With respect to such people the Psalmist says: "They shall leave their riches to strangers, and their sepulchers shall be their houses forever" [Psalm 48:11–12]. And in Job 27[:19] it is written: "The rich man when he sleeps will take away nothing with him; he will open his eyes and find nothing," because people found none of his riches in his hands. Sometimes people who pull a tree, that is, those who pray for such a person, are not strong enough for the weight of the branches, and thus they who pull him labor in vain. A person who is thus pulled can say the words of Proverbs 23[:35]: "They pulled me, and I did not feel it." And sometimes the rope breaks in many places or is tied to different trees, that is, prayers or alms are scattered and go to people to whom the goods he has bequeathed or given had belonged in the first place, for alms that come from theft or from unjust gain do not help the person who has stolen them but rather help those who have deserved them. In this way, those who pray pull to the south people whom they do not know, while those whom they believe they are pulling are left behind. For men cannot pull anything unless God the Father will pull with them, after the true word of John 6[:44]: "No man can come to me unless the Father, who has sent me, draws him." But what ropes or bands God the Father draws with, he himself shows us, speaking through the mouth of the prophet in Hosea 11[:4]: "I will draw them with the cords of Adam, with the bands of love." A rope must be firmly tied to the tree it is supposed to pull. But a person who has lived without love and dies in this state, does not have the binding rope of love, and therefore he cannot possibly be pulled to the south with this or any other rope. Since according to the Savior's words in Matthew 24[:12], "iniquity will abound and the charity of many will grow cold," it is no wonder that few people are drawn to Christ. But whoever holds the end of this rope of charity firmly in his life will, at his death, be drawn by it to the south. But since I do not know whether or not anyone has this love perfectly, I still ask, **Where has Simon gone?**

In these words that have thus been introduced, two things can be briefly discerned, according to their logical order, and can be applied to this man:

the preeminence of love and obedience,
and the evidence of stupor and sadness.

The first is shown by the meaning of his name, when "Simon" comes [logically] first in the question, for "Simon" means obedient or obedience.[7] The second is hinted at by this man's, or Simon's, withdrawal, when "Where has he gone?" is added to his name. About these two together the spouse in Canticles 5[:17] asks: "Where has your beloved gone, O most beautiful among women?" But since Simon has died and gone from us, I fear that his memory fades and his oblivion grows strong. Therefore I still ask, if anyone will answer me, as I asked in the beginning when I said: "Where has Simon gone?" This question has been repeated again and again, and not at all answered. Therefore I will now in reply give a threefold answer as the threefold matter of this brief sermon.

---

7. Like so many name etymologies, derived from Jerome.

First then, if anyone asks where Simon has gone now, I say: from pain to rest.

Second, he has gone from exile and pilgrimage to his homeland.

And third and last, he has gone from wretchedness, tribulation, and grief to eternal happiness.

I now finally answer that with God's grace Simon has gone to these three, as will become clear in the development. And these three points will briefly form the matter of my collation.[8]

[1]

First I say that this Simon has gone from pain to rest. This I show by natural reason. You know, and reason teaches us, that any natural motion is from a beginning to an end, or from one extremity to its opposite, and the more it leaves the beginning behind, the more it approaches the end. When it has left the beginning totally behind, it will rest in the end of its motion, because it is against logic that action should end in action, and rest in rest. Now, since in the world, as the starting point of motion, is continuous action, and in heaven, as the final point of motion, is unending rest, and since Simon has now left the starting point, namely, this world, totally behind, it would follow that he is at perfect rest in the final point, that is, heaven. And thus Simon has now gone from labor unto rest. In Job 5[:7] it is written: "Man is born to labor as the bird to fly." Therefore, as it is natural for a bird to fly, according to the law of its nature, so it is natural for man to labor, as from his original condition. But many people refuse to labor and thereby deviate from the law of their own nature. Of these the Psalmist says: "They are not in the labor of men, neither shall they be scourged like other men. Therefore pride has held them fast" [Psalm 72:5]. Augustine glosses this text by saying that "people who are not scourged with other men here in time will be scourged with the devils in eternity."[9] And yet there are many who, while they are here, labor continuously and yet will never arrive at the goal of eternal rest. Such are people who are prompt and strong in things that belong to this world, but slow and weak in things that belong to God.

8. On "collation" see above, p. 136.
9. Cf. Augustine, *Enarrationes in Psalmos* 72.10.

Of these, Gregory says on his *Moral Commentary* 10: "All those who love this world are strong in worldly things but weak in heavenly ones. Because for worldly glory they want to sweat to death, but for eternal hope they persist not a whit in laboring. For earthly gains they endure any harm whatever, but for the reward of heaven they refuse to endure even the slightest verbal insult. They are strong enough to assist earthly judgment all day long, but in prayer before God they are tired out in the span of a single hour. To acquire riches and honors they often suffer nakedness, adversity, hunger, and thirst; but to seek heavenly goals with their labor they delay the more, the later they believe that these will be given them."[10] Thus Gregory. Whence the prophet Isaiah in chapter 49[:4] says in the person of one who labors in such fashion and does his work with half-hearted dedication: "I have labored in vain and have spent my strength without cause and in vain." And in Jeremiah 45[:3]: "I am wearied with my groans, and I find no rest." But, beloved, *this* man did not labor thus in vain. Quite in contrast to lovers of this world, he was weak in earthly things and ready in heavenly ones, and strong to fulfill the observance of everything that belongs to the divine law by carrying out the precepts and his obedience. According to the original meaning of his name he is obedient, for he was always obedient to God, in whose commandments and service he labored continuously till the end of his life. For that labor he has now, I trust, received the full reward of eternal rest and can truly say the words of Sirach 51[:35]: "I have labored a little and have found much rest for myself."

[2]

For the second main part I said that he went from exile and pilgrimage to his own homeland. We all, as long as we live in this life, are pilgrims and strangers—as the Psalmist says: "I am a stranger with you and a pilgrim as all my fathers were," Psalm 38[:13]. And at Zephaniah 1[:8] it is written: "In the day of the victim of the Lord I will visit upon all that are clothed with pilgrim's apparel." "Pilgrim's apparel" is this corruptible body, in complete contrast to the apparel of our homeland. In this apparel, while and as long as we are "in the body,

---

10. Gregory, *Moralia* 19.27.

we are absent from the Lord," 2 Corinthians 5[:6]. On this verse the Gloss says: "He who is absent is not yet in his homeland." But alas, there are many who do not consider themselves to be pilgrims in this world but rather its natives and citizens, who put and exhaust all their hope, love, and labor in earthly things. Over these the Apostle in Philippians 3[:18–19] weeps, calling them "enemies of the cross of Christ, whose God is their belly, whose end is destruction, and whose glory is in their shame; those who mind earthly things." On this authority Augustine writes, in the third part of his sermons, *Sermon 43*: "The belly is a god to him who believes his exile to be his homeland, death to be life, who seeks his distinction not in good morals but in clothes, who would never exchange this life for eternity if he could prolong it."[11] Whereas Gregory in the exposition of a homily on a single martyr says: "If we diligently reflect on what and how great are the things we are promised in heaven, everything on earth becomes vile to our mind. In comparison to the eternal life, this earthly life should rather be called death than life," etc.[12] From this exile, pilgrimage, and death Simon has now gone, and thus he now rests safely in his proper homeland. "Our homeland," says Augustine in the first part of *Sermon 1*, "is heaven, whose citizens are the angels," whose temple is God, whose brightness the Son, whose love the Holy Spirit. All heavenly dwelling is secure. There no friend is ever lost, none becomes another's enemy, nobody dies or becomes ill.[13] This city will not need the light of the moon or the sun, for God, the Lord, will give it light, and its lamp will be the Lamb, at the end of Revelation [22:5]. Our Simon, drawn by the sweetness of this heavenly homeland, always longed for it, in prosperity and in adversity, in health and in illness, saying with the Psalmist: "For better is one day in your courts above thousands." And thus "I have loved the beauty of your house and the place where your glory dwells" [Psalms 83:11 and 25:8]. Simon has now traveled to that place, and thus he has gone from the exile of this world to his own homeland. This was my second part.

---

11. Augustine, *Sermo 208* (PL 39:2132).

12. Gregory, *Homiliae in evangelia* II, homily 37.1 (PL 76:1275).

13. Cf. Augustine, *Sermo 378* (PL 39:1674).

[3]

In the third and last place I said that Simon has gone from grief and sadness, wretchedness and tribulation, to everlasting happiness and eternal glory. Blessed Bernard says, on the words of Job 5[:19], "In six troubles he shall deliver you," etc., as follows: "The first trouble and wretchedness of man is his painful concern with the needs of his wretched body, which now craves food, now drink, now sleep, now being awake. Now the cold bites him, then the heat; now leisure is a burden, then hard work. Now his head hurts, then his stomach, and next his blood, they annoy and trouble us without ceasing. Second, we are troubled by the vices of the heart, impatience and anger and the bite of envy, the desire for praise, and an infinite number of others that attack us every day and make us unhappy. Third and fourth are prosperity and adversity. Fifth, ignorance and blindness, in which we do not know in many situations what we are to do. The sixth tribulation is our adversary the devil, who 'as a roaring lion, goes about seeking whom he may devour,' 1 Peter 5[:8]."[14] Of these and similar tribulations and anxieties that befall man day in, day out, Job speaks in chapter 14[:1–2] when he says: "Man born of a woman, living for a short time," etc., and then adds: "and flees as a shadow." Boethius presents the same beautifully and clearly in book 2, prosa 4 of his *Consolation*: "Who," he says, "is so completely happy that he does not at some point struggle against his condition?" as if to say, no one. "Human goods are by their nature a matter of anxiety. Either they are not ever fully achieved or they do not last forever. One man has plenty of wealth but is ashamed of his family origin; another is well known for his noble family but is so oppressed by poverty that he would rather be unknown. One man is surrounded by wealth and a noble family but weeps that he is not married; another is happily married but has no children, so that he gathers his wealth for a stranger to inherit, and yet another has children but in sadness weeps over the crimes of his son or daughter. Hence no one is easily satisfied with his fortune."[15] Thus Boethius. But all these miseries, griefs, tribulations, and anxieties **Simon** has now left behind and **has gone** safely to the future and perpetual glory. Amen.

14. Bernard of Clairvaux, *In Septuagesima*, sermon 1.5 (PL 183:165–66).
15. Boethius, *De consolatione philosophiae* 2, prosa 4.

21

CONVOCATION (THOMAS BRINTON)

ON BRINTON, SEE ABOVE, selection 11. As bishop of Rochester—next door to London and Westminster—Brinton was much involved in larger political and ecclesiastical issues of his day. He is, in this regard, perhaps best known for the following sermon, which he seems to have preached during the meeting of the Good Parliament (end of April to May 1376). The sermon was delivered to the convocation of the clergy of the province of Canterbury and would be dated to May 18. It has attracted the attention of students of Middle English literature for its social criticism as well as Brinton's mentioning the fable of belling the cat, the latter presumably echoed in Langland's *Piers Plowman* (B Prologue, 146–210). For Langland's putative historical references and allusions to this sermon, see G. R. Owst, "The 'Angel' and the 'Goliardeys' of Langland's Prologue," *Modern Language Review* 20 (1925): 270–79.

The quantitative imbalance in this sermon between the introductory matter and the development of the three principals is characteristic of Brinton's longer sermons, discussed in *Collections*, 366–67.

SOURCE:

Thomas Brinton, *Sermons,* ed. Mary Aquinas Devlin, O.P., Camden Third Series 85–86 (London: Royal Historical Society, 1954), 2:315–21. Parts of this sermon have been translated in F. A. Gasquet, *The Old English Bible and Other Essays,* new ed. (London: George Bell and Sons, 1897), essay 3, "A Forgotten English Preacher," 54–86, at 60–67.

LITERATURE:

Wenzel, *Collections*, 45–49.

Anna P. Baldwin, "The Historical Context," in *A Companion to Piers Plowman*, ed. John A. Alford (Berkeley and Los Angeles: University of California Press, 1988), 67–86, at 78–79.

George Holmes, *The Good Parliament* (Oxford: Clarendon Press, 1975), 103–4.

Andrew Galloway, *The Penn Commentary on "Piers Plowman,"* (Philadelphia: University of Pennsylvania Press, 2006), 133–40 (misdating Bromyard).

꙳

Fifth Sunday after Easter.

The doer of the work shall be blessed, James 1[:25].

Among the works that man's industry dares undertake I consider preaching to be the most fearsome and dangerous. For what is more fearsome than to preach the word of God, when Jeremiah, who had been sanctified in the womb, refused to become its carrier, Jeremiah 1[:5]? It is a common failing that almost everybody would rather hear a sermon against the vices of others than his own. Clerics want one to preach against lay people who give their tithes poorly; lay people want one to preach against clerics and churchmen who give the worst example to others. Husbands are pleased when one preaches against the pomp and ornaments of their wives; wives are pleased when one preaches against their husbands' excessive expenses. Prelates are pleased when one preaches against their subjects' disobedience; their subjects are pleased when one preaches against the prelates' vices and negligence. And thus, what one group dislikes [to hear] tends to please the other. I dare say it firmly, to carry out this work of preaching worthily is divine rather than human, after the words of Nehemiah 6[:16]: "This was the work of God." What is more precious than to preach the gospel? Preachers of the word of God urge and convert so many souls to do good, they explain and show them so many fruitful examples of virtue, and in return they promise them so many eternal rewards from God. In a *figura* of this, the Apostle in 2 Timothy 4[:5] enjoins on every preacher: "But you be vigilant, labor in all things, do the work of an evangelist, fulfill your ministry," as if to say: You, prelate or curate, be watchful in your concern with holy preaching; labor in carrying out meritorious deeds; do the work of an evangelist by preaching the firm truth; and fulfill your ministry by showing constant holiness. Therefore, that I may today carry out such a laborious and fruitful work for the praise of God and your edification, at the beginning of the sermon say the Lord's Prayer.

The doer of the work shall be blessed. A Christian may well know how to recite the articles of faith: how six refer to Christ's divinity and six to his human nature. The first article referring to his divinity is that that there are three persons in one godhead. The second is to believe that the Son of God is God. The third is to believe that the Holy Spirit is God. The fourth, that the Catholic church and her sacraments have the power from the Holy Spirit to forgive all sins. The fifth is to believe that we all shall rise again in the same flesh in which we live. The sixth, that after the resurrection the just will receive eternal life with both choirs.[1] Now, if any Christian does not believe this explicitly and in detail, yet believes that the church holds these things, he will be saved in the faith of the church, just as the daughter of the Canaanite woman was healed in the faith of her mother.[2] As the Psalmist says, "all his works are done with faithfulness" [Psalm 32:4]. With respect to the human nature of Christ, the first article is to believe that the Son of God was conceived by the Holy Spirit. The second, that he was born God and man from an undefiled virgin. The third, that he suffered and died on the cross, and that he then descended in his soul to hell, while his body rested in the tomb. The fourth, that on the third day he rose from the dead. The fifth, that he ascended to heaven and is sitting at the right hand of God the Father. And the sixth, that he will come at the end of time to judge the living and the dead.

Now, even if a Christian knows these articles, it will not be enough for his salvation unless he has manifest works of faith in him, for as the Apostle says in James 2[:20], "Faith without works is dead." But some Christian will say: "Come what may,[3] I shall be saved on the words of our Savior that 'He who believes and is baptized shall be saved,' at the end of Mark [16:16]. Now, every Christian has these

---

1. *Cum vtraque scola* in the edition.   2. Mark 7:25–30.

3. *Quacumque via data.*

two [i.e., faith and baptism]; therefore, etc." To this I answer: It is one thing to believe God, another to believe that God exists, and yet another to believe in God. To believe that God exists is something that devils and unbelievers do too. To believe God means that whatever he has promised us, he will fulfill in us. But we believe in God when we put our hope in him and love him truly and carry out our faith in deeds. Whence Augustine says in chapter 7 of his book *On the Christian Life:* "Since we do not recognize a title without the activity it denotes (for every title is based on a certain activity), how can anyone be called 'Christian' unless the activity of Christ appears in him? The title 'Christian' denotes justice, humility, and innocence. If one does not have these in oneself, one appropriates somebody else's name to one's own damnation. Only he can be called 'Christian' who follows Christ in his actions."[4] From these things follows as a conclusion what our thema says, that **The doer of the work shall be blessed.**

Now, among the institutions that were established in England in the past, one practice of great renown and excellence is still in use: the Lords and Commons are called together to Parliament to discuss and legislate for the good state of the country. But of what use is it to discuss affairs in Parliament and publicly denounce transgressors of the law, if such denunciation is not followed by due correction? Laws are worthless unless they are correctly enforced. But is it not known, and almost everywhere publicly acknowledged, that it is not people who incline to virtue but those who lead vicious and scandalous lives who have long had the chief share in the government of this kingdom? We universally grumble and protest against the rule of such men, yet we do not have the courage to speak the truth as to the proper remedy.

St. Augustine tells us the real reason of our silence in the following passage: "When the Egyptians desired, in spite of considerable opposition, to deify Isis and Serapis, they first ordered that anyone who called them human or discussed their existence should be put to death. And that no one should be ignorant of this law, in every place where images of these gods were set up they erected a statue that held a finger to its mouth, so that by this image of silence all who entered

---

4. Pseudo-Augustine, *De vita christiana* 6 (PL 40:1036–37).

the temple might know that the truth was to be concealed."[5] In the same way, our modern rulers—those overthrowers of truth and justice—wishing to raise their lords to the altars, as best they know how, have proclaimed that a coward is a hero, the weak man strong, the fool a wise man, the adulterer and the pursuer of lechery, a man chaste and holy. And in order to completely gain their own interests and to encourage their king in notorious crimes, they put before all who come to court an image of worldly fear, so that no one, of whatever rank and condition he may be, should dare to stand up against or castigate the evildoers.

But whose duty is it to speak of these matters? Most certainly, it is the duty of the prelates, of the lords temporal, of confessors, and even of preachers. As to the prelates, who ought to support the church on their shoulders like columns and lay down their lives in defense of its liberties—why do they remain silent when they see Christ daily crucified in his members? Why are they silent when they see the innocent condemned, poor ecclesiastics deprived of their benefices, and the church's rights so outraged that today the holy church of God is in greater slavery than it was under Pharaoh, who did not know the divine law? In all these things they show that they are hirelings and not shepherds. And the reason is that they are seeking preferment and are aspiring to be translated to richer sees. The lords temporal are silent because they shrink in dread from offending their king, trembling where in fact there is no reason to tremble, because it may well be believed that if [the king] were told the truth, he is so yielding and easily led that he would by no means tolerate such things in the realm. Confessors are silent because, so long as they can easily have their own comforts, conveniences, and honors, they do not care for souls. Therefore, they ought not to be called confessors but confusers, not teachers but rather traitors—traitors first to God, whose authority and commission they notoriously abuse; second, to their temporal lords, to whom they ought not to hesitate to speak the truth, that they may reclaim them from their errors; and third, to themselves, because they lose their souls for the sake of a little gain, authority, or fa-

---

5. Based on Augustine, *De civitate Dei* 18:5. See the similar development and application in *Fasciculus morum* IV.iii (p. 324).

vor that they acquire in this world. And preachers are silent because many of those who have touched upon the vices of the lords before this time, in sermons given at the Cross of St. Paul's,[6] have at once been arrested and taken before the king's council as malefactors. After being examined there, they have been condemned and banished or suspended from further exercise of their office of preaching. To conclude: Of these has become true what the Psalmist says: "They are all gone aside, they are become unprofitable together; there is none that does good, none but one" [Psalm 13:3],[7] namely, the commoners, who, like the foundations of the common weal, effectively support the king and the Parliament.

Let it not be this way, reverend sirs, lest our Parliament be compared to that parliament of rats and mice in a fable. We read that the mice had strictly ordained in their assembly that every cat should have a bell attached to its neck, so that when they were warned by its sound, the mice might safely escape to their holes. An ancient rat met a mouse returning from the parliament and asked what news there was. When the mouse had explained to him the gist of the business, the rat remarked: "This is a most excellent law, provided someone is appointed by your parliament to carry it into execution." The mouse replied that no such arrangement had been made by parliament. And so the law remained useless and inoperative. For the love of Christ, and in defense of our country that has been brought to such straits, let us be not merely talkers but doers! Let us "cast off the works of darkness, and put on the armor of light," Romans 13[:12], so that our

6. Sermons preached at the cross outside St. Paul's Cathedral, London, were frequently vehicles for the discussion of major social, theological, or ecclesial issues; see Patrick J. Horner, "Preachers at Paul's Cross: Religion, Society, and Politics in Late Medieval England," in *Medieval Sermons and Society: Cloister, City, University*, ed. Jacqueline Hamesse et al. (Louvain-la-Neuve: Féderation Internationale des Instituts d'Études Médiévales, 1998), 261–82.

7. The last phrase of the psalm verse, *non usque ad unum*, is normally translated as "not a single one" and thus reinforces the preceding statement. But, as Augustine points out, it may also be read as *non praeter unum*, "not up to one" or "none except one" (*Enarrationes in Psalmos*, on Psalm 13:2), the "one" in Augustine's commentary being Christ. It seems that Brinton is here using that meaning to accuse all social classes up to, or rather down to—that is, except—the commoners.

life may be amended and our kingdom governed in justice, recalling the words of the Psalmist: "Blessed are they who keep judgment and do justice" [Psalm 105:3]. And so, after the words of our thema, **the doer of the work shall be blessed.**

For the development of our sermon we should notice that it is commonly said in a proverb: "Do well and have well."[8] May every sermon be to that end, so that those who hear it may learn how they should do well and be rewarded according to their good works, because God will "render to everyone according to his works," as is said in the Psalm [61:13]. But since it is plain that the kingdom of England—

which formerly abounded in wealth, is now poor and penniless;

which formerly was resplendent with grace is now graceless and shameful;

which formerly ruled itself in justice is now full of vice without rule—

so that every one of you who has separated himself from God through sin and evil deeds may be reconciled with God through good works, I can put before him the words of Revelation 2[:5]: **"Be mindful from whence you have fallen and do penance, and do the first works,"** as if scripture were saying: O you sinner, while you stood in grace, you were the companion of angels and the devout servant of Jesus Christ, who were before you by giving direction, above you by infusion, beneath you by supporting you, within you by spiritual indwelling, and around you by defending you, for "works please God," Ecclesiastes 9[:7]. As you have fallen from such great grace, **be mindful from whence you have fallen,** namely, from the highest to the lowest, from paradise as it were into hell, from peace and prosperity into tribulation. And this is no wonder, since according to the Apostle in Romans 2[:8–9], "indignation, tribulation, and anguish upon every soul of man that works evil." But then follows [in our text]: **"Do penance"** [Revelation 2:5], because penance is health to the soul, the forgiveness of sins, the joy of

8. The manuscript gives "Bene fac et bene habe." See Bartlett Jere Whiting and Helen Whiting, *Proverbs, Sentences, and Proverbial Phrases from English Writings Mainly before 1500* (Cambridge, Mass.: Belknap Press of Harvard University Press, 1968), D278.

angels, the putting to flight of demons, the closing of the mouth of hell, and the opening of paradise. And our text says further: **"Do the first works."** But what were those first works of the English through which they stood in grace, peace, and quiet? Surely, works—

of cleanness with respect to themselves;
of holiness with respect to God;
and of justice with respect to their neighbor.

[1]

With regard to the first, namely, works of cleanness, the realm of England is not only polluted but disgraced by three sins especially, namely, lechery, and adultery, and also simony. That stinking sin of lechery, while it eats up the possessions of anyone in whom it rules, confounds his person, takes away grace, condemns his soul, buries his knowledge, and ruins his name and reputation, it can yet so rule in a person of higher rank that it exceeds the adultery and incest in a person of lower estate. Hence it is no wonder that, if a person from among the people falls, he falls by himself, but if a prince or prelate falls, as many other people fall with him as he rules over. This sin has so scandalously prevailed among our temporal lords that I can conclude with what the Psalmist says: "The earth is contaminated by their works" [Psalm 105:39].

Regarding adultery, there is no nation under heaven that is so disgraced on account of its adultery as England. This is clearly shown in distinction 56 [of the *Decretum*], where Boniface, pope and martyr, writes to the king of the English as follows: "If the English people, as is widely reported in the provinces, treat their legitimate marriages with contempt and lead vile lives in adultery, we must believe that that nation will not be strong in battle nor steadfast in faith, honorable before the world, or beloved by God, but it will rather engender sons who are degenerate and lepers," and so on.[9] Are we strong and fortunate in battle? Tell how.[10] Are we steadfast in faith? Do we have

9. *Decretum*, distinctio 56, 10 (Friedberg, *Corpus iuris canonici*, 1:222).

10. *Dic quomodo*, a tag that occurs frequently in Brinton's sermons, as a signal for the preacher (Brinton or whoever might use his sermons) to elaborate the point just made. See the discussion in *Collections*, 48.

honor in the world? Indeed, we are more false than anybody else and hence not lovable to God. Why are there so many illegitimate heirs and illegitimate divorces in the realm of England, unless it is because there is so much lechery and adultery everywhere that few men, and especially few lords, are content with their wives, but everyone neighs in lust after his neighbor's wife or maintains a concubine in place of his own wife, however beautiful and honorable she may be—which is horrible, detestable, and deserving of death. There is a story about an English nobleman who, when he was warned some morning in a melee of nobles that he would die a shameful death that same day, fell to the ground and exclaimed: "Woe to me that I have never loved my wife!" He thus acknowledged publicly that the cause of his death was his adultery.[11] Of him we can say in conclusion as the Psalmist says: "The sinner has been caught in the works of his own hands" [Psalm 9:17]. Do not act this way, you adulterers, that you may not become the ruin of this land. Look at the privileges and worthiness that marriage has. First the worthiness of its institution. For whereas other orders were instituted by holy men, the order of matrimony was instituted by God himself. So, if an apostate from the Order of St. Benedict or of St. Augustine commits a sin, surely someone who transgresses the order instituted by God commits an even greater one. Second, other orders were founded outside paradise, but this one in paradise, as is affirmed in the *Liber sextus,* "On vows," canon 1.[12] Third, at the time of the flood God saved the order of matrimony. Fourth, God honored the order of matrimony when, in the presence of his mother and disciples, he blessed marriage by miraculously changing water into wine.[13] Fifth, the virtue of matrimony renders a deed venial that without it [i.e., the sacrament] is horrible and a mortal sin. Reflect on these things and be pure, remembering what is written in Proverbs 21[:8]: "As he is pure, his work is right."

With regard to simony, how dangerous it is for lords to promote their relatives by simony can be seen in the chronicles.[14] While his fa-

---

11. The same story occurs verbatim in Bromyard, *Summa praedicantium* A.XVII.7, fol. 39rb.

12. *Decretals, Liber sextus,* 15.1 (Friedberg, *Corpus iuris canonici,* 2:1053).

13. John 2:1–11.

14. Helinand of Froidmont, *Chronica,* for the year 1040 (PL 212:933).

ther Conrad was still alive, the emperor Henry accepted a silver whistle from some cleric with the understanding that when he became
emperor he would advance the cleric to a bishopric. When Henry suc-
ceeded his father to the empire, he fulfilled his promise to the cleric. But soon thereafter he fell seriously ill, took to his bed, and lay
still for three days without spirit and voice as if he were in a trance,
and his spirit of life only pulsed in his breast. When the prelates and
other friends invoked God's clemency for his health, he at last came
to himself and recovered. Then he called the cleric to himself whom
he had promoted for that silver whistle and degraded him through a
decree of his council. Having done this, he confessed before all who
were within his hearing that during the three days that he had been lying without sign of life, he was held down by demons, whom he felt
to be so violent that, as they were blowing flames of fire in his face
through that whistle, they burned his whole body inside and outside.
Among these flames a young man appeared who had been roasted
in fire, who brought a wondrously large chalice and gave him relief,
and so his burning was extinguished and he returned to his former
health. That young man was St. Lawrence, whose monastery the emperor himself had rebuilt after it had been destroyed by pagans, and
to which, among other ornaments, he had given a golden chalice. By
that good deed he was freed from the fire, and so one can fittingly say
to this emperor what is written in 2 Chronicles [19:2–3]: "You deserved the wrath of God, but good works have been found in you." So
much for the first part.

[2]

Second, we must do works of holiness with respect to God. Such
works are attendance at Mass, at sermons, and in devout processions.
For the first we have the examples of Kings Henry III of England and
Louis of France, who ruled at the same time.[15] The king of England
was most devout in hearing Mass, while the king of France was the
same in listening to sermons. Some day, as the king of England was
about to dine with the king of France and was coming late to table
because he had been hearing so many masses, the king of France said

15. Cf. Tubach, no. 2526.

to him: "Lord king, you know no measure in hearing masses." And England replied: "Neither do you in hearing sermons." Both are to be greatly commended. The first, because people who hear Mass devoutly are granted these privileges: on that day, first, they will have what they need for their livelihood; second, trivial speech and oaths are forgiven; third, they will not lose the light of their eyes; fourth, sudden death will not overcome them; fifth, while they are hearing Mass, they do not age; and sixth, every single step of theirs from and to Mass is counted by the angels.[16] Thus, it is "the work of the just unto life," Proverbs 10[:16]. The other king is to be commended because "Blessed are they who hear the word of God," etc. [Luke 11:28]. When temporal lords were pleasing to God in such deeds, they had glory and honor and peace, for as the Apostle says in Romans 2[:10], "Glory, and honor, and peace to every one who does good works."

With respect to processions: When a procession is made because of some pressing tribulation, it seems that those who have grievously sinned are more urgently obligated to participate in the procession. Now, the iniquities of the rich and the nobles are greater than are those of the middle class and the poor, for whereas the latter commonly live honestly on their own earnings, the former, for the most part, live upon the goods of other people—as by violent seizures, exactions, extortions, and expensive pleasures. As a result, when all things are considered, those who should be richer than everyone else are through their bad self-rule the poorer. For what rule of justice and equity is it that, when processions are ordered to avert common tribulations, ecclesiastics, religious, and a few of the middle class should come, who have, relatively speaking, offended God only slightly, while the rich people and the nobility, who are the main cause of these afflictions, neither come, nor pray, nor do penance for their iniquities, but sport in their beds and in other luxuries to their heart's content? Now, someone might say: "The bishop of Rochester tries to prove

---

16. These so-called virtues or merits or Meeds of the Mass formed a widespread medieval commonplace found in Latin and vernacular languages, often even rhymed. A good collection of instances is given by Adolph Franz, *Die Messe im deutschen Mittelalter* (Freiburg: Herder, 1902; repr., Darmstadt: Wissenschaftliche Buchgesellschaft, 1963), 336–72.

in his sermon that kings and their offspring are obliged to go in processions, something that has not been commonly seen before these times." I answer: I do not intend to compel anyone to go in procession, but rather to persuade him to lead a devout life. Doesn't it seem abominable that, if there were a duel in the city of London tomorrow, which is forbidden by every law, so many rich and great men would come together that the place could hardly hold their crowd? But if a procession were ordered in London in prayer for the king and the peace of the realm, even if the bishop were there with his clergy, there would hardly be a hundred men from the common people to follow him. So, I conclude: if the king or the prince were to set an example of humility by showing his bodily presence in processions, he would glorify God and be held in greater reverence by the world, for our Savior says to all men of higher rank: "Let your light shine before men, that they may see your good works and glorify," etc., Matthew 5[:16].

[3]

To the third point [i.e., works of justice with respect to our neighbor]: Since according to Augustine kingdoms are but dens of thieves unless they are ruled in justice,[17] does it seem to you a just order when the king and his sons are so led by their counselors that they themselves are poor and wretched, given their rank, while those who lead them are so rolling in riches that, if a fourth of the kingdom's temporal possessions were for sale, they would have the money on hand to buy them? Moreover, the king is held to reward in a noble way those who serve him, who should be noblemen and the sons of noblemen. But this should be done according to their rank, so that he will put his own children above his servants. For it is neither fitting nor just that the servants become lords and their lords remain in poverty. Unless the king and his children are well provided with what they require, they must needs spoil the church and devour the people. Does it seem a just order that unworthy and low-born people have access to the king for furthering their affairs, while the nobles and prelates, when they come to the court for business and for the needs of their churches, are not granted an audience but are forced to remain out-

---

17. Augustine, *Ad fratres in eremo* 31 (PL 40:1292).

side among the poor, and after being catechized by people who are not really sent to them by the king, are compelled to go away without a useful reply? Alas! The king of France grants audience to his people three times a week and personally gives full justice to all who ask for it, while the noblemen of England cannot get their rights, though they ask for them with all their power. Moreover, if foreigners and especially the lords of Aquitaine who on behalf of England have lost their dominions and castles, come to this country for help, they are not received with honor, nor are they consoled or receive a pledge— they hardly meet with even a pleasant look or a kind word.

Further, is it a just order when the king of France has for his privy council seventy men chosen from every state of life, by whose advice all difficult matters are settled, while the king of England, though he has prudent and faithful councilors and officials, acts in like difficulties by the counsel of only one, so that the words of scripture "One works" have come true?[18] Nor is it proper or safe that all the keys of the kingdom should hang at the girdle of one woman.[19] Such a rule is against the advice of Jethro, who counseled Moses, the victor of the people, in Exodus 18[:21] as follows: "Provide out of all the people able men, such as fear God, in whom there is truth, and who hate avarice," and so on. Councilors should indeed be men, not boys, youths, and lewd people, since by rejecting the advice of the aged and following that of the young, Rehoboam lost his kingdom.[20] Neither should they be women, who are shrewd in looking after their own advantages; but men of uprightness, maturity, and holiness, for "the wicked man makes an unsteady work," Proverbs 11[:18]. Then follows [in Jethro's advice], "such as fear God." People from the middle and lower classes suffer punishments in the present life through which they are cleansed, but lords and counselors usually go scot-free, however many injuries they inflict on the church or the common weal. For this, they are left entirely to God's judgment. Hence, there should be a three-

---

18. 1 Corinthians 12:11: "All these things one and the same Spirit works." Probably a reference to John of Gaunt.

19. Literally "wife" (*ad vnius uxoris cingulum*). It is thought that Brinton is here referring to Alice Perrers, who was Edward III's influential mistress, but not his wife.

20. 1 Kings 12:1–11.

fold fidelity in counselors, namely, in their life, in their justice, and in their counseling: in their life with regard to themselves, in their justice with respect to the people, and in their counseling with regard to their lords, that they tell them the solid truth. And it follows further "who hate avarice." For unless counselors hate, nay, even destroy avarice, first in themselves, that they do not look out too much for their own advantage or even for that of their lords, and second in their lords, that the latter do not extort the goods of their subjects—unless counselors do this, they will burn so much with the fire of their greed that they cannot see the sun of justice. And so "the work of iniquity is in their hands," Isaiah 59[:6]. According to Bernard in a sermon, "a good deed speaks to the secret ears of God, for whether we sleep or are awake, whether we eat or drink or do something else, a good deed always calls out to God."[21]

"Therefore, while we have time, let us work good" [Galatians 6:10], that on the day of judgment we may be rewarded with the good workers for all eternity, when the Father will say to the Son, "Call the laborers and pay them their hire" [Matthew 20:8].

21. Perhaps Gregory, *Epistula 44* (PL 77:1154).

22

TO THE CLERGY

THIS SERMON BEARS NO RUBRIC that would indicate its occasion
or audience, but internal addresses as well as its entire subject matter
show that it was directed to priests who had the cure of souls; it may
therefore have been given at a synod or visitation. The manuscript
in which it uniquely occurs (see selection 8) also contains a copy of
Wimbledon's famous sermon *Redde rationem vilicationis tuae*, in one of
its two different Latin forms. The present selection shares Wimbledon's concern for priestly morals and accountability and his lament
at abuses, and beyond this uses the three questions on which *Redde rationem* is based and echoes its sense that the end of the world is near.
It is thus possible that *Take heed* is by Wimbledon also.

SOURCE:
Cambridge, University Library, MS Ii.3.8, fols. 134v–138v (A-42).

LITERATURE:
Wenzel, *Collections*, 175–81.

⌁

Take heed, watch, and pray, Mark 13:33.
  Our high priest, Jesus Christ, who came down from heaven that he
might offer himself on the altar of the cross as a living host to placate
God the Father for the redemption of mankind, when he had fulfilled
the mysteries of our redemption in his suffering, death, and resurrec-

tion, and was about to remove his bodily presence from this world, instituted and ordained his disciples as ministers and dispensers of grace in many forms in the Church Militant. These disciples he ordained as his ministers especially that they should rule his house and family, the church of the faithful; that they should faithfully guard his vineyard; that they should become vigilant shepherds of his flock; and that they should bring in the Lord's harvest. And—to touch on these things lightly—he chose and foreordained them to be faithful dispensers of all his mysteries in the church of the faithful so that they could say the words of the Apostle in [1] Corinthians 4[:1]: "Let a man so account of us as of the ministers of Christ, and the dispensers of the mysteries of God." He distinguished their orders, degrees, and conditions according to the distinction and diversity of the offices to which they had been sent and ordained. Reflecting on this, the Apostle says in Ephesians 4[:11]: "He gave some as apostles, and some as prophets, and others as evangelists, and yet others as pastors and doctors for the perfecting of the saints, for the work of the ministry, for the edifying of the body of Christ." But you, rectors of souls, priests, and pastors, to whom this sermon[1] is especially directed, are the successors of the aforesaid ministers and disciples of God, representing them in God's church and taking their places. From them and through them spiritual power in God's church has flown to you, namely, that of binding, loosing, and dispensing the church's sacraments to the faithful. As Christ's disciples, therefore, you have been set apart from the people, adopted to the holy mystery, chosen into the royal priesthood, and called out of darkness into God's marvelous light, so that of you can be truthfully said what is written in 1 Peter 2[:9]: "You are a chosen generation, a kingly priesthood, a holy nation, a purchased people, that you may declare his virtues, who has called you out of darkness into his marvelous light." You, my beloved, who have been adopted to have care and solicitude for the church, must understand what great and lofty ministries in the Church Militant have been entrusted to you, which are full of sacred mysteries. For you have been made, and have been set in God's church as watchmen, shepherds, and mediators—watchmen of the house of God, shepherds of the Lord's flock,

---

1. *Presens collacio.*

and mediators between men and God. Now, it is a watchman's office to take heed, a shepherd's to watch, and a mediator's to pray. Therefore, that all laziness in your office may be rejected and all diligence be sought, all you watchmen of the church, shepherds, and mediators between God and men must hear the words of our Savior which I have taken as the thema for this collation: **Take heed, watch, and pray.**

And in these words which I have thus introduced, all who have a cure in the church are admonished in three things—in the quoted words they are exhorted to be

provident,
solicitous,
and fervent.

Provident in their keen and discreet circumspection, in the words **Take heed;** solicitous in their vigilance in guarding the Lord's flock, in the following word **Watch;** and fervent through their holy devotion of prayer, in the final word **Pray. Take heed, watch, and pray.** It behooves the watchmen of the church to take heed with keenness; the shepherds of souls, to watch with zeal; and the mediators between God and men, to pray with earnestness. With regard to the first it is written in Ezekiel 3[:17]: "Son of man, I have made you a watchman to the house of Israel." With regard to the second, in Luke 2[:8]: "There were shepherds watching, and keeping the night watches over their flock." And with regard to the third, in Deuteronomy 5[:5]: "I was the mediator and stood between the Lord and you." The first quotation implies the keenness of the ministers of the church, the second, their zeal; and the third, the need or usefulness of their prayer.

[1]

The first main part is that churchmen must be provident in their keen and discreet watchfulness, as watchmen and eyes of the church. Beloved, you should know that churchmen are meaningfully understood to be the eyes and watchmen of the church on account of several properties of eyes that must morally belong to churchmen:

One is that eyes are set in the top part of one's body, the head;

another, that eyes weep in suffering with other parts of the body when they hurt;

and a third, that when the body grows old, the eyes fail and become weak.

[a]

The first property of bodily eyes is that they are set in the top part of the body, namely, the head. The same is true of the spiritual eyes of the church, namely, the churchmen, who morally speaking hold in God's church a higher dignity than the other members of the church, as a sign that, as they stand above others in the height of their dignity, they must surpass them in the holiness of their life. On which Gregory says in book 1 of his *Pastoral Rule,* chapter 4: "As a prelate or priest surpasses the members of his flock in the honor of his order, so must he transcend them in his moral virtutes."[2] Beloved, you should know that among all dignities that of a priest is the most noble and eminent. As much as an angel is beyond man, spirit beyond the body, heaven beyond earth, or sun beyond moon, so much is the dignity of a priest beyond any temporal dignity. Whence Chrysostom says in homily 5 of his work *On Matthew:* "A priest's dignity is the highest dignity if one keeps it immaculate." And he adds: "For if God esteems the souls of human beings more precious than all his goods, how much more believable is it that a priest is higher than all his other goods when he brings God the gain of these souls?"[3] It is commonly said that "The higher one's place, the holier must one's life be." Hence it certainly behooves priests of the church, on account of their priestly dignity, to have a clean conscience, a spotless life, and a holy behavior. A clean conscience with respect to God, a spotless life with respect to themselves, and a holy behavior with respect to their fellow human beings. You know that the more eminent one's dignity is, the more honorable one's standing, the more heavenly one's behavior, and the more spiritual one's actions—the more one must keep oneself from sin or vice, which drags down one's dignity, dishonors one's person, disgraces one's behavior, and frustrates one's due actions. For in holy scripture, priest are more often and more repeatedly commanded than lay people that, before all else, they be

2. Gregory, *Regula pastoralis* 2.3; also *Registrum* 1.25.
3. Pseudo-Chrysostom, *Opus imperfectum,* homily 51 (PG 56:928).

holy,
pure,
and spotless—

holy because they have been especially singled out to serve God; pure because they are the chosen vessels of God and have been ordained to cleanse the people; and scripture commands them to be spotless because they have been set as an example and put on show for the whole world—"we have been put on show in front of angels and men," [1] Corinthinans 4[:9].

It behooves God's priests to be holy. Thus it is written in Exodus 19[:22]: "The priests that come to me, let them be sanctified, lest I strike them." And in Leviticus priests of the Law are often commanded: "Be holy, because I am holy" [11:44, etc.]. It also behooves priests to be pure, because they are ordained to cleanse the people; whence Sirach 34[:4]: "Who can be made clean by the unclean?" as if to say, no one. And it behooves priests to be spotless, that is, without stain of sin. Whence the Apostle writes in Ephesians 1[:4]: "God chose us before the foundation of the world, that we should be holy and spotless in his sight"; and in [1] Maccabees 4[:42–43] it is written that Judas "chose priests without blemish, whose will was set upon the law of God, and they cleansed the holy places." Beloved, it is good for priests to be wholly spotless, for they deal with holy mysteries and are objects of reverence even to the angelic spirits. Even if perhaps they cannot be without spot on their fleece,[4] that is, without venial sin, let them nevertheless be without spot in their body, that is, without mortal sin. They must not be swollen with pride, livid with envy, troubled by anger, dry with spiritual sloth, grasping in avarice, stinking with lechery; rather, they must always have their desire set on the law of the Lord and be zealous for the souls and for the flock they rule, whom they have received to rule as patrons, to heal as physicians, and to instruct as teachers. In truth, if all our priests were such as I have just described, without doubt they would be feared by all the faithful of the church as their leaders, loved as their fathers, and worshipped as saints.

4. The preacher may be thinking of Genesis 30:32–43, Jacob's trick of getting lambs with spotted fleece.

But, alas! It seems to many that we have fallen into these unhappy times in which the lights of the church seem to have become darkness and the stars of heaven have fallen to the ground, as in the prophetic words of the gospel: "The stars shall fall from heaven," Matthew 24[:29]. For now the watchmen of the church, our priests, have become blind, shrouded in darkness, and befogged. Our stars, that is, our clerics, have fallen from the height of their clerical honor as from heaven to the earth, so much so that they know nothing but the earth, love only the earth, think of the earth, and speak of the earth, and thus are contentious, querulous, envious of another, and slandering each other. There is almost such confusion in God's church that the priests, who should be "the light of the world," according to Matthew 5[:14], are now in greater darkness than the lay people and dissolute in every kind of vices. Behold, nowadays there is no tonsure on their heads, no mark of religion in their garments, no modesty in their words, no moderation in their eating, no shame in their gestures, and no restraint in their actions. What more? Certainly, many of them are like lay people in acquiring temporal goods, like merchants in business dealings of any kind. They are like knights in the costliness of their garments and like women in the inconstancy of their minds. Such priests or clerics, indeed, hardly deserve to be called watchmen of the church, since they are all blind and in darkness, according to Isaiah 56[:10]: "His watchmen are all blind." Such men do not adorn God's church but rather disfigure it like monsters, as Bernard says in his treatise *On Consideration, to Pope Eugenius:* "A monstrous thing in God's church is the blind watchman, the mute herald, and the teacher without knowledge."[5]

Oh, beloved, that our watchmen would be so keenly watchful that they see the ugliness of their own sin in front of them, the calamity of other people's misery next to them, the sharp pain of everlasting punishment beneath them, and the reward of eternal glory above them! Then they would have eyes on every side, like the animals that John says he saw, in Revelation 4[:6]: "And the animals were full of

---

5. A sequence of such oxymorons following "monstruosa res" can be found in several twelfth-century spiritual writers, including Bernard, *De consideratione ad papam Eugenium* 2.17, but not this precise quotation.

eyes before and behind." For with his right eye man must look at his rewards, with his left at his punishments, with the one behind at the misery of his neighbors, and with the one in front at his own guilt. Moses in Deuteronomy 3[:27–28] prefigures this: "Go up to the top of Pisgah, and cast your eyes round about to the west, and to the north, and to the south, and to the east, and behold": in the east your eternal reward, which will always be rising and, as it were, be new; in the west your everlasting pain, in which all temporal happiness will set and fail; in the south the burning of your sin; and in the north the wretchedness of your neighbor.

[b]
The second property of the bodily eye is that it weeps as if suffering with other parts of the body when they hurt. Likewise, priests and those who have the cure of souls, who are the spiritual eyes of the church, must break out in tears of compassion when they see and reflect on the wretchedness of their flock, after the example of Paul, who wept with those who were weeping and was weak in compassion with the weak.[6] For he wrote of himself in 2 Corinthians 11[:29]: "Who is weak, and I am not weak? Who is burning, and I am not on fire?" as if to say, I suffer with everyone. Let therefore those rectors of souls and shepherds of the Lord's flock be ashamed whose eyes have become so dry that they cannot shed one tear for the people who are weak and perishing or want to have compassion with them. Nowadays the Gospel of Luke 10[:31–32] seems to come true, which says that when they see the wounded man, the priest and the Levite go by. Beloved, you must know that we priests have been set in the church as fathers, judges, and physicians. Like devoted fathers we must have pity on the misery of our children; like just judges we must have pity on the poor when they are oppressed; and like good physicians we must have pity on the sick in their illness, so that we may be all things to all men: a foot to the lame, an eye to the blind, a staff to the weak, and a shield to the oppressed. But there are many fathers in the Church Militant who nowadays have no compassion on their children. They could well be prefigured in the ostriches of Job 39[:16], of whom is said: "They

6. Cf. Romans 12:15 and 1 Corinthians 9:22.

are hardened against their young ones, as though they were not theirs." Similarly, there are many judges in the church who have no compassion on those who live under their rule. Of these the words of Ezekiel 22[:27–29] have come true: "The princes, the judges, in the midst of the people are like wolves ravishing the prey. They run after gains through covetousness. They oppress the needy and poor and afflict the stranger." Isidore says in his work *On the Greatest Good*, book 3, chapter 99: "The poor are more grievously torn to pieces by evil judges than by the most cruel enemies."[7] There are many spiritual physicians of the church who have no compassion with the infirm. For our physicians pay no attention to the well-being of the souls, nor do they give the infirm the salutary medicine required by the nature of their diseases or the need of their sins. Instead, now the physicians of souls certainly do just like unskilled physicians of the body: an unskilled physician thinks he can heal any disease of the body with a single plaster, and physicians of the soul think they can heal every spiritual sickness with a single remedy or a single kind of remedy. So they order only a single remedy against every vice and sin, and this, in the vernacular, is called "pain-money."[8] It can indeed be called "pain," for to many people it is very painful. But whether it is to be called a remedy I don't know. In truth I believe that, if it is a remedy, it should rather be called a laxative of the purse than a remedy for souls. So it seems that in God's church there is little compassion of fathers for their children, of princes for the oppressed, or of physicians for the sick. And thus the words of Bernard to Pope Eugenius, in book 3, have become true: "A donkey falls down, and there is someone to help him up; but a soul perishes and there is no one to cure it," morally speaking.[9]

[c]

The third property of the eye is that when the body grows old, the eyes fail and become weak. In similar fashion, morally speaking, as the Church Militant is growing old,[10] her eyes now seem to be grow-

---

7. Isidore, *De summo bono*, also called *Sententiae*, 3.52 (PL 83:724).

8. *Pena pecuniaria*, a gift of money as penance or for the forgiveness of sins.

9. Bernard, *De consideratione* 4.6 (PL 182:786).

10. For the motif of the church on earth or the world grown old, see *Collections*,

ing dark, since spiritual men and ecclesiastics now fall into spiritual
blindness more than they used to. For we see that our priests and clerics today are worse than lay people, so that the words of Isaiah 24[:2]
are proven true: "The priest shall be like the people." A biblical figure
occurs in Genesis 27[:1]: "Isaac was old, and his eyes were dim, and
he could not see." The state of the church today can be seen prefigured in the statue of Nebuchadnezzar, which is described in Daniel
2[:32–33]. Its head was of gold, its breast and arms of silver, its belly
and thighs of brass, but part of its feet [of iron and part of clay. This
statue was of gold through][11] wisdom, of silver through purity of life,
and of brass through eloquence. These three things are necessary to
a prelate and preacher: brightness of wisdom, purity of life, and clarity of eloquence. But one part of the feet, that is, of the lowest rank
of the clergy, namely, today's rectors, is of iron in their hardness of
heart, and another part is of clay in their carnal impurity. And thus it
goes with the church today, if one compares olden times with modern. Once Moses hid his face because the children of Israel could not
look at him for the brightness of his face, as is said in [2] Corinthians 3[:7]. But today our Moses, that is, the priests of the modern age,
could hide their faces because of their shame. For nowadays the children of Israel and the common faithful despise to look at them and
instead blush, at times wagging their heads[12] because they see nothing in them that is commendable. The priests of the church used to
be undefiled in holiness, adorned with virtues, gifted with heavenly
knowledge, grown perfect in the gravity of their manners, detached
from secular business, and set aside for use by God. But in our time
they do not deserve being called priests of God but rather priests of
Dagon, on account of their greed (see 1 Samuel 5), priests of Baal because of their pride (see Kings 28),[13] priests of Belphegor because of
their lust (see 1 Samuel 2),[14] or priests of Nanaea for their ignorance

---

177–79, and James M. Dean, *The World Grown Old in Later Medieval Literature* (Cambridge,
Mass.: Medieval Academy of America, 1997).

11. Evidently a line has dropped out of the text.

12. Cf. Matthew 27:39.

13. Perhaps 2 Kings 10:19, or rather Jeremiah 2:8?

14. Could the preacher have been thinking of Hophni and Phinehas, the sons of
Eli? See especially 1 Samuel 2:12, 22.

(see 2 Maccabees 1[:13]). So today, "as the world's evening declines"[15] and the church is growing old, the church can rightly say the words of the Psalmist: "The light of my eyes is not with me" [Psalm 37:11]. It is reported that when Archbishop Peter of Sens once came to the abbey of Clairvaux to visit a lay brother in that house who often fell into ecstatic raptures and to converse with him, he urged him to tell him about some vision he had seen in his ecstasy. And the lay brother replied: "I saw a lady beautiful of face and adorned with gold and gems, and as I was awed and admired her beauty, she said to me: 'What do you think, who am I?' I answered: 'I think you are the blessed and glorious Virgin, Our Lady.' And she said: 'No, my son, no. Look at my back.' When I looked at her back, I saw that she was decayed, stinking, and crawling with snakes, toads, and worms. 'Now,' she said, 'you can see that I am not the glorious Virgin. I am not the Virgin Mary but Mother Church. In my first state, as in my front, I was most beautiful and fittingly adorned in the apostles, martyrs, confessors, and virgins, but in my back, that is, in the last age, I have become decayed, corrupted, and full of shame in today's churchmen. My "silver is turned into dross" (Isaiah 1:[22]).'"[16]

[2]

The second part is that churchmen are admonished to watch solicitously in keeping the Lord's flock, as watchful shepherds of the sheep. This is indicated in the word **Watch**. Beloved, as it is proper for a watchman to be keenly watchful, so it should be proper for a shepherd to watch solicitously; as in Luke 2[:8]: "Shepherds were watching," etc. You should know that a shepherd's zeal about the Lord's flock consists in three things: shepherds must feed their flock with word, example, and temporal aid. Whence every shepherd of the church is held to be a lesson to his sheep in his salutary preaching; an example for them in his holy way of life; and a help for them in merciful giving. To prefigure this, Peter, the prince of the shepherds, was told three times: "Peter, feed my sheep," at the end of John [21:15–17]. But any

---

15. *Vergente mundi vespere*, from the hymn *Conditor alme siderum*, sung at vespers for the first Sunday in Advent.

16. This seems to be a version of the common vision of Lady World. See Tubach, no. 5390 (with literature) and 1051.

shepherd must feed his sheep with the word in three ways: with the word of correction about the judgment to be feared; with the word of exhortation about penance that is to be done; and with the word of consolation about the glory of heaven that is to be desired. For all of these the shepherds are held to watch: to preach about pains and punishments so that their flock may fear God; to call them to penance so that they may bring fruit; and to promise them heavenly goods so that they may love God above all things. And as they do this with a threefold word, so also with a threefold example. On which Gregory says in book 1 of his *Pastoral Rule,* chapter 14: "Who by virtue of his office is of necessity held to preach the highest things by word is also of necessity held to show forth the highest things by his example."[17] The shepherds of the church are held to feed the Lord's flock with their example of penitence, of humility and patience, and of charity and friendship. With their example of penitence, the shepherds must watch to feed the Lord's flock against the fleshly desire of pleasure seekers. With their example of humility and patience, they must feed the Lord's flock against the vainglory of the proud. And with their example of charity and friendship they must feed the Lord's flock against the cupidity of the greedy, in whom charity is so dead that they love no one but themselves. These three evils, namely, fleshly desires, pride, and avarice, are three kinds of seed that an enemy, the devil, has sown most abundantly in the Lord's field.[18] Wherefore the Lord's harvesters, such as priests and those who have the cure of souls, are held to watch solicitously in order to root up, cleanse, and destroy this cockle from God's field with their word and example, and to sow, set, and plant in God's people examples of penitence, charity, and patience, after the words of Jeremiah 1[:10]: "I have set you to root up, and to destroy, and to plant, and to build." With such examples the ancient shepherds fed God's people eagerly. And above them all, our Savior Jesus Christ fed them even more eagerly, who as an example of penitence suffered the pain of the cross; as an example of patience endured shameful reproaches; and as an example of charity gave his soul for his friends, after John 15[:13]: "Greater love than this has no man,

17. Gregory, *Regula pastoralis* 2.3.
18. Cf. Matthew 13:28.

that a man lay down his life for his friends." Our shepherd Jesus thus offered himself entirely as an example for us that he could say more truly than others what is written in John 13[:15]: "I have given you an example, that as I have done to you, so you do also." Beloved, as has already been said that a shepherd of the church must feed his flock with a threefold word and a threefold example, so is he likewise held to feed this flock with a threefold aid, namely, temporal, bodily, and spiritual. With temporal aid, by giving generous relief for the needs of his flock from his own possessions and the patrimony of the church; with bodily aid, that if need be he offer himself bravely to physical death for the sake of his flock; and with spiritual aid, that he eagerly intercede and pray to God for the salvation of his flock, so that in all these things the words of the Apostle in [2] Timothy 4[:5] can be applied to every shepherd of the church: "But be you vigilant, labor in all things, and do the work of an evangelist."

But it is to be feared, beloved, that nowadays many shepherds do not feed the flock of the church in these ways. Since the shepherds lack knowledge, they do not feed with the word; since they are fleshly, they do not feed with their example; and as covetous and greedy shepherds, they do not feed with their aid. It is to be lamented that with such shepherds the word of correction has become an easy forgiveness; the word of exhortation, silence; and the word of consolation, rebuke. About the flock of such shepherds one can say with Jeremiah 50[:6]: "The flock has become lost, for their shepherds have caused them to go astray." Truly, flocks are led astray by their shepherds when the nourishment of word, example, and aid which is owed the flock is withheld or taken away through the shepherds' lack of knowledge, pride, and negligence. Such are the shepherds and priests whom blessed Gregory rebukes in his *Homilies*, homily 7, where he says: "Behold, the whole world is full of priests, but rare is the laborer found in the Lord's harvest."[19] We, therefore, beloved, who carry out the cure of Christ's sheep, let us eagerly watch in our cure, first examining our own lives and then attending vigilantly to the salvation of our flock and prudently dispending the goods that have been en-

---

19. Gregory, *Homiliae in evangelia* 1.17.3.

trusted to us. Of these three things we churchmen especially will have to give a reckoning on the day of judgment. As Aquinas says on the Psalm [10:6] "The Lord tries the just and the wicked": "In the future judgment, the judge will ask first about yourself, how you have lived; second about those entrusted to you, how you have ruled; and third, about your goods, how you have spent them."[20] On the first question is written in Wisdom 6[:4]: "He who will examine your works and your thoughts." On the second, in Ezekiel 34[:10]: "Behold, I myself come upon the shepherds and will require my sheep," for then the words of Jeremiah 13[:20] will be said: "Where is the flock that is given you, your beautiful cattle?" And on the third, in Luke 16[:2]: "How is it that I hear this of you? Give an account of your stewardship!" Any wise shepherd of the church who reflects on this examination by his judge, if perhaps he has formerly been vigilant in order to oppress his flock, will from now on be vigilant about their edification, and he will perhaps apply to himself the words of Jeremiah 31[:28]: "As I have watched over them to pluck up, to throw down, to scatter, to destroy, and to afflict, so will I watch over them to build up and to plant them." So, since you, beloved, do not know when the Lord will come to demand an account from you, be vigilant in your cures, lest when he comes he find you asleep. **Watch.** Which was the second part.

[3]

The third main part was or is that, on account of their office, churchmen are held to be fervent in devout prayer, for they are mediators between God and men. Beloved, as it behooves a shepherd to watch eagerly that the flock entrusted to him is not diminished, that

20. The three questions are a commonplace that occurs in many medieval sermons and handbooks. It seems to have been begun by William Peraldus, in his sermon on the parable of the wedding feast, where a man without the proper wedding clothes is asked, "Friend, how did you come in here not having a wedding garment?" (Matthew 22:12; Peraldus, *Sermo 119* on the Sunday gospels). The Peraldus passage, which applies the three questions to prelates at the Last Judgment, was copied verbatim by Repingdon (RE-49) and its derived cycle (N-5). It occurs in expanded form in Felton (FE-26) and similarly in other sermons, including A-41 and A-42. Wimbledon's famous sermon *Redde rationem vilicationis tuae* (a copy appears as A-48) uses the three questions as the topic of its first part and applies them to all three estates (priests, knights, and the laity).

it is multiplied, and that it is given back to its lord, so it behooves a mediator between God and men to soften God's wrath by his prayers, to appease the offense done to God, and to reconcile souls to God. All and every one of these, the mediators between God and men, that is, devout churchmen, carry out every day through the service of their devout prayer. So did Moses, Aaron, the prophets, and all the holy fathers as mediators between God and men in their prayer appease the offense done to God, reconcile souls with God, and procure his grace and glory, as the scriptures of both the Old and the New Testament report and show in many places. Therefore, you priests of God, to all and every one of whom has been enjoined by virtue of your office to offer a sacrifice of prayer to God the Father on behalf of God's people, persist in your devotion and prayer, watchfully carrying out the command of scripture which admonishes and says in the first letter of Peter 4[:7]: "Watch in prayers." "Watch therefore and pray," Matthew 26[:41]. It is to be feared, beloved, that nowadays the hearts of the priests and ministers of holy church are so dried up through the pestilence of pride, ambition, and greed, and have become so arid and cold for lack of the dew of grace and devotion, that their prayers, petitions, and shouts to God seem to be inaudible. It is written that "God does not hear the sinners" [John 9:31]. Bernard writes to Pope Eugenius, in book 3: "Does not ambition wear out the threshold of the apostles[21] more than prayer?"[22] as if to say, It does indeed. But how can there be devotion in God's church where so much ambition is the rule? And in the same book it says: "You see how all ecclesiastical zeal is aimed at gaining some honorable position. Everything is given to preferment, nothing to holiness and devotion."[23] Beloved, priests and ministers who are thus ambitious and arid through their lack of devotion do not deserve to be called mediators between God and men, as their mediation provokes God's wrath rather than elic-

---

21. *Limina apostolorum,* the papal curia in Rome, where the chief apostles (Peter and Paul) lay buried. In St. Bernard's words, visits to their tombs, i.e., the curia, were made more in order to gain an ecclesiastical advancement than for true devotion, as observed in a pilgrimage.

22. Bernard, *De consideratione* 3.5.

23. Ibid., 4.5.

its his forgiveness. On this, Gregory says in his *Pastoral Rule*, book 1, chapter 10: "When one who is in disfavor is sent to intercede with an angry person, the mind of the latter is provoked to greater severity."[24] And the Lord speaks against them when he says in Isaiah 1[:15]: "When you stretch forth your hands, I will turn away my eyes from you; and when you multiply your prayers, I will not hear; for your hands are full of blood," that is, your deeds are full of sins.

It is to be greatly feared, beloved, that such priests and shepherds of souls, who now are the first, will then be the last; they who now are fishermen of men will in the future be thrown out with the bad fish; they who now are herdsmen of sheep will in the future be numbered among the goats;[25] and they who now are laborers in the Lord's harvest will then, it must be feared, be burnt with the chaff.[26] For the love of Jesus Christ, therefore, let us priests, who have been accepted to carry the burden of the ecclesiastical cure without our deserts, who have received the name of priest and shepherd against our merit, and who preside over the flocks and sheep of Christ, let us fear that terrible sentence spoken in Wisdom 6[:6]: "A most severe judgment shall be for them who bear rule." And let us in prayer say with blessed Gregory the devout words that are written in his *Homilies on the Gospels*, in homily 17: "Just God, who have willed to call us as shepherds or priests in your people, grant, we pray, that what we are said to be by human speech we may truly be in your eyes."[27] Which God may grant us, who in the perfect Trinity lives and reigns. Amen.

---

24. Gregory, *Regula pastoralis* 1.10. 25. Cf. Matthew 25:33.
26. Cf. Matthew 3:12.
27. Gregory, *Homiliae in evangelia* 1.17 (PL 76:1149).

23

VISITATION OF A MONASTERY

LIKE THE CHURCHES IN A DIOCESE, monasteries were required to be visited regularly by the bishop or a religious from another house of the order. During the visitation, the visitator would inquire about the congregation's spiritual and moral life and about such external features as the performance of the liturgy, the sufficiency of provisions, availability of service books, the state of the buildings, etc. As a rule, the visitation began with a sermon preached by the visitator or a person delegated for this function.

The following anonymous sermon is uniquely preserved in a fifteenth-century monastic sermon collection from Worcester Priory (see above, selection 9). Besides the constant balanced triads, it shows such characteristic features of a traditional monastic style (going back to the twelfth century) as a complex, highly wrought syntax (for instance, in the opening sentences of the second paragraph and note 4) and punning (at notes 16–17).

SOURCE:

Worcester, Cathedral Library MS. F.10, fols. 248vb–250va (W-130).

LITERATURE:

Wenzel, *Collections,* 257–63 and 151–58.

﹏

Let us see if the vineyard flourishes, Canticles 7[:12].

Reverend fathers and lords, three things in particular are required in a preacher of God's word: wisdom in his speech, pleasingness, and strength in virtue or grace. Wisdom is required in a preacher so that he may teach those who hear him; pleasingness, to attract them; and strength in virtue or grace, to be able to call them from evil and lead them back to the good. For these three things it is necessary that a preacher is fluent and eloquent, for according to Augustine, in book 4 of his book *On Christian Doctrine*, chapter 11, an orator must speak in such a fashion that he teaches through his wisdom, delights through his sermon's pleasingness, and molds his audience through his virtuous strength or grace. And Augustine adds to this: teaching is a matter of necessity; delighting, of sweetness; but molding the audience; of victory.[1] But as I, who am to announce the word of God, lack these things, I am compelled to cry to the Lord and say with the prophet, "Ah, ah, ah, Lord God, I do not know how to speak, for I am a child," Jeremiah 1[:6]. In this authority three failings are noted with respect to me. First a lack of knowledge, for "I do not know." Second my lack of pleasingness in words, for "I do not know how to speak." And third, my lack of virtuous strength, for "I am a child." Therefore, aware of my weakness and insufficiency, I find no other help than to place my hope wholly in my God, who kindly inspired his servant Moses, whom he was about to send to the people in Egypt and who made excuses because he had no eloquence, as is told in Exodus 4[:10]. God said to Moses, as is reported in the same chapter: "Who made man's mouth? or who made the mute and the deaf, the seeing and the blind? did not I? Go therefore and I will be in your mouth: and I will teach you, and you will speak" [:11–12]. Him I therefore invoke at the beginning of this collation and pray that he, who has created me deaf and mute, may be with me in this work, giving me strength of virtue, and that he may be in my mouth granting me pleasingness of speech, and that he may teach me what to say by pouring wisdom into me. And I commend to your devout prayers, etc.

Let us see if the vineyard flourishes, as before. The heavenly husbandman—mover and measure of the whole sublunary world and of the eternal mansion—who from the first light until evening pours in-

---

1. Augustine, *De doctrina christiana* 4.12.

crease into his creation, once planted a choice vineyard, namely, the saintly monastic estate, in a fruitful place, in the vines of our holy fathers in Egypt. Later, saving it with his right hand from the hostile wolf's rapaciousness, he moved and transferred it to the ends of the entire Christian world.[2] The little plants of this monastic vineyard strengthened the soil of the Militant Church's garden so much that, before all other orders, it buds forth in its vines, blossoms in its branches, and brings fruit in its grapes without let. It is frequently bound up with the ties of obedience, diligently cleaned by giving up property, deeply dug up through mortification of one's flesh, and propagated through salutary rules and counsels. Therefore, at the beginning of our visitation, let us diligently inquire and **see if this vineyard flourishes.** Let us see if it has been planted with enough shoots, if the plants have been fenced in as necessary, if the fenced-in vineyard is being diligently cleaned by the vinicultor, whether after cleaning it is cared for by its vigilant guard and preserved from the attacks of the wild wolf, so that in its time it may overflow with abundant fruit where before hardly any flowers were growing. Thus, let us first, with careful diligence, **see if the vineyard flourishes.**

In these words, briefly, three things are shown:[3]

the work of solicitous visitation, in **"Let us see"**;
the beauty of a monastic congregation, in **"vineyard"**;
and the sweet smell of good conduct, in **"flourishes."**

2. These two introductory sentences—in the Latin text a single one—are a good example of the complex monastic style of the later Middle Ages: "Celestis quidem agricola, metrum et mensura tocius ordinis sublunaris et etheree mansionis, a luce prima in vesperam sue fabrice influens incrementa, vineam quandam electam in loco vberi, sanctam scilicet religionem monasticam, in vitibus sanctorum patrum nostrorum primo in Egipti partibus plantatam ad horam quam postea ab inimici lupi rapacitate sua dextera adquisitam in tocius Christianissimi [*read* Christianismi?] terminos transtulit et transduxit." For other examples, see *Collections*, 400–402, and Wenzel, *Macaronic Sermons: Bilingualism and Preaching in Late Medieval England* (Ann Arbor: University of Michigan Press, 1994), 128–29.

3. The preacher gives two separate divisions. The first is technically a *divisio ab intus*, dividing the *words of the thema* into three parts and confirming the first two with different scriptural quotations. This is followed by a *divisio ab extra*, in which the preacher takes the *notion* of the monastic community, imaged as a vineyard, and divides it into several features. This second division is then used "for the further development."

If it **flourishes,** the work of solicitous visitation must diligently look into the state of the brethren, so that we may **see;** the beauty of the monastic congregation must sprout abundantly to produce fruit, in **the vineyard;** and the sweet smell of good conduct must spread as a good example, **if it flourishes.** On the first it is written in Genesis 37[:14]: "See (in Shechem) if all things are well with your brothers and bring me word again." Shechem means, etc. On the second is written in Canticles 2[:13]: "The vines in flower yield their sweet smell." And so, that our work may come to an end, let us see if beauty is shown in the vineyard and sweet smell found in the blossom if it flourishes. Let us start our business and **see if it flourishes.**

But for the further development of this short sermon, we should briefly notice that:

this religious vineyard is to be protected with a hedge, that is, by its officials;[4]

it is to be planted or extended with virtuous vines, namely, with cloistered, that is, contemplative, monks;

and third it is to be cleansed of evil rot, which must be inspected by superiors and visitators.

Thus the vineyard must flourish in the contemplative monks through their willing obedience, holy life, and keeping the discipline of their Rule, through sufficient relief in what is necessary, and through reform of excesses that need to be corrected. And so, the vineyard must stand strong in the active monks, blossom in the contemplatives, and give forth a sweet smell in the superiors. And thus, by carrying out the business of this visitation, not hastily and prematurely, not in ignorance and impropriety, but with diligence and discretion, **let us see if the vineyard flourishes.**

---

4. "Officials" here refers to the officers or obedientiaries of a monastery, such as cellarer, kitchener, guest-master, sacrist, and so on. The preacher speaks of three segments of a monastic community: its officials or active monks, its contemplative monks, and the superiors or *prelati,* such as the abbot or prior.

[1]

First, for my first main part, I said: let us see if the vineyard that is to be protected with a hedge, that is, active (monastic) officials, is flourishing in

> their honest conduct,
> their faithful administration,
> and their fervent devotion.

For as "the world is seated in the wickedness" [1 John 5:19] of avarice, the sower of that evil, the "boar out of the wood" [Psalm 79:14], is trying to lay waste our vineyard, the religious life, in its temporal goods and bring it to ruin. Unless it is guarded by circumspect and provident officials as by a hedge, the grasping hand of the world will, in armed theft, not only carry off the goods of this vineyard in its leaves and branches but take away its livelihood in the roots. Therefore, you officials must hedge in this vineyard and throw out the enemies of Christ and the church like thorn bushes. And against the foxlike deceit of your enemies you must prudently devise, set up, and prepare for yourselves such snares and stratagems as may be necessary. Hence we say, striking your hearts, "Catch us the little foxes that destroy the vines," Canticles 2[:15]. According to the Philosopher in book 12 of *On Animals*, the sweet smell of a vineyard in bloom and bearing fruit antagonizes all poisonous animals, so when it blossoms and bears fruit, snakes flee from it and toads cannot bear its fragrance.[5] Hence, if holy and devout officials flourish in this world in purity of life, and if they bring fruit in their actions through good religious behavior, the poisonous tongue will stop wagging, the evil snake of scandal will flee, and the smell of a good reputation will spread most sweetly, so that one can finally say about such officials what is written in Sirach 24[:23]: "Like the vine I have brought forth a pleasant odor, and my flowers are the fruit of honor and riches." Let us inquire about such things more closely and see if **this vineyard flourishes.**

Second, I said that we want to see if this religious vineyard flourishes in its officials through their faithful administration. The author

5. See Bartholomew, *De proprietatibus rerum* 17.180 (p. 953).

of *On the Properties of Things* writes that a vine that is planted in moist or rich soil is lush with branches and leaves but only rarely brings forth blossoms and fruit.[6] Thus our officials: when they grow in too much richness of earthly desires or in too much moisture of carnal lust and wantonness, they do not blossom or bring fruit in their vowed poverty but rather burgeon with forbidden things, like Achan, who took "a scarlet garment exceeding good, and two hundred shekels of silver, and a golden rule" against the anathema at Jericho [cf. Joshua 7], or like Ananias and Sapphira, who hid the money from what they had sold [Acts 5], and in the end they receive divine vengeance, like that barren fig tree that spouted leaves but had no fruit [Matthew 21:19]. An official must carry out evenhanded justice to others and live a strict life in himself, and so he will bring lots of fruit. Whence the prophet says in Psalm 91[:13]: "The just shall flourish like the palm tree." According to Augustine on the same Psalm, in the palm tree we can find bitterness in the rind, beauty in the branches, and abundant fruit in its top.[7] Therefore, Christ says to such officials, in Matthew 20[:4]: "Go you also into my vineyard." Go, that is, in faithful administration, a strict way of life, and overabundant fruit bearing. And as we intend to inquire if this is the case, **Let us see if the vineyard flourishes.**

In the third place I said that we want to see if this vineyard flourishes in its officials through their fervent devotion. Albert says that a vine blossoms and bears fruit well in warm and dry soil.[8] In the same fashion, when an official blossoms with warm devotion, is dried out in his restrained desires, and shines forth in fruitful charity, then it becomes clear that such a person flourishes in his vineyard, and he may say the words of Canticles 2[:1]: "I am a flower of the field, and a lily of the valleys." A flower of the field, according to Avicenna, is graceful of stem, and red in color (because of its blood-colored corolla), and adorned in its leaves.[9] Just so a person of religion must be flex-

---

6. Ibid.

7. Augustine, *Enarrationes in Psalmos,* Psalm 91, 13.

8. Presumably the Dominican theologian Albert the Great (d. 1280), who wrote a good deal on natural science.

9. Avicenna (d. 1037) was an Arabic physician and theologian translated into Latin and widely studied for his medical knowledge as well as his theological views.

ible in his humble stem, red in his devotion of fervent charity, and well adorned with the leaves of his five senses. A lily of the valley naturally grows among rocks, yet it remains unharmed among them; thus, though a person of religion should often communicate with his students, the hardness of the world will not be able to hurt the flower of his devotion. Then the diligent and solicitous visitator can say the words of Canticles 6[:10]: "I went down into my garden to see the fruits of the valleys, and to look if the vineyard had flourished and the pomegranates budded." I went down, I say, into the garden of this visitation that I may see the fruits of the valleys, that is, the officials, with respect to their honorable way of life—that was the first part; and to see if the vineyard flourished, in the faithful administration—the second part; and to see if the pomegranates budded, with fervent devotion—the third part. That we may inquire about these three things with certainty, **Let us see if the vineyard flourishes.** In these words are indicated the diligence of the visitators, in **Let us see;** the growth of the active monks, in **vineyard;** and the pleasingness of the contemplatives, in **flourishes.**

[2]

For my second main part I said that we want to see if this vineyard is flourishing in observing the discipline of our Rule. Everyday experience teaches us that a vine is small, and the more flowers, grapes, and fruit it carries, the more it gives and bends down to the ground. So it is also with good men of religion. The more gifts of virtues they possess, the more they are ready to obey and willing to humble themselves before their superiors. Blessed Bernard writes about this memorably in a sermon on St. Andrew as follows: "He who is perfectly obedient knows no delay in carrying out the will of the one who bids him."[10] Hence we efficiently carry out—

first the precepts of the gospel and others to which we are obligated,

then the commands of our superiors, in everything that is licit and honorable,

---

10. Probably Bernard, *Sermones de diversis* 41.7.

so that we may truly say what is written in Exodus 24[:7]: "All things that the Lord has spoken we will do, we will be obedient." The author of the book *On the Nature [of Things]* teaches that water lilies and heliotropes open their leaves when the sun rises, but when it sets they close them, and in this way they follow the course of the sun.[11] In the same way, a true monk must open all the powers of his mind to do his work when his superior bids him, and when he forbids it, he must close his desire to transgress, and thereby obey his superior in all things, so that he may flourish through his ready obedience "as the flower of roses in the days of the spring, and as the lilies that are on the brink of the water" Sirach 54[:8]. And as we wish to inquire about the good will of the cloistered monks, **Let us see if the vineyard flourishes** in them, the vineyard of religion, through their whole life and pure innocence. Doctor De Lyra, in his commentary on Numbers, reports that the ministers of Solomon had their garments distinguished by different flowers according to their several offices, by which one could at once perceive the office of each minister.[12] So truly, whatever obedience and humility is within our monks must flourish outside in the purity of their exemplary action, so that they may not only acquire merit for themselves through their humility but become a shining light for their neighbor through the external purity of their holy life. Palladius, in his book *On Agriculture,* says that when an almond tree is carefully cultivated and planted in a vineyard, it bears more fruit than in other gardens or in the fields.[13] For according to Isidore, it blossoms more abundantly than all the other trees.[14] Thus, without doubt, when the garden of the cloister is tilled with the hoe of the observances of the Rule, by offering the tree of one's self with its root, one bears fruit that is more pleasing to God, burgeons more than [when living] in the world, and offers God pleasing first fruits in the flowers of one's holy way of life. Of such a one is written in the last chapter of Ecclesias-

11. Pliny, *Historia naturalis* 2.109; 18.252; 22.57; Isidore, *Etymologiae* 17.9.37.

12. The Fransciscan Nicholas de Lyra (or of Lyre; d. 1340) was the most learned biblical exegete of the fourteenth century, whose biblical commentaries are collected in his *Postillae,* first printed in 1471–72.

13. Perhaps Palladius, *De agricultura* 2.6.

14. Isidore, *Etymologiae* 17.7.24, with "earlier" instead of "more abundantly."

tes [12:5]: "The almond tree shall flourish," namely, in the purity of
a holy life; "and the locust shall be made fat," in giving an example
of good acts. For thus "with the fruit of her hands she has planted a
vineyard," last chapter of Proverbs [31:16]. And thus, **Let us see if** in
the purity of the cloistered monks and their holy way of life **the vineyard flourishes.**

Second I said that we want to see if this vineyard is flourishing
in the contemplatives by their eagerness to observe the discipline of
the Rule. In olden times the elders of the cloister together with the
younger monks made the vineyards and vines of books with their own
hands. Many of them wrote many books, as they took advantage of
the time between the canonical hours and devoted the times set aside
for the rest of their bodies to writing codices. From their labors, until this very day, some sacred treasuries shine forth in many monasteries, full of many books that give the knowledge of salvation to those
who wish to study them, and a pleasing light to the paths of others. Oh happy foresight, so useful to their untold future offspring, to
which no planting of shrubs, no sowing of grain can be compared!
There has not been such a number of men armed with these who in
their times were great hunters of the spiritual foxes, men who now
have left their nets to others that they might catch the evil little foxes that do not cease to demolish the flourishing vineyards of our order. But alas, nowadays, it is said, booze is sought and tossed in one's
stomach while books are despised and thrown away.[15] And thus, many
men's study today lies in emptying cups, not emending codices.[16] The
vineyard of study is left desolate, just like another "field of the slothful man" and another "vineyard of the foolish man" [Proverbs 24:30].
In Job 15[:32–33] it is said: "His hands shall wither away. He shall be
blasted as a vine when its grapes are in the first flower, and as an ol-
ive tree that casts forth its flower." Let it not be thus, reverend sirs,
but rather as the Wise Man says in Sirach 39:19, "Send forth flow-

15. I have tried to imitate the Latin wordplay here: "Liber Bachus respicitur et in
ventrem trahicitur, liber codex despicitur et a manu reicitur." The pun rests on *Liber*,
the Latin name for Bacchus, and *liber*, i.e., book.

16. The sentence continues the punning: "Calicibus epotandis non codicibus
emendandis indulget hodie studium plurimorum."

ers, as the lily, and yield a sweet smell, and bring forth leaves in grace, and praise with canticles, and bless the Lord in all his works." For lilies have sallow roots, white blossoms, green leaves, and sweet-smelling sap and seeds. Just so monks should be sallow in the fruitful recitation of scripture, green in composing books, and sweet-smelling in acquiring knowledge, so that the words of Ezekiel 17[:6] may apply to them: "It became a vine, and grew into fruit-bearing branches, and shot forth sprigs." "It became a vine," green through their ready obedience, with respect to the first part of the verse; "it grew into fruit-bearing branches," white through their holy life, with respect to the second; "and it shot forth sprigs," sweet-smelling through their eager pursuit of discipline, with respect to the third. Therefore, with watchful skill **Let us see if the vineyard flourishes.** Behold, the work of investigators, in "let us see"; the dwelling of monks, in "the vineyard"; and the blossoming of good habits, in "flourishes."

[3]
For my third main point, and now more briefly, I said that we want to see if this religious vineyard is flourishing in its superiors, in:

their caring attention to their monks,
the sufficient provision with what is needed,
and the discreet guidance in correcting their defects.

Regarding the first, the vineyard must be carefully cultivated; regarding the second, it must be frequently visited; and regarding the third, it must be purged of what is superfluous. A superior must, with provident circumspection and circumspect providence, cultivate the vineyard that has been entrusted to his care, by watering what is dry, cutting off what is rotten, and strengthening what is weak. The dry ones he must water with special zeal. The faltering ones he must correct by means of the Rule. Let him correct those who have failed with the whip of discipline,[17] refresh those who are ignorant with the food of knowledge, and protect those who are innocent from ruin. In this way he will glue together what has been broken, straighten out what

---

17. The Latin *disciplina* can mean not only "teaching" and "discipline" but also the concrete practicing of penance: scourging or self-mortification.

is crooked, and bring to peaceful rest what is at strife. Whence he is commanded, as was the angel in Revelation 14[:18]: "Thrust in your sharp sickle and gather the clusters of the vineyard of the earth, because the grapes thereof are ripe." The vineyard of the earth is harvested when the superiors hasten to cherish it and cultivate it devoutly by giving caring attention to their monks. Nonetheless, **let us see** with respect to still other things **if the vineyard flourishes.**

I also said that we want to see if this vineyard flourishes in the superiors in their providing sufficiently what is needed. In the first chapter of Canticles is written about the superior: "A cluster of cypress is my love to me, in the vineyards" [1:13]. According to natural philosophers, the seed of the cypress is white and sweet-smelling, and when it is cooked in oil, it makes a delicious ointment that comforts and restores.[18] Thus must the superior's diligence bring with its ointment the salve of pious help and comfort, so that to those who lead a good life he may not use a cautery but a salve, not a stinging plaster but rather a comforting confection. So Christ commands him in Matthew 21[:28]: "Son, go and work in my vineyard"—"son," meaning, through imitation, "go" to a pious work, and "work" through salutary relief in what is necessary. And pious devotion stirs us to **see if the vineyard flourishes.**

Third, I said, and this is the end, that we want to see if this religious vineyard is flourishing in its superiors through their discreet guidance in correcting defects. Many weak persons are more efficiently drawn to take upon them the yoke of observing the Rule by gentleness of compassion rather than the steel or sword of austerity. And indeed, if a superior looks at the innermost secrets of his own weakness, he will show himself more gentle in correcting the failings of others. This matter is heeded in canon law: distinction 45, canons *Licet, Disciplina,* and *Recedite;* and distinction 50, canon *Ponderet.*[19] Thus, "with regard to their monks, superiors must have mercy that gives

18. Bartholomew, *De proprietatibus rerum* 17.25.

19. *Decretum,* distinctio 45, canons 4 or 6, 9, and 16; distinctio 50, canon 14 (Friedberg, *Corpus iuris canonici,* 1:161 or 162, 163, 166; 182). The remainder of the paragraph quotes from or paraphrases Dist. 45, cc. 9–10, 14 (Friedberg, *Corpus iuris canonici,* 1:163–66).

counsel with justice, and discipline that punishes with piety." For that reason, when a man is half dead, he is given wine and oil, so that through wine his festering wounds may be cleansed and through oil his great pain softly eased.[20] A superior, therefore, must show stinging discipline, the wine, with which he must mix the softness of well-meaning sympathy, the oil. Thus severity must be mixed with leniency, that from both together a well-proportioned mixture may come, so that the monks under his care are not harmed by great austerity nor grow slack by too great leniency. Thus, in judging rightly, the superior holds a balance in his hand, with justice in one scale and mercy in the other, so that in his just deliberation he may correct some actions in equity, and allow others to the delinquent in mercy. From this it is clear that neither mild leniency without severity, nor righteous zeal without mildness, should be found in a superior. Let then the rigor of discipline rule mildness, and let mildness in speech clothe the rigor, and so one is commended by the other, so that strictness is not rigid, nor sympathy remiss. Thus in canon law.

Let then the superiors say the words of Canticles 2[:15]: "Our vineyard has flourished"—through their caring attention to their monks, with regard to the first point; their sufficient provision with what is needed, with regard to the second; and their discreet guidance in correcting their defects, with regard to the third. Of this vineyard is written in Matthew 21[:33]: "There was a man, a householder," add: Christ; "who planted a vineyard, and made a hedge round about it, and dug in it a press, and built a tower, and let it out to husbandmen." The hedge stands for the active officials to whom the vineyard is entrusted that the foxes do not steal its grapes, as was said in the first main part. The building of the tower indicates the contemplative monks, who contemplate God daily with devout prayers, and this in the second main part. The press stands for the superiors, in whose ruling the grapes of the entire vineyard are prudently trodden and their juice carefully pressed out, and this in the third main part. For all of these is written in Ezekiel 28[:26]: "They shall build houses," that is, the active monks; "and shall plant a vineyard," the superiors; "and shall

---

20. Cf. Luke 10:34.

dwell with confidence," the contemplatives—here with grace and in the future in glory.[21] May he who lives and reigns without end give us this glory. Amen.

21. In this final paragraph the preacher has devised a twofold summation of the sermon, in a figure called *unitio* or *connexio partium*. The quotation of Ezekiel 28:26 verbally unites the three main parts of the sermon, while the quotation of Matthew 21:33 unites the three sections of main part 3. This sophisticated rhetorical figure was already used at the ends of the preceding main parts.

24

ENCLOSURE OF A NUN

THIS SERMON HAS NO RUBRIC, but as the text makes clear, it was preached at the enclosure of Alice Huntingfield in a religious order. If the phrase "in today's epistle" at its head refers to the reading in the sanctoral cycle (rather than a Mass for the enclosure of a nun), the sermon could have been given on the feast of the Conversion of St. Paul, January 25. The anonymous preacher's punning on the name of the woman to be enclosed raises this rhetorical device to heights beyond what one normally finds in funeral and academic sermons (cf. 20 and 25), and his use of Ovid as well shows him to be an unusually learned and witty speaker.

SOURCE:
Cambridge, Jesus College, MS 13, part 5, fols. 79v–83v (J/5-18).

LITERATURE:
Wenzel, *Collections*, 140–45.
Wenzel, "The Classics in Late-Medieval Preaching," in *Mediaeval Antiquity*, ed. Andries Welkenhuysen, Herman Braet, and Werner Verbeke (Leuven: Leuven University Press, 1995), 127–43, at 135–42.

❧

Enter the city, Acts 9[:7], and in today's epistle.

My reverend sirs, Aegidius in his book *The Rule of Princes*, book 3, part 1, chapter 2, says that a material city is set up for three purposes:

to live, to live well, and to live virtuously, and the most important is to live well and happily. The same is said in the same work, book 3, part 2, chapter 32.[1] The first purpose is to live. Everyone in this world lives either without law, and in this case he lives like a beast—for a human being who is not ruled by positive law or the law of reason is counted among the beasts, according to Boethius, *The Consolation of Philosophy*;[2] or he lives above the law, and in this case he lives like a god and is called a divine person—for God and virtues are not subject to laws; or he lives according to the law of princes and magnates, and in this case he lives a citizen's life like a human being. And since this last way of living is more often found in a city than elsewhere, life in a city is a more authentic way of life. Second, the city was set up in order to live well. To live well as a human being requires many things, such as food and clothes and other things that are necessary to human beings. These are more readily and easily found in a city rather than elsewhere, for if a person cannot find food and clothes in rural villages, he will find them quickly in cities. Third, the city was set up in order to live virtuously. For the greatest virtue is that a human being is governed and ruled by reason and virtues. Through what he observes in his experience, through good communication between one man and another, and through an exemplary life, a person will perceive and learn many reasonable rules in a city which he would not perceive if he lived by himself in the country. Since, then, material cities of this world were established mainly for the sake of living virtuously, this applies even more to the city of holy religion, which in scripture is called a city of strength. For as the Wise Man says in Proverbs 18[:19]: "A brother who is helped by his brother is like a strong city." Yet a city would not be strong unless it be strong in virtues. For Augustine says, in book 1 of *The City of God*, chapter 23, that a city's strength lies more in virtues than in men's physical strength. For that reason, he says, "that wise man Scipio forbade to build theaters in the city of Rome, for he did not judge that commonwealth to be a happy one whose walls were standing while its morals were falling."[3] As a sign of this,

---

1. Aegidius (Giles of Rome, d. 1316), *De regimine principum* 3.1.2 and 3.2.32.

2. A general teaching of Boethius's *De consolatione philosophiae.*

3. Augustine, *De civitate Dei* 1.33. Notice the punning: "pocius stat in virtutibus quam viris" and "stantibus moenibus, ruentibus moribus."

the commentator on Fulgentius, book 2, says that the city of Troy was not captured as long as the goddess Pallas, who is the goddess of reason and virtue, stayed in the city; but as soon as she was carried off, the city was captured.[4] And therefore it is said in the Psalm [126:1]: "Unless the Lord keep the city, he watches in vain who keeps it." Since, then, in scripture the city of religion is called strong, and since it would not be strong unless it be strong in virtues, it necessarily follows that it is virtuous.

And that this city is very virtuous and perfect, I show in the following way. St. Thomas [Aquinas], in part 2–2 of his *Summa*, question 87, affirms a threefold perfection.[5] The first is that God is loved as much as he is lovable, and this love is not possible for any creature but belongs only to God. The second kind of perfection is that one's affect in all its ability always, in actuality, tends to God; and this perfection is not possible for any creature in this life but only in heaven. The third kind of perfection is that everything that goes against the motion of love toward God be excluded with all one's power. And this perfection is twofold: one is to shun mortal sin, which directly destroys charity and the love of God. To this perfection every human being is held, out of necessity for his salvation. The second kind of this perfection is to shun, for the love of God, all those things that are not sinful and can coexist with charity, such as temporal goods, marriage, and honors, with which charity can coexist. This is the highest degree of perfection that in this kind is possible to creatures. Now, since men and women in the religious state not only shun sin but also those things that may become an occasion for sin and diminish love in their hearts, and voluntarily bind themselves to Christ through a solemn vow, these hold the highest degree of perfection of this kind in this world. Moreover, it is a greater virtue to observe both Christ's commandments and his counsels than to observe only one of these. But the religious observe both, others do not. Therefore, the state of

---

4. While the Palladium, an image sent by Pallas (Athena, or Minerva) to Troy, remained in the city, Troy was safe. The image was stolen, and Troy fell. Cf. Dionysius of Halicarnassus, *Roman Antiquities* 1.68.

5. Thomas Aquinas, *Summa theologiae*, 2-2, q. 24, art. 8, resp., and art. 9. See also 2-2, q. 186.

the religious is more perfect than that of other people. And thus, in order to show that perfection exists mainly in the city of religion, Grosseteste offers the conceit that the city of the religious is neither in heaven nor on earth but between the two. For in as much as one is lifted from the earth through the contemplative life, one approaches heaven; and in as much as one is engaged on earth in the active life, one remains on earth. Hence Jeremiah prophesied about this city, in chapter 30[:18–19]: "The city shall be built in her place, and out of her shall come praise and the voice." For St. Thomas says, as above, question 433,[6] that the religious life directly does what is to God's honor, and therefore it takes first place among the other moral virtues.

A figure of all that has been said we have in blessed Paul, in today's epistle. For there we read about him that, when he traveled to Damascus to persecute Christ's servants, the Holy Spirit punished his evil deed on the way and cast him to the ground. And when blessed Paul asked, "Lord, what do you want me to do?" as the best remedy for his soul the Lord sent him to the city and told him to **enter the city.** And when he had entered the city, he learned a new religion, and then he became from an enemy of Christ his most famous friend, as a sign that, if a person cannot save his soul in the world, he should go into the city of religion. There, if ever, he will be saved. And so Lot said that he would escape the peril of Sodom: "There is this city here at hand, a small one, to which I may flee and I shall be saved in it," Genesis 19[:20].

Considering then this lady, who today has professed this religion, laying aside the vanity of the worldly city so that she might begin a new life: with blessed Paul she has today entered this city. Whence the words of Ruth 3[:15] apply to her: "She went into the city." But that in entering this city she may not be afraid of her new experience, I will comfort her in her entrance and say, "Bravely **enter the city!**"

For the further development of our sermon, beloved, you should know that among other cities I find in holy scripture three good ones, of which I will now speak:

---

6. Thus in the manuscript. The reference is to Thomas Aquinas, *Summa theologiae* 2-2, q. 81, art. 6, resp.

the city of man's mind,
the city of holy religion,
and the city of the joy of heaven.

Since I wish the best of these cities for this lady who has now made her profession, I say as I said before, **Enter the city.**

[1]
The first city of which we shall speak, then, is the city of man's mind. Beloved, in book 2 of his *Metamorphoses* Ovid imagines that the sun had a house built with tall columns, whose walls were of gold, the doors of silver, and the roof of ivory. In this house were painted the heaven, the earth, the sea, and the twelve signs of the zodiac. There was also a changeable god depicted in this house, who was called Protheus, who had an indeterminate appearance because he would suddenly change into different shapes.[7] This city, this palace, this house of the sun is nothing else but the city of man's mind. This city is raised in three high columns, which are the three theological virtues, namely, faith, hope, and love, which correspond to the three powers of the soul. For faith stirs our rational part to assent to God and believe in him; hope urges our irascible part to trust in God; and love causes the concupiscible part of man's mind to desire and love God. And as these columns raise man's mind to heaven, to God, they are called the high columns of this city. The city must also be surrounded with walls of gold, which are the four [cardinal] virtues. The first wall will be prudence, through which man should rule himself in God's honor. The second will be justice, so that man may have the proper relation to his neighbor. The third will be temperance, so that man may not glory too much in this world's prosperity. And the fourth will be fortitude, so that man may not be overcome by adversities. In addition it is necessary for this city to have gates of silver. The gates of the city of man's mind, beloved, are man's five senses. Silver, in holy scripture, indicates good discretion. This, then, means that the gates of the five senses must needs be guarded with good discretion in order to keep the city of the soul safe. For Gregory says that through these

7. Ovid, *Metamorphoses* 2.1–18.

gates either death or life enters into your soul.[8] Therefore, to let life in and keep death out, they must be well guarded. In addition to all this, the house must have a roof of ivory. Now, the roof of a house, as you well know, withstands rain and various kinds of tempests. So the roof of the house of the soul will be patience, through which man will overcome all the tribulations of this world. Furthermore, in the house of the sun were depicted heaven, earth, sea, and the twelve signs of the zodiac. This, beloved, indicates nothing else than the dignity of man's soul. This dignity is so great that it is shown in the image of heaven, earth, and all creatures. Whence Augustine says in *On Spirit and Soul* (and this is put into book 3, chapter 2, by the Master on Properties): "The soul, made in the likeness of all knowledge, holds in itself the image of all things. It is like the earth in its senses, like water in its imagination, like air in its reason, like the firmament in its intellect, and like the empyreum in its intelligence. Thus man's soul offers the image of all the elements and of all the major creatures."[9] And above all these, our soul holds the image of the most blessed Trinity more truly than any other creature. No angel, no archangel, none of the angels in heaven has the image and likeness of God as does man, as the Master of the *Sentences* says in book 2, distinction 16, chapter 1.[10] In this, man is the worthiest of all creatures, as is seen in the same place, distinction 39, chapter 1.[11] If we, then, consider how gloriously the Sun of Justice has fashioned the city of man's soul, how he has chosen it for his throne, seat, and tabernacle in which this sun would reside in this world, and how he has adorned it with his blessed image, it is clear that man is much beholden to God. For the Sun of Justice has no other dwelling on earth than in man's soul.

And thus, to make the city of our soul a likeness of the city of the sun as described by Ovid, and to demonstrate that the Sun of Justice does not reside on earth anywhere but in man's soul, "one shall be called the city of the sun," Isaiah 19[:18]. But alas, beloved, that in this

---

8. Perhaps Gregory, *Moralia* 21.2.

9. Pseudo-Augustine, *De spiritu et anima* 4 (PL 40:782), quoted in Bartholomew, *De proprietatibus rerum* 3.3 (p. 49).

10. Peter Lombard, *Sententiae*, apparently 2.16.2, last sentence (1:406).

11. Perhaps *Sententiae* 2.39.1 (1:553).

house was also depicted Protheus, the changeable god, who had an indeterminate shape. This god denotes nothing else but the sinners of this world, who through mortal sin change God's likeness into a different form, namely, into an image of the devil. Chrysostom proves this in his *Imperfect Work*, homily 31: "As a good person shows God's image, so an evil one, without God's image, has the image of the devil."[12] And this, beloved, is a great danger. Consider: if a man were to despise or to falsify the seal of an earthly king, he would be worthy to be hanged. Even more so, one who falsifies the seal of the eternal king would be worthy of eternal punishment. Consider, I pray, how strong the city of your soul is when it is in the state of grace and adorned as I said before, and how wretched it is in mortal sin. Chrysostom says in his book *On the Return of the Fallen:* "As the evil spirits are given no access to the secrets of heaven, so no defilement could penetrate into a pure mind."[13] So that, in the view of this teacher, the devil could as easily enter heaven as man's soul when it is in the state of grace. Whereas, he says further, our soul is stripped of all its ornaments through mortal sin and remains deformed and vile, and all its guard is gone from it, so that, as he says, when the soul is in the state of mortal sin, the demons can enter it as easily as hell. We find a figure for the strength of man's soul that is in the state of grace in Ecclesiastes 5[:14–15], where the Wise Man says that there was "a little city, and few men in it. There came against it a great king, built bulwarks round about it, and the siege was perfect. Now there was found in it a man poor and wise, and he delivered the city by his wisdom." This little city is man's soul. Against her comes the devil with seven armies of the deadly sins. But certainly, a wise man does not fear, for through his goodness, through his good prayer he will keep the devil out and put him to flight and guard his city. And so [God] ordained seven petitions in the Lord's Prayer to put the seven armies to flight. So, if you feel the devil approaching, say the Lord's Prayer, and all the demons of hell cannot harm you.

12. On this work, see above, selection 7, note 15.

13. Cf. John Chrysostom, *Ad Theodorum lapsum* 1.1 (PG 47:278). The manuscript's quotation agrees with the medieval Latin translation of *De reparatione lapsi* in Hereford Cathedral, MS O.iii.8, fol. 67vb.

From all that we have said we can infer that there are four main things that support the city of man's soul: the love of God, the praise of God, the image of God, and wisdom. These four powers are indicated in the name of this lady, for she is called Alys in English. The first letter, A, denotes *amorem Dei,* the love of God; the second, L, *laudem Dei,* the praise of God; the third, Y, *ymaginem,* his image; and the fourth, S, *sapienciam,* wisdom. Through the mystery of her name, therefore, she would be a great supporter of this city. Certainly, the more virtuous a person is, the better she is disposed to guard the city of her soul. Now, Alys is all goodness; therefore, etc. This is manifest when we divide her name in two parts, Al-Ys: she is "all there is," and only that. But nothing is except the good, for evil has no existence. Therefore, she would be all goodness. In addition she is called Alicia, as in *alliciens,* alluring. Now, since she is all good, as was said, she cannot allure to evil. Therefore, she necessarily allures God to herself and everyone to good. In this way, by the power of her name, she is a worthy dweller in the city, a true guardian. And that she may worthily guard the city of her soul to the honor of God, I say to her the words that I spoke at the beginning: **Enter the city.**

[2]

The second city we must speak of is that of holy religion. In book 8 of the *Metamorphoses* Ovid says that the city of Alchose[14] had a very strong tower, in which Nisus, the king of that city, enclosed his daughter named Silla. That woman who was thus enclosed had nothing to bring her comfort except that Apollo, the god of truth, sometimes flew through the air and on that tower struck his lyre so sweetly that the woman took great delight and comfort from that tune. This city Alchose is the city of religion; the strong tower is the place of this particular religious order, namely, of these enclosed ladies. That woman Silla, who was enclosed in that city, is this venerable lady who has today been enclosed in the tower of this order. For when you read her name backwards, it becomes the vernacular name of this lady,

14. Ovid says *in urbe Alcathoi,* "in the city of Alcathous," the king of Megara. The preacher evidently understood Alcathous, or as he says "Alchose," to be the name of the city rather than the king; Ovid, *Metamorphoses* 8.7–8, 14–18. Scylla's name, obviously pronounced "Silla" by the preacher, appears in *Metamorphoses* 8.91.

Allys or Alis, in Latin Alicia. Therefore their names in some way agree with each other. And what consolation will this woman who was thus enclosed have? Without doubt, the almighty God of Truth will comfort her with his harp. As you know, a harp is, first of all, made of wood that is elegantly fashioned and adorned and also painted with several shields of lords. This wood signifies nothing else but the contemplation this lady should have of several benefits from God, which exceed any benefits given to any creature. For God never gave any creature such great benefits as he gave to human beings. A faithful person should reflect on how God made him or her human when he could have made him an animal; how he made man clean whom he could have made a leper; how he made man healthy whom he could have made diseased; how he gave him all the members of his body whom he could have made a monster. And above all he should reflect that when he commits a mortal sin, he denies God, all the saints, his baptism, and the whole fellowship of heaven, and we commit ourselves to the devil. And still it is God's goodness that when we deny him, he guards us and gives us time to redeem our sins, while the one whom we have committed ourselves to would destroy us. And certainly, in waiting for us God did more for us than he did for that glorious Lucifer, who at a mere breath of pride fell and will forever be a devil. Also Adam, our first parent, was cast out of paradise for the mere taste of an apple. We in contrast commit sin, not once as they did, but every day, and yet God has pity on us. This is a great benefit from God, no doubt. And therefore Chrysostom says in the first book of *On Compunction:* "If we die a thousand times, and even if we fulfill all virtues of the soul, we do nothing worthwhile in comparison with what we have received from God."[15] If this lady will reflect on these things, she will find matter of great consolation in her God, and she will see that she can do nothing in this world that compares to what God has done for her. And in this way she will have very good wood for her harp.

On the wood of this harp one puts black leather, and this signifies contemplation of Christ's Passion, whose flesh became black for the salvation of mankind. In this one must reflect on God's goodness, for

---

15. John Chrysostom, *Ad Stelechium de compunctione* (PG 47:418).

as Anselm says in a meditation, God did not want to send to us an angel or archangel to redeem us, but he himself came down to man from heaven, out of the unique love he had for mankind, that he might heal man of his sickness and reinstall him in his kingdom.[16] We have an example of this in everyday experience. If the king of England had a servant of his stable who was sick and who could only be healed if the king wore the wretched clothes of that servant on his own body for three days, surely, if the king did this for the love of his servant, one would say that the king loved him tenderly. In like fashion, beloved, that Christ might heal mankind, he not only took the clothes of our nature and wore them for thirty-three years, but he died for us a most bitter death in that same garment. Let the faithful soul reflect on this, and she will find that for God's love there is nothing too great that she cannot endure.

The strings of this harp are good works and God's praise here on earth. As the strings are connected to the wood of a harp, so must all our works be anchored in God. The pins then will be the virtues and good qualities that link our works to God. The plectrum[17] will be charity, which perfects all our works and our virtues and completes them in God. If, then, this lady has such a harp and joyfully plays on it throughout this city, she will no doubt find much consolation in God. In order for her to do so, it is written in Isaiah 23[:16–17]: "Take a harp, go about the city; sing well, sing many a song, that you may be remembered. And it shall come to pass after seventy years," that is, if you serve God well by praising him in this world, you will be remembered not only here but in the future world.

Beloved, now we have placed this lady Alice in the tower of religion and given her a harp with which to make joy and gain comfort. But she has yet another name, namely, Huntingfield, which indicates that she should hunt in the field. But how, since she is enclosed, shall we take her into the field to hunt, especially since I have never read in scripture that a person's good lies in hunting? Therefore it would be a miracle if we could make a woman into a good huntress. But, beloved, there is a great difference between literal hunters and spiritual ones. A

16. Anselm, *Meditatio 4* (PL 158:733).
17. The English word *wrest* is used.

literal hunter, as you know, needs certain things: hunting dogs, a collar, a leash, and a horn. In the same way, in order to hunt spiritually and to engage in this sport spiritually, this lady must have three hunting dogs, namely, obedience, poverty, and chastity. Let us not wonder that these virtues are likened to hunting dogs. For the Master of the *Properties* says that among the animals the dog is most prudent, grateful, and faithful.[18] Prudence is related to obedience, gratitude to poverty, and faithfulness to chastity.[19] These dogs must have collars of good discretion. They must be led well with the leash of reason and be governed with the horn of good knowledge. Having these, she must, as her name declares, go into the field to hunt there. Papias lists sixteen different kinds of fields, among which there is one called "a field that is measured out, which is an enclosed field and assigned to a town."[20] Experience teaches us that hunting is better in enclosed fields and in parks than it is in forests, because in the former no animal can escape, while from the latter it can. And thus, that this lady may not grow weary in her desire to hunt, she is placed in an enclosed field. This field is adjacent to the city of holy religion. And so, noble lady, hunt happily in this field according to your name! If you do so, I dare promise that you will not miss the end you are striving for, which is life eternal. Of her is said over several verses in 1 Maccabees 3[:4, 6, 8, 7]: "In the hunt . . . salvation prospered in her hand . . . ; she went through the city . . . and her memory is blessed forever."

But since these three virtues—obedience, poverty, and chastity— are the chief ones on which the religious life rests, they are symbolized in the garments of these noble sisters, so that we may reflect better on them. Blessed John says that everything in the world that keeps man away from God lies in three things: in riches, lustful pleasures, and honors [cf. 1 John 2:16]. That in their desire to serve God fully these sisters may not be hampered by riches, they have scorned

18. Cf. Bartholomew, *De proprietatibus rerum* 18.24 (p. 1035).

19. Obedience, poverty, and chastity are the three basic vows of the religious life, by which Alice Huntingfield would have bound herself on this occasion. See the following paragraph.

20. *Papiae Elementarium—Litera A,* edited by V. de Angelis, Testi e documenti per lo studio dell'antichita (Milan: Cisalpino-Goliardica, 1977), 144. Papias was a lexicographer, whose Latin dictionary was made in 1053.

them in their voluntary poverty. This is symbolized in their black veil, whose black color says they are dead to the world. Second, that they may not be hampered by fleshly desires, they have renounced them in their complete chastity. This is symbolized in their habit, which covers their whole body like a cross and expresses mortification of the flesh. And third, that they may not be kept away from God by worldly honors, they have forsaken them in their great humility and obedience. This is symbolized by their cord, which is tied in the bend of their body and shows that a woman of holy religion must in obedience bend before her superior. This cord also has five knots that pertain to true obedience. The first is patience without grumbling, the second reverence without groveling,[21] the third fear without displeasure, the fourth love without flattery, and the fifth good will without deception. Whatever sister is thus bound in her mind with this cord and its knots will no doubt be fully obedient. But the wimple that covers her breast and is tied with the jaw band symbolizes two things. First, in so far as it covers her breast, it shows purity in thought; and insofar as it is tied with the jaw band so that it cannot be moved too far, temperance in speech. For the Apostle commands holy virgins not to be loquacious.[22]

From all that has been said in this main part, three points can be taken. First, since this lady is called Alice, she should, like Silla, be enclosed in the tower of religion, where she is to comfort herself with the harp of contemplating God's gifts and praising him. Second, since she is called Huntingfield, she should be busy in the enclosed field of this city with good works. And third, since she has been clothed in the sacred garments of this order, she should reflect on what they stand for and eagerly practice it, so that she may receive God's blessing. For there is no doubt that, when her inner *habitus* corresponds to her external habit, she will have virtue in this world and glory in the next. And so, to exhort her to this, as the prophet says, "put on the garments of your glory, O holy city," Isaiah 52[:1]. That she may do this, I exhort her as I did in the beginning: **Enter the city.**

21. "Reuerencia wytowtyn snowtyng."
22. Perhaps 1 Corinthians 14:34–35? Evidently a line has dropped out of the Latin text.

[3]

The third city we speak of is the joy of heaven. Of this city the prophet says that it is "the glorious city that dwells in security" [Zephaniah 2:15]. In as much as this city is gifted with virtues and all goodness, in which lies her strength, as I said before, it follows that it is the model of cities, especially since there is no city that cannot be much emptied of her virtues except this one. For experience teaches us that a city that cannot be won over by betrayal from within or by attack from without can be said to be a strong city indeed. So it was with this heavenly city. For one dweller of this city attempted to assail it as a traitor, and this was Lucifer when he wanted to be equal to God in power. As he was already very powerful through God's gift, he still wanted to be more powerful, and so Power resisted him and cast him out of the city of heaven as a traitor into hell. This city was further assailed by another being who lived, as it were, in its suburb, and this was our forefather when he wanted to be like God in knowledge. And since his will was evil, he was not only deprived of this city of heaven but also of his own dwelling place, that is, paradise. From these things it is clear that this city cannot be won through power, as Lucifer tried, nor through knowledge, as Adam attempted. What, then, will win this city? Certainly, nothing else but goodness and a virtuous life. Therefore the Wise Man says in Proverbs 21[:22]: "The wise man has scaled the city of the strong." Be good, and you will of necessity win the city.

To speak some more of the glory and strength of this city: Experts tell us that four things make a city strong. First, that it is well walled and surrounded by water, to resist enemies from outside. Second, that it is at peace inside. Third, that it is well stocked with victuals. And fourth, that it is placed in a well-aired location, to better avoid pestilence, for pestilence does more harm in a city than elsewhere for the greater contagion in close dwellings. To apply this to the city of heaven: First, this city is so well surrounded by walls and water that it cannot be won by any enemy. It once used to be said in a popular song:

> We shall make a jolly castle
> On a bank beside a brim;

None shall e'er come to it
Unless he knows to swim,
Or else he has a boat of love
For to sail therein.[23]

This castle on the bank is the castle of the heavenly city, of which Ezekiel 48[:2] says: "on a very high mountain there was the building of a city." But that you may not think it is insecure since it stands on high: you know that any object that has four sides stands most firmly, for a stone cube will stand firm on whatever side you turn it. So, in order to stand firm, the heavenly city "lies in a foursquare" [Revelation 21:16]. The water that surrounds it is the water of penitence. Every human being is either a just person or a sinner. If he is a sinner, he cannot enter this city unless he swims in the water of penance. If he is just and without sin, he sails over this water in the boat of love. But whether he swims or sails, he is a friend of the heavenly one. None can enter in any other way. Therefore, obviously no enemy can harm this city. This is "a great city strongly fortified," 1 Maccabees 5[:46]. In this city, moreover, is perpetual peace and eternal rest, and therefore it is said in Sirach 24[:15]: "In the holy city I rested," so that he who had sought rest in all things could not find it except in the heavenly city, which alone is perfectly holy. In addition, no pestilence can enter this city. Avicenna in his *Canon*, fen 2, says that in order to assure good health in a city, doors and windows must face east.[24] Therefore one must take the greatest care in a city that breezes from the east can enter the houses. Now, to show that the city of heaven is free from such pestilence, John says that it has three gates facing east, Revelation 21[:13]. And there will be no lack of victuals in this city, for John says in Revelation 22[:1–2] that he saw in the heavenly city "a river of the water of life, clear as crystal, proceeding from the throne of God; and

23. "Dicebatur enim aliquando in cantico wlgari: We schun maken a ioly castel on a bank bysyden a brymme, schal no man comyn theryn but ʒyf he kun swymme or buth be [*read* he] haue a both of loue for to seylyn ynne," fol. 83. This "canticum vulgare" seems not to be recorded elsewhere.

24. Avicenna, Liber 1, fen 2, doctr. 2, chap. 11; in *Avicennae . . . Libri canonis quinque . . .* (Venice, 1564), 100. The Arabic word *fen* designates a section in Avicenna's *Canon* and was known to medieval Latin writers and to Chaucer.

on both sides of the river was the tree of life, bearing its fruits every month." This clear river of water, proceeding from the throne, indicates nothing else but the joy the saints will have in contemplating the Godhead. And therefore it is said in the Psalms [45:5]: "The stream of the river makes the city of God joyful." The tree of life standing on both sides of the river symbolizes Christ's human nature, in which his divinity is enclosed, and it brings forth the joy the saints will have in contemplating his human nature with their bodily eyes. If we then consider the properties of the city as set forth in what has been said, it is clear that the dwelling in this city is good for mankind. And thus it is said in 2 Kings [2:19]: "And the dwelling of this city is very good." To this city may he bring us who lives and reigns forever. Amen.

25

ACADEMIC SERMON/
LECTURE (FRISBY)

THE MEDIEVAL UNIVERSITY originated as a church institution, whose primary aim was to form theologians, preachers, and priests. In the theological faculty, though there was no formal course in "homiletics," preaching was a required and ongoing activity, and often young men were sent to university to learn how to preach even if they were not pursuing a degree. Both graduate students and masters in theology had to give sermons on various occasions: for purposes of examination, to the general (university) public, and at special academic events, such as inception, the beginning of a lecture course, or the presentation of degree candidates. In all these cases, during the later Middle Ages, the scholastic sermon form was used, and it was imitated even in academic speeches in the faculties of arts (including philosophy) and law. Some European universities have preserved these customs down to the present day.

The following example of academic preaching—or speech making in the form of a sermon—has been preserved together with three introductory sermons on Peter Lombard's *Sentences* that in the manuscript are ascribed to "Frysbi," perhaps the Dominican Ralph Frisby, who lectured at Oxford in the 1330s. All four lectures use the same thema. The *Sentences* formed the major textbook for systematic theology (in contrast to Bible studies, composed probably 1155–58) in the later Middle Ages, and all theology students had to "read" and eventually to lecture on it. The subject matter of its four books is alluded to at least twice in this final lecture of Master Frisby's course.

The present sermon was delivered at the end of the course. It begins at once with an announcement of the three topics the preacher will develop: his own gratitude for the attention and work of his students, an introduction of his academic successor, and a warning against dangerous idleness during the coming vacation. The members of the division and the respective parts of the development are again and again verbally linked to the terms of the thema (with "freedom" often standing for the will). Particularly at the end of major and often minor sections the preacher is at pains to connect his points to these terms, and he often does so with the help of rhyme. The resulting verbal texture is impossible to reproduce in English, and hence I have added the respective Latin passages in the notes. Such summation and connection with the thema is typical of refined preaching in the fifteenth century and can even be found in the English sermons given by Hugh Legat (see D. M. Grisdale, ed., *Three Middle English Sermons from the Worc. Chapter MS. F.10* [Leeds: Leeds University Press, 1939], 13, 17, 20), though Legat uses Latin hexameters instead of rhymed prose.

Another characteristic of academic speeches in sermon form of this time is the speaker's punning on the name of a degree candidate or, as here, of his successor, whom he presents to his audience. Punning is usually accompanied by remarks about personal traits—here the man's corpulence, his taking powders, his hailing from Scotland—and in the fifteenth century these formed a peculiar kind of academic wit that often amounted to ribbing rather than polite deference. The present selection keeps to a nice middle way in its depiction of the corpulent Scotsman Thomas, who whistles when he gets angry.

SOURCE:

Padua, Biblioteca Antoniana MS 515, fols. 123v–126v (Padua-61).

LITERATURE:

Wenzel, *Collections*, 126–27 (on this manuscript) and 297–304 (on university preaching).

S[trickland] G[ibson], "The Order of Disputations," *Bodleian Quarterly Review*
6 (1929–31): 107–12, with translated excerpts from a presentation speech
of degree candidates.

Katherine H. Tachau, "Looking Gravely at Dominican Puns: The 'Sermons'
of Robert Holcot and Ralph Friseby," *Traditio* 46 (1991): 337–45.

J. C. Wey, C.S.B., "The *Sermo Finalis* of Robert Holcot," *Mediaeval Studies* 11
(1949): 219–24. A close parallel to this sermon, preached in the 1330s.

❧

Final Lecture.

Where the spirit of the Lord is, there is freedom, 2 Corinthians
3[:17].

Reverend fathers:

The charity of the audience here in attendance, which is especially
appropriate to the **spirit;**

the profound learning of the bachelor who succeeds me, which is
the possession of the **Lord** because God is the lord of all knowledge;

and the opportunity for misbehavior during the coming vacation,
which rises out of the **freedom** of the will,

move me to commit you to God's rule, so that [your] **freedom may be
where the spirit of the Lord is.**

[1]

I place first the fraternal charity of the present audience that is appropriate to the spirit, for I have always found you to be affectionate,
intelligent, and studious, because you have been benevolent, docile,
and attentive—qualities that render a student perfect, according to
Augustine in book 4 of his *Christian Doctrine,* chapter one.[1] I say, I have
found in you

the greatest benevolence and courtesy,

the greatest industriousness and ability,

and the greatest diligence and zeal.

---

1. Cf. Augustine, *De doctrina christiana* 4.2 or 4.

Regarding my first point, according to the venerable Fulgentius in his *Mythology*, Benevolence or Friendship is described in a picture of Jupiter, who in Greek is called Zeus.[2] It is depicted as having its head bowed, veiled in gold, with a pleasing face, and of bright color. Charity is depicted with bowed head, as with the head of a ram—the ram, *aries*, is so called from the Greek word *ares*, which in Latin means "virtue"; and the head of this virtue is like that of a ram to indicate the supreme degree of worthiness and perfection that charity holds in the ranks of the soul's virtues. Second, it is clothed in a cloak of gold, for it has the quality of gold, which can be hammered out more than any other metal. This indicates that charity stretches out to God, to one's own self, to one's friend, and to one's enemy. That cloak is wide, in the words of the Psalm [118:96]: "Your commandment is exceeding wide." Third, it has a joyful and pleasing face. Astrologers say that Jupiter rules people of sanguine temper, the "children of Jupiter," whose temperament is joyful by nature.[3] This disposition is appropriate to charity, which according to the Apostle is "patient and kind" [1 Corinthians 13:4]. And fourth, it has a bright color. For this reason Jupiter is called *Diespiter* by the poets, that is, "father of the day's brightness"[4]—*dian* in Greek means "bright" in Latin. And this too is quite appropriate to charity, which cannot hide, for friendship is a gift that does not hide itself in adversities. And as in the words of the Wise Man, "wisdom will not enter into a malicious soul" [Wisdom 1:4], so on the contrary "when the Spirit comes"—to whom is linked the goodness of charity—"he will teach you all truth," John 16[:13].

Now, with respect to this first quality of Jupiter and of Friendship, I have found that each one of you has studied well what the Master of the *Sentences* taught: in his first book, [he taught of] the most perfect Father of All, who eternally creates and inspires; in the second, the most powerful Creator, who brought into being and rules all things; in the third, the most generous Redeemer, who has redeemed

2. Hans Liebeschütz, *Fulgentius Metaphoralis: Ein Beitrag zur Geschichte der antiken Mythologie im Mittelalter*, Studien der Bibliothek Warburg 4 (Leipzig: B. G. Teubner, 1926), 78–87.

3. Or "jovial," as we still say.

4. *Diespiter*, that is, "diei claritas pater."

and preserves man; and in the fourth, the Restorer, who cures and heals him who was grievously wounded. With the virtue of a ram's humility, your life has worshipped the majesty that exists equally in the three [divine persons]; has praised the power in his works; has fervently loved the shining piety that for our sins suffered pain; and has merited the cure needed for the wounds he suffered. And thus your love of all-powerful God has had its head bowed. Second, it was clothed in gold. Now, each of you should have a teacher who would teach others to apply themselves to their studies with courage, to direct their hearts to think and imagine with subtlety, to dispute and examine with keenness, and to discern and pronounce with truthfulness. But I have observed things crudely, have lectured obtusely and lazily, have achieved very little in my ineptness, have made assertions lightly and not completely, have not based my conclusions on clear arguments, have formulated and announced my syllogisms in language that was not distinct, or not very sharp, or lukewarm, and without a sound and solid wealth of words, and have sought vain and frivolous things. In all this, out of your golden charity, which "covers a multitude of sins" [James 5:20], you have supported, excused, accepted and praised [me]. And thus your friendship has been with its head bowed and clothed with gold. Third, with the ability and diligence of your minds, which showed forth its pleasing face smiling with learning, you have perceived, discussed, argued, retained, and thus made progress, for according to blessed Jerome, "a docile mind even without a teacher is worthy of praise."[5] But since humility of mind is not sufficient without eagerness in exercising it, in order to have the fourth quality of charity, a bright color in what is to be learned, you have eagerly come to school, heard my lectures, listened with your ears, and put what you have learned in your hearts. For these things I declare without feigning that I am forever obliged to each one of you. For which I cannot thank you enough, yet I offer you as many thanks as there are atoms in a large body, crumbs in a loaf, shining stars in the sky, drops in the whole ocean, leaves in a dense forest, and individual moments in the whole of time.

And just as Christ, before he went from this world to his Father,

5. Jerome, *Epistula 53*.

promised his disciples that he would send them the Holy Spirit—as he was saying, "I shall send him to you" [John 16:7]—so I, as I am about to leave this lectern and give my place to another, pray for you to the Father that he may send you another comforter. Luke 22[:28]: "You are the ones who have continued with me in my temptations," and thus I leave for you, just as my own father left for me, a regency[6] of the greatest consolation and pray that your freedom may be there where the spirit of the Lord is. For Hugh of St. Victor says in book 4, chapter 16 of his work *On Noah's Ark:* "God calls us to his land, to his country, because this [our] land is not worthy of such love—the lowliness of the land diminishes his love. A joyful love requires a pleasing place."[7] And since the spirit of the Lord moved upward where there is the peak of happiness and the fountain of all joy, I pray that [your] freedom may be where the spirit of the Lord is. Ecclesiastes 3[:21]: "Who knows if the spirit of the children of Adam ascends upward?" Isaiah 30[:28]: "The spirit of the Lord like a torrent overflowing to the midst of the neck." Into this promised river some are led to their ankles, others to their knees, some to their kidneys, and still others to their necks. The ankles support our bodies, the knees make us walk, from the kidneys comes our concupiscence, and from the necks our speech. Those who are led into the river of the Holy Spirit to their ankles are people strong to bear adversity; as the Psalmist says: "By the spirit of his mouth all their powers [were established]" [Psalm 32:6]. Those who are led to their knees are people who are high-minded to undertake virtuous labors; Ezekiel 1[:12]: "Where the impulse of the spirit was, thither they went." Those who are led to their kidneys are people in whom all fleshly desires are quenched. And those who are led to their necks are those who also have useful words in their mouths; Matthew 10[:20]: "It is not you who speak, but the Spirit of your Father who speaks in you." That these four features of the spirit may be in you, I pray that where the spirit of the Lord is, there may your freedom be—simplicity of life, in the **spirit;** authority of rule, of the **Lord;** and prosperity without ills is where the spirit of the Lord is. Behold:

6. The manuscript can be read as either *regnum* or *regimen.* "Regency" would refer to the tenure or office of a regent master.

7. Hugh of St. Victor, *De archa Noe* 4.4 (PL 176:669).

the love given to us, **spirit;**
the gracious giver, of the **Lord** (for "lord" means "gift giver");[8]
the strength bestowed on us, **freedom;**
and the sweetness we desire, **where the spirit of the Lord is.**

The healer of the body is shown in the **spirit;** the leader whom I always follow is the **Lord;** my mind and heart are ruled through **freedom;** and the goal I pray for is to be **where the spirit of the Lord is.**[9]

[2]
Second, the profound learning of the bachelor who succeeds me, which is the possession of the **Lord,** is shown in

the meaning of his name,
the good proportion of his figure,
and the evidence of his work.

[a]
Aegidius, in book 3, part 2, chapter 5 of his *Rule of Princes,* says that the honor of dominion should rather be given to men than to women, because a man ranks higher by his reason, is bolder in his courage, less swayed by passions, applies his mind powerfully, and is naturally guided by the rule of prudence.[10] But Thomas,[11] whose name as it were means "all man,"[12] gifted with the just mentioned characteristics, is worthy to rule because of the depth of his knowledge. For

8. One medieval etymology of *dominus* is *dans munus.*

9. In Latin this triple connection runs as follows: "Simplicitas vitalis—**spiritus;** auctoritas regalis—**Domini;** prosperitas absque malis—**est ibi vbi est spiritus Domini.** Videte amorem datum—**spiritus;** datorem gratum—**Domini** . . . ; vigorem latum—**in libertate;** dulcoremque peroptatum—**illi vbi est spiritus Domini.** Corporis patet doctor—per **spiritum;** dux quem semper sequor—est **dominus;** regitur mens atque cor—per **libertatem;** finis pro quo precor—est esse **ibi vbi est spiritus Domini,**" fol. 124v.

10. Aegidius (Giles of Rome), *De regimine principum* 3.2.5.

11. Obviously the first name of the preacher's successor.

12. Thomas, that is, *totus mas.* This "etymology" occurs in contemporary sermons for St. Thomas Becket (FI-70, B/2-19). The following "etymologies" are standard medieval lore and can be found, for example, in the *Catholicon* by Johannes Balbi of Genua, or in the *Legenda aurea* (p. 32).

Thomas means "abyss," which is the impenetrable depth of waters from which wellsprings arise and flow. Thus Thomas will be a wellspring of wisdom, according to the Psalm: "Your judgments are a great deep" [Psalm 35:7]. The name Thomas also means "twin." According to Master [Bartholomew], *On the Properties of Things*, book 8, the sign of Twins *(Gemini)* is the sign of man, and "when Mercury in his happy aspect is joined with it, it renders man able in his judgment and speech, for it is the house of kindred and closeness, of counsel, of religion, and of food and dreams."[13] In this fashion, Thomas, who was engendered under the rule of Mercury, should and does have a twofold learning: speculative and practical, human and divine. For that reason his soul can say, with a pleasant heart: "I alone have compassed the circuit of heaven and have penetrated into the bottom of the deep" [Sirach 24:8]. The word *abyss* comes from *a*, "without," and *bissus*, which is a kind of white linen; hence it means "without whiteness." And since a cleric that has no learning is commonly called a white or blank cleric, in my successor, in contrast, you can see how "darkness was upon the face of the abyss" [Genesis 1:1], so that he may be capable of holding my office, and you can see how he progressed in the study that calls us back from evil. Thus "the abyss" of holy theology "calls unto the abyss" [Psalm 41:8], namely, unto Thomas. I could report other specific things that my successor has done for his special friends, but I pass them over, for "Thomas was not with them when Jesus came" [John 20:24], that is, "my salvation," which will gain its strength from my ending. The name Thomas can also come from *tomos*, which means "cutting off," because he will cut me off from my many labors, as I deserve. Thomas further means *totus means*, "all-going," that he may enjoy a similar honor. Cicero says, in book 3 of his *Offices*, that if two wise men were in the ocean on a plank that could not carry both together, one of them should yield to the wiser one, so that the latter could be of greater use to the common weal.[14] Specialists in optics say that deep-set eyes see farther and more clearly than protruding ones, because they derive a greater strength from being closer to the common nerve in which lies the

13. Bartholomew, *De proprietatibus rerum* 8.12.
14. Cicero, *De officiis* 3.90.

power to see as in their wellspring; they are also farther removed from being hurt, and their power to see is more concentrated together.[15] As proof of this, a person at the bottom of a deep well can see the stars by day, which he would not see if he were above on the surface. So, since my successor's intellectual eye is deep-seated, it follows that from the clarity of his vision he is worthy to hold the lecturer's office. According to Gregory, in book 1 of his *Dialogues*, "a mind that is filled with God's spirit shows open signs of that, namely, truth and humility, so that, if these come together perfectly in a mind, they give testimony of the presence of the Holy Spirit."[16] Hence, since in my successor is the depth of humility and of truth, it follows that **where the spirit of the Lord is, there is freedom.**

[b]

The same is proven by the good proportion of his figure, which is round. Roundness seems to be so perfect that he whose wisdom turns heaven in a circle, created heaven so that it should perform a circular motion in the most convenient way. Thus, the sun and the moon and all the stars turn the heavens in a sphere, and with the turning of their glory they illumine all things.[17] And in the end they return in their circuit, so that a ray that issues from them assumes a circular figure. And if it encounters some impediment, it wants and tries to return to circular motion. So also ...[18] because the parts of a circle are less distant. And so all things conform themselves to a circle as much as they can, so that they may retain their greatest power. Also man, as he was originally created, had this circular figure reasonably assigned to him, that in his being created in the image and likeness of God he, as the lord and head of all creation, should through his legitimate use of creatures return to his Creator, perfect in his virtues and fulfilled in his happiness, so that God would be Alpha and Omega, the beginning and the end. It further seems that a spherical body, among all figures, is the most inclusive and the most perfect, the most widely connected,

15. Cf. Bartholomew, *De proprietatibus rerum* 5.6, with reference to "Auctor perspectiue."

16. Gregory, *Dialogi* 1.1 (PL 77:156).

17. Cf. Job 37:12.

18. I cannot make sense of the manuscript reading: *de viuo exeunte'de vale.*

and the most harmoniously unified. Thus, in his spherical figure, my successor through his amplitude comprehends the immensity of the divine attributes, according to Book 1 [of Peter Lombard's *Sentences*]; through his completeness he measures the universality of perfection of all creatures, according to Book 2; through his ability to connect he knows the distance of natures that are united, according to Book 3. And in the fourth place, through his close harmony he retains the infusion of graces, according to Book 4. Now, according to Aristotle in his *Problems*, part 16, problem 11, when a round body is thrown on a flat one, it first moves in a straight line, but when it reaches the end of its motion and rest, it moves in a circle.[19] So, as the spirit moves in a circle, it will perform the course of its exercise so that **its freedom will be where the spirit of the Lord is.**

[c]

Third, the same is the case in the evidence of his work. Study and learning are fostered mainly by three things, which are humility, poverty, and a foreign land, as Hugh puts it in his *Didascalicon*, book 3, chapter 12, when he says: "When some wise man was asked about the way and form of learning, he answered,

> A humble mind, eager search, a quiet life,
> Silent investigation, poverty, and a foreign land,
> These will open up for many the secrets of learning."[20]

Now, as a sign of his humility, my successor uses many powders in his food and drink, so that he may recall to his mind the words of Genesis 3[:19]: Remember, man, that "you are dust, and to dust you shall return." In 1 Kings 19 it is written how, as Elijah (whose name means "robust ruler" or "God's rule") was standing on the mountain, first a great and strong spirit passed in front of him, that is, a wind that tore up mountains and shattered rocks, but God was not in the wind. Next came an earthquake, but God was not in the earthquake. Then came fire, but God was not in the fire. But after the fire came the whistling

19. Aristotle, *Problemata* 16.11.

20. Hugh of St. Victor, *Didascalicon* 3.13 (PL 176:772). Cf. Hugh of St. Victor, *The Didascalicon*, trans. Jerome Taylor (New York: Columbia University Press, 1961), 3.12, p. 94. Taylor gives other occurrences of these verses on p. 214.

of a gentle air, and God was in that. In this way, when Thomas, who like Elijah is a robust ruler of his passions, gets angry at some injuries, he does not emit a spirit of pride in presumptuous words, nor does he shake his companions with clamorous words, nor does he start or flare up in the fire of wrath, for in none of these is the Lord. But in his humility he will only whistle, not quarrel, for he emits "the whistling of a gentle air," and therein is the Lord. Thus, the freedom of his will is, not where there is the spirit of pride, but the spirit of the Lord. In the second place, he lives in the strictest poverty. He is called poor, *pauper*, not because he can do little *(parum potens)* in his powerlessness, for he is square and compact;[21] nor because he prepares little *(parum parat)* for his delight; but because he owns little *(parum possidet)* in wealth. This is also shown in his name, whose first syllable, *tom*, denotes emptiness, and the second is *as*, which is the same as an obolus. I firmly believe that in the purse of his servant the sun must be shining, for it is bright without any obolus in it. Wherefore he can say about gold and silver, with a clear conscience: "Silver and gold I have none; but what I have, I give you willingly" [Acts 3:6]. For "the abyss says, 'It is not with me,'" Job 28[:14]. Further, if a lower body is empty, a higher body flows down to fill it. So, since the desire or freedom of my successor is empty as it lacks the desire for earthly things, it follows that the goodness of the Holy Spirit with its sevenfold gift will flow down to him, and in this way he will have **the freedom where the spirit of the Lord is.**

In order for this indeed to happen, he left his own land and his kindred for a foreign land.[22] John 16[:7]: "If I do not go, the Paraclete will not come to you; but if I go, I will send him to you." On this text it may be asked: since the Holy Spirit cannot be separated from the Son and was not impotent in Christ's presence, why did the presence of Jesus Christ not allow the Holy Spirit to be present with him? In its sense the Interlinear Gloss (and it comes from Augustine)[23] an-

---

21. The square figure or cube denotes robustness, perfection, immovability; cf. Revelation 21:16.

22. Cf. Genesis 12:1.

23. The Interlinear Gloss on John 16:7 only says, "If you cling to the flesh, you will not be able to receive the Spirit," a quote from Augustine's commentary on the Gospel of John (PL 35:1869).

swers that the apostles had a certain natural affection for Christ's human nature, whether on account of the miracles he had worked, or the good deeds he had done, or the pleasure of his conversation, or the beauty of his body. Of this affection Christ disapproved when Peter, as Christ was foretelling his Passion, said with affection, "Lord, be it far from you, this shall not happen to you!" and Christ answered: "Go behind me, Satan, you do not savor the things that are of God, but the things that are of men" [Matthew 16:22–23]. [Our] Thomas the Twin considered this, that is, the impediment to the Holy Spirit, and fearing that his affection for his parents and friends might prevent him from progressing in his studies, he left Scotland and came to this university from far away. For as far as heaven is from earth, so are his ways far from yours, and his thoughts far from yours.[24] He further passed through Cheviot,[25] the door of hell, which is a horrible place and of vast solitude, so that by his effort he may acquire the splendor of learning, after the words of Wisdom [Ecclesiastes 1:18]: "He who adds knowledge, adds also labor." And further, according to Master [Bartholomew] *On the Nature of Things*, book 10, the north wind is a purging air and brings serenity,[26] I do not doubt that the spirit of the Lord will rest on him, the spirit of wisdom and understanding, of counsel and strength, of knowledge and piety. And that pride may not destroy everything,[27] the spirit of the fear of the Lord will fill him. And in this way "you shall receive the power of the Holy Ghost coming upon you, and you shall be witnesses unto me" of his herald [Acts 1:8], for his learning in things that are necessary will not be lacking, but any wise listener who hears him will be even wiser.

And so, in my desire that you may progress in your studies, after acknowledging my faults and giving thanks I support his replacing my

24. Cf. Isaiah 55:8–9.

25. The manuscript reads *ciuiot*, which must be a reference to the Cheviot Hills, on the border between England and Scotland.

26. Bartholomew, *De proprietatibus rerum* 11.3.

27. Possibly the preacher was thinking of a common Latin tag:

> Si tibi copia, si sapiencia formaque detur,
> Sola superbia destruit omnia si comitetur.

("If you have plenty, if you have received wisdom and beauty, pride alone ruins everything if it comes with it"). Cf. Wenzel, *Verses in Sermons*, 141–42.

person, a man who is not a lightweight though he is short,[28] one who is not without learning but full of the prudence of the Holy Spirit. And I wish, out of my great love, that your affection and freedom may be with him where the spirit of the Lord is.

He gladdens those who are of one mind—the **spirit;**
he strengthens the faint of heart—the **Lord** who "gives hands";[29]
he does not admit but rejects impurity of the mind—**freedom.**
He fills many hearts—the **spirit;**
he rules the laws of the land—the **Lord;**
no pressure does harm—**freedom;**
the mind rejoices that will stay—**where the spirit of the Lord is.**
I see a simple nature—**spirit;**
he makes me humble—the **Lord;**
ready for a twofold act—**freedom;**
draws me to extend myself—the place **where the spirit of the Lord is.**[30]

[3]

In the third and last place I say that the opportunity [you have] for misbehavior during the coming vacation, which rises out of the **freedom** of the will, moves me [to say] that your freedom may be where **the spirit of the Lord** is. Cicero, in his book *On Offices,* understands that freedom is but the power to live as you will.[31] But now you are in a state, not of virtuous work, but of idle vacation. According to the grammarians, the word *vacation* comes from *vacuum.* A person who is free *(vacat)* for something—that is, to do something—at times does not do anything. To be free for rest means that being free from other

---

28. "Non leuis quamuis breuis."

29. "Dat manus," apparently another etymology of *Dominus;* though perhaps a scribal error for the more usual etymology *dat munus* given earlier.

30. "Letificat concordes—**spiritus;** fortificat vecordes—**Dominus** qui dat manus; non permittit set abdicat mentis sordes—**libertas.** Replet corda plura—**spiritus;** regit regni iura—**Dominus;** non nocet pressura—**libertas;** gaudet mens mansura— **ibi vbi est spiritus Domini.** Naturam cerno simplicem—**spiritus;** me facit sibi supplicem—**Dominus;** potest [*read* potens?] in actum duplicem—**libertas;** trahit vt me amplicem—locus **ibi, vbi est spiritus Domini,**" fol. 125v.

31. Cicero, *De officiis* 1.70.

labors one gives oneself to rest and leisure.[32] Now Vacuna rules, who according to the poets is the goddess of *vacatio.*[33] Since idleness leads to need (Proverbs 28[:19]: "He who follows idleness shall be filled with poverty") and brings foolishness (Proverbs 12[:11]: "He who pursues idleness is very foolish"), he who applies his body to pleasures is foolish; he who does not apply his mind to gaining knowledge is more foolish; but he who does not apply himself in either body or mind to good works can be declined[34] by school boys in grammar schools as: he who lives in idleness is foolish, foolisher, foolishest. Third, idleness that lacks any good leads to perversity; Sirach 33[:29]: "Idleness has taught much evil." Therefore, since the spirit is sometimes ready for healthy exercises but the flesh is always weak, do not pay attention to spirit and flesh [together] but **let your freedom be where the spirit of the Lord is.** For Seneca says, in his *Letter* 86 to Lucilius: "Leisure without letters is death and a living man's burial."[35] Also, according to Bernard in book 2 of his *On Consideration:* "Idleness is the mother of strife and the stepmother of virtues."[36] Hence a rhymester says:

> For loss of goods I weep, but more for the loss of days.
> Things anyone can gain again, but no one regains time.[37]

Now, since according to the rules of law, where a greater danger lurks one must act with greater caution, let your affection not be attached to earthly things, which are at rest, but rather like heavenly bodies, which are moved by angelic spirits, **let your freedom be where the spirit of the Lord is.** The Philosopher asks in his book on *Problems,* part 10, problem 7, why we cannot move our eyes at the same time in different directions whereas we can move them together in one and

32. In classical and medieval Latin, the verb *vacare,* from *vacuus,* "empty," means both to be free from doing something, i.e., without occupation or obligation, and to be free to do something, i.e., to devote oneself to.

33. See, for instance, Ovid, *Fasti* 6.307.

34. *Declined:* the writer clearly means *compared,* i.e., the adjective *foolish* can be put in the comparative and superlative degrees.

35. Seneca, *Epistula* 82.3.

36. Bernard, *De consideratione* 2.22.

37. A very popular proverbial saying; see Walther, *Proverbia* 4893, and Wenzel, *Preachers, Poets, and the Early English Lyric,* 133 and 253.

the same direction. For we can move both of them simultaneously up or down, but we cannot move one up and the other down. And he answers that things that are linked in their origin have the same motion. Though the eyes' movement comes from two nerves, these nerves come together in one cross-section in the forepart of the brain, so that their origin and consequently their movement is one and the same. (This must be understood of normal people, not of those with only one eye.)[38] In moral terms: Reason and freedom [of the will] are the two eyes of the soul. Now, the movement of reason is circular: it begins with God and tends toward God, since God is Alpha and Omega, the beginning and the end. Therefore, so that no deformity of nature may appear, our **freedom must be where the sprit of the Lord is.** The Philosopher further asks in the book just mentioned, part 2, problem 9, why prizes are promised and given in victories of the body but not in those of the spirit, that is, in philosophical disputes. And he answers in two ways. First, because in physical victories it is certain who gains the better part, but in philosophical disputes we do not have such certainty, as there are different opinions for either side. He also gives a second and better reason for the same: the prize given for a bodily combat is insufficient for acts that concern wisdom.[39] As scripture testifies: "All the things that are desired are not to be compared with her" [Proverbs 3:15], and her prize must exceed one's merit. Therefore, wise men were not promised a temporal prize but an eternal one. And thus, although man's spirit, like my own, has often held false opinions, maintained improbable questions, offered false reasons, and given useless responses, yet the spirit of the Lord cannot deceive or be deceived. Therefore, in view of that infinite prize, **let freedom be where the spirit of the Lord is.**

Seneca says in his *Letter 49:* "The mind of a wise man is like the world above the moon: there is always tranquillity. Here you have the reason why you want to be wise, because a wise man never lacks joy. This joy is born only from a virtuous conscience."[40] Equally, Sextus the Pythagorean in his proposition 404: "A philosopher's enormous freedom lies not in his name or fame but in his soul."[41] But accord-

38. Aristotle, *Problemata* 31.7.   39. Ibid., 30.11.
40. Seneca, *Epistulae* 59.16.
41. Perhaps referring to the *Sentences* of Sextus the Pythagorean, 309: "Next to God

ing to blessed Gregory in his *Moral Commentary*, book 18, on the words of Job [27:10], "Or can he delight himself in the Almighty?": "The mind can never be without some delight; it takes it either in the lowest things or in the highest." And then follows: "The greater its care in burning for the lowest things, the more painful the time it freezes away from the highest ones."[42] For according to blessed Augustine in book 8, chapter 4 of his *City of God*—and he recites the view of Plato—"A wise person is he who is so closely linked to God in his mind," as partner[43] and lover, "that nothing comes in between to separate them."[44] And since in the Apostle's words "he who is joined to the Lord, is one spirit with him" [1 Corinthians 6:17], that your intellectual humility may be strong, **let your freedom be where the spirit of the Lord is.** In his *On the Trinity*, book 4, chapter 3, Augustine says: "What is love"—which is the act of freedom appropriate to the Holy Spirit—"if not a life that couples or seeks to couple together two beings, namely, the lover with his beloved?"[45] This bond is most strong. For of the several unions: between accident and subject, form and matter, the rational soul and its body, one's understanding with what is being understood, and a beloved object with is lover, the last union is the strongest. The next to the last is stronger than those that precede, as the Philosopher has it, but the last is the strongest, because it presupposes the next to the last within itself, since nothing is loved unless it is understood. From this follows that "love is strong as death" [Canticles 8:6]. But according to Gregory, *On the Gospels*, homily 25, on the word of John, "Mary stood at the sepulcher without, weeping" [John 20:11]: "For a lover it is not enough to have seen [his love] only once, for the power of his love makes the desire of his love even greater."[46]

Therefore, that in your vacation your comprehension of learning

---

nothing is as free as a wise man," or 264b: "You will be free from all things if you serve God." *The Sentences of Sextus,* ed. and trans. Richard A. Edwards and Robert A. Wild, S.J. (Chico, Calif.: Scholars Press, 1981).

42. Gregory, *Moralia* 18.9.

43. The manuscript reads *coniutor,* perhaps for *coniunctor?*

44. Cf. Augustine, *De civitate Dei* 8.1, but the quoted passage comes from *De utilitate credendi* 15.33.

45. Augustine, *De Trinitate* 8.10.

46. Gregory, *Super evangelia* 2.25.2.

may not become void, and hence your love may not cool, **let freedom be where the spirit of the Lord is.**

> A breathing of the heart inspired in us through the **spirit;**
> the highest power is generous and gracious, through the **Lord;**
> the strength given to you is not limited at all, since he is **freedom;**
> a place wide and beautiful on high, **where the spirit of the Lord is.**

For the first and second, Wisdom 12[:1]: "Oh, how good and sweet is your spirit, O Lord!" But since Lady Theology is not a slave woman but freeborn (cf. Galatians 4[:7]), one may ask as in Job 28[:12]: "Where is wisdom to be found, and where is the place of understanding?" And Wisdom answers for herself: "I dwell in the highest places," Sirach 24[:7], so that the freedom of our will may seek her there, where the spirit of the Lord is.

> Subtle understanding is opened to us through the **spirit;**
> the regard of honor to which I am subject is [directed] to the **Lord;**
> the mind's affect is upright, not bent down, since it is **freedom;**
> the place is perfect where God is loved, **where the spirit of the Lord is.**

Behold:

> what makes the heart devout, the **spirit;**
> enhances him who is promoted, the **Lord;**
> rules the body in its entirety, **freedom;**
> and all evil is cast off, **where the spirit of the Lord is.**

Behold:

> what penetrates human minds, the **spirit;**
> what helps all on earth, the **Lord;**
> what is absolved of worldly ways, **freedom;**
> and thus rejoices in the sweetness of pure glory, **where the spirit of the Lord is.**

And thus:

the emanation of love and awakening of fervor for the infinite God is the **spirit;**

the declaration of his worth and proclamation of his honor is shown to him who is the **Lord;**

the brightness of knowledge and approval of work in an intellectual being proceed from **freedom;**

the spreading of sweetness and the contemplation of its author without end of our hope, **where the spirit of the Lord is.**[47]

So then, let your hearts be fixed on where your joys are. Which he may grant us who with the Father, etc.

47. "Pectoralis flatus et nobis inspiratus—per **spiritum;** summus potentatus largus est aut gratus—per **Dominum,** qui dat minus vigor tibi datus in nullo est artatus—cum iste sit **libertas;** locus pulcher et latus in alto situatus—**est ibi vbi est spiritus Domini.** . . . Subtilis intellectus nobis est detectus—per **spiritum;** honoris respectus cui sum subiectus est ad Dominum; mentalis affectus est rectus non deiectus, cum sit **libertas;** locus est perfectus quo Deus est dilectus, **ibi vbi est spiritus Domini.** Ecce: quid facit cor deuotum—**spiritus;** magnificat promotum—**Dominus;** regit corpus totum—**libertas;** omne malum est amotum—**ibi vbi est spiritus Domini.** Ecce quid illabitur mentibus humanis—**spiritus;** ecce quid proficitur omnibus mundanis—**Dominus;** ecce quid absoluitur a moribus prophanis—**libertas;** et ideo dulcore letabitur glorie non inanis—**ibi vbi est spiritus Domini.** Et sic: amoris emanacio, feruoris excitacio, infiniti Dei est **spiritus;** valoris protestacio, honoris proclamacio exibetur ei qui est **Dominus;** splendoris informacio, laboris approbacio intellectualis rei in procedunt a **libertate;** dulcoris pululacio, auctoris speculacio sine fine nostre spei, **ibi vbi est spiritus Domini.**" fol. 126v.

FREQUENTLY QUOTED
SOURCES

Aegidius Columna (Aegidius Romanus, Giles of Rome). *De regimine principum.* Rome: Hieronymus Samaritanius, 1607. Facsimile reprint, Aalen: Scientia Verlag, 1967.

Bromyard, John. *Summa praedicantium.* London, MS Royal 7.E.iv. Quotations are to the alphabetical chapter (as Bromyard calls it), paragraph, and folio in this manuscript (e.g., A.XVII.7, fol. 39rb, referring to chapter A.XVII on *Adulterium*, paragraph 7).

Burleigh, Walter. *Liber de vita et moribus philosophorum.* Ed. Hermann Knust. Litterarischer Verein in Stuttgart 177. Tübingen: Litterarischer Verein in Stuttgart, 1886. Reprint, Frankfurt am Main: Minerva, 1964.

Caesarius of Heisterbach. *Dialogus miraculorum.* Ed. Joseph Strange. 2 vols. in 1. Cologne: Heberle, 1851.

Fasciculus Morum: A Fourteenth-Century Preacher's Handbook. Ed. and trans. Siegfried Wenzel. University Park: Pennsylvania State University Press, 1989.

Friedberg, Aemilius [Emil]. *Corpus iuris canonici.* 2 vols. Leipzig: B. Tauchnitz, 1879. Reprint, Graz: Akademische Druck- und Verlagsanstalt, 1959.

Jacobus a Voragine ["Januensis"]. *Legenda aurea.* 3d ed. Ed. Th. Graesse. 1890. Reprint. Osnabrück: Otto Zeller Verlag, 1967.

———. *Sermones de tempore et de sanctis.* Basel: Johann de Amerbach, 1488.

John of Salisbury. *Policraticus.* Ed. Clement C. G. Webb. 2 vols. Oxford: Clarendon Press, 1909.

Justinian. *Corpus iuris civilis Iustinianei.* Ed. Johannes Fehe. 6 vols. Lyons, 1627. Facsimile edition, Osnabrück: Otto Zeller Verlag, 1965–66.

Peter Lombard. *Sententiae.* 3d edition. Ed. Patres Collegii S. Bonaventurae, 2 vols. Grottaferrata: Collegio San Bonaventura, 1971–82.

The Sarum Missal. Ed. J. Wickham Legg. Oxford: Clarendon Press, 1916.

Tubach, Frederic C. *Index Exemplorum: A Handbook of Medieval Religious Tales.* Folklore Fellows Communications 204. Helsinki: Akademia scientiarum fennica, 1969. Cited by number.

Valerius Maximus. *Factorum et dictorum memorabilium liber.* Ed. C. Kempf. Leipzig: B. G. Teubner, 1888.

Walther, Hans. *Proverbia sententiaeque latinitatis medii aevi.* 6 vols. Göttingen: Vandenhoeck & Ruprecht, 1963–1967.

Wenzel, Siegfried. *Preachers, Poets, and the Early English Lyric.* Princeton: Princeton University Press, 1986.

————. *Verses in Sermons: "Fasciculus Morum" and Its Middle English Poems.* Cambridge, Mass.: Medieval Academy of America, 1978.

William (Guilielmus) Peraldus. *Sermones.* Tübingen: Johann Otmar, 1499.

FURTHER READINGS

The collaborative volume *The Sermon*, edited by Beverly Mayne Kienzle in the series Typologie des sources du Moyen Âge occidental (fasc. 81–83 [Turnhout: Brepols, 2000]), provides good discussions of the major problems of the medieval sermon together with extensive bibliographies that include individual preachers and indicate available translations. O. C. Edwards Jr., *A History of Preaching* (Nashville: Abingdon Press, 2004), is a fine and comprehensive history of preaching and homiletic rhetoric in Christianity from its origins to contemporary practices. Its second volume, on CD, offers a number of patristic, Carolingian, and medieval sermons in translation. For more detailed lists of individual preachers, especially in the Middle Ages, one will have to consult such older histories as Jean Longère, *La prédication médiévale* (Paris: Etudes Augustiniennes, 1983), and Johannes Baptist Schneyer, *Geschichte der katholischen Predigt* (Freiburg im Breisgau: Seelsorgeverlag, 1969).

From later medieval England, translations of Latin sermons occur in the following works:

Fletcher, Alan J. *Preaching, Politics and Poetry in Late-Medieval England.* Dublin: Four Courts Press, 1998. *Eamus hinc* (Ascension, pp. 32–39); *Sequuntur agnum* (Innocents, pp. 86–99); *Relictis omnibus* (5 Trinity, pp. 100–113).

Horner, Patrick J. *A Macaronic Sermon Collection from Late Medieval England: Oxford, MS Bodley 649.* Toronto: Pontifical Institute of Mediaeval Studies, 2006. Edition of twenty-three macaronic sermons with modern translations.

Johnson, Holly. "Preaching the Passion: Good Friday Sermons in Late Medieval England." Ph.D. diss., English Department, University of North Carolina at Chapel Hill, 2001. *Dilexit nos* (pp. 118–77); *Christus passus est* (pp. 235–87); and *Quare rubrum* (pp. 307–22), all sermons on the Passion.

Wenzel, Siegfried. *Macaronic Sermons: Bilingualism and Preaching in Late Medieval England.* Ann Arbor: University of Michigan Press, 1994. *Amore langueo* (Good Friday, pp. 212–67); *De caelo quaerebant* (3 Lent, pp. 270–307); *Quem teipsum facis* (Passion Sunday, pp. 310–45).

GENERAL INDEX

Aaron, 268

Abbéville, John of, xii

Abraham, 113, 125, 156–58, 176, 197, 231

Absalom, 129

Abuses, 124, 179, 255

Achab, 145

Achan, 275

Active, 57, 185, 186, 188–90, 192, 273, 274, 276, 281, 286

Adam, 38, 60, 70, 73, 98, 99, 101, 111, 113, 116, 173, 231, 236, 291, 295, 303

Address, 14, 33, 62, 122, 136, 154, 220

Adultery, 36, 217, 248, 249

Advent, iv, xii, 53, 55, 170, 264

Aegidius, 283, 284, 304, 316

Age, 26, 116, 125, 173, 188, 199, 207, 209, 224, 251, 263, 264

Alanus, 140

Albert the Great, 275

Albumasar, 67

Alexander Nequam, 67, 189

Alexander the Great, 222

Alford, John A., 126, 242

Alkerton, xiv

Alliteration, 77

Almond, 277, 278

Alms, 16, 17, 86, 93, 94, 109, 159, 161, 234, 235

Amasa, 119

Ambrose, St., 16, 115, 131, 143

Ananias, 275

Andrew, St., 53, 276

Annas, 103, 114, 115

Annunciation, iv, xii, 165–73

Anselm, St., 50, 73, 126, 292

Antichrist, 144, 146, 151, 161

Anticlaudianus, 140

Antiphanes, 44

Antiphon, 102, 170

Antony, St., 88, 209

Apollo, 290

Apostle, the (Paul), 20, 32, 33, 36, 47, 58, 89, 99, 100, 110, 111, 115, 125, 129, 146, 148, 159, 194, 196, 201–6, 208–10, 213, 217, 231–233, 239, 242, 243, 247, 251, 256, 259, 266, 294, 301. *See also* Paul

Apostles, 8, 10, 34, 49, 83, 114, 115, 122, 126, 145, 147, 148, 158–60, 167, 177, 203, 256, 264, 268, 309

Aquinas, Thomas, St., 135, 285, 286

Aquitaine, 253

Aristotle, 12, 41, 61, 78, 151, 208, 210, 307, 312

Arithmetic, 137

Armagh, 168, 191, 192, 196

Arnaud of Bonneval, 121

Arrow, 150

Artes praedicandi, 32

Articles of Faith, 80, 147, 151, 202–4, 209, 243. *See also* Creed

Ascension, 53, 185, 318

Ash Wednesday, iv, 82

INDEX OF BIBLICAL QUOTATIONS

Preaching in the Age of Chaucer: Selected Sermons in Translation was designed and typeset in Centaur by Kachergis Book Design of Pittsboro, North Carolina. It was printed on 60-pound Natures Natural and bound by Thomson-Shore of Dexter, Michigan.